D0724844

# Financial and Accounting Guide for Not-for-Profit Organizations

## Seventh Edition
## 2010 Cumulative Supplement

**Malvern J. Gross Jr., CPA**
*Retired Partner, PricewaterhouseCoopers LLP*

**John H. McCarthy, CPA**
*Retired Partner, PricewaterhouseCoopers LLP*

**Nancy E. Shelmon, CPA**
*Partner, PricewaterhouseCoopers LLP*

WILEY
John Wiley & Sons, Inc.

Copyright © 2010 by PricewaterhouseCoopers. PricewaterhouseCoopers refers to the individual member firms of the worldwide PricewaterhouseCoopers organization. All rights reserved.

Published by John Wiley & Sons, Inc., Hoboken, New Jersey.

Published simultaneously in Canada.

No part of this publication may be reproduced, stored in a retrieval system, or transmitted in any form or by any means, electronic, mechanical, photocopying, recording, scanning, or otherwise, except as permitted under Section 107 or 108 of the 1976 United States Copyright Act, without either the prior written permission of the Publisher, or authorization through payment of the appropriate per-copy fee to the Copyright Clearance Center, Inc., 222 Rosewood Drive, Danvers, MA 01923, 978-750-8400, fax 978-646-8600, or on the Web at www.copyright.com. Requests to the Publisher for permission should be addressed to the Permissions Department, John Wiley & Sons, Inc., 111 River Street, Hoboken, NJ 07030, 201-748-6011, fax 201-748-6008, or online at www.wiley.com/go/permissions.

Limit of Liability/Disclaimer of Warranty: While the publisher and author have used their best efforts in preparing this book, they make no representations or warranties with respect to the accuracy or completeness of the contents of this book and specifically disclaim any implied warranties of merchantability or fitness for a particular purpose. No warranty may be created or extended by sales representatives or written sales materials. The advice and strategies contained herein may not be suitable for your situation. You should consult with a professional where appropriate. Neither the publisher nor author shall be liable for any loss of profit or any other commercial damages, including but not limited to special, incidental, consequential, or other damages.

For general information on our other products and services, or technical support, please contact our Customer Care Department within the United States at 800-762-2974, outside the United States at 317-572-3993 or fax 317-572-4002.

Wiley also publishes its books in a variety of electronic formats. Some content that appears in print may not be available in electronic books.

For more information about Wiley products, visit our Web site at http://www.wiley.com.

*Library of Congress Cataloging-in-Publication Data:*
Financial and accounting guide for not-for-profit organizations/
Malvern J. Gross, Jr., . . . [et al.].—7th ed.
    p. cm.
  Malvern J. Gross's name appears as main author entry in earlier ed.
  Includes index.
  ISBN 978-0-470-45706-1 (supplement)
  1. Nonprofit organizations—Accounting.  I. Gross, Malvern J.
   HF5686.N56G76 2005
   657.98–dc22

                                        2005000045

Printed in the United States of America

10 9 8 7 6 5 4 3 2 1

# About the Authors

**Malvern J. Gross, Jr.,** was the author of the first edition of this text and a significant contributor to many of the subsequent editions. He is a retired partner of Price Waterhouse (a predecessor to Pricewaterhouse-Coopers LLP) and a nationally recognized authority on accounting and financial reporting for not-for-profit organizations. He was chairman of the AICPA Subcommittee on Nonprofit Organizations that wrote the 1978 landmark Statement of Position for Certain Nonprofit Organizations and of the Accounting Advisory Committee to the Commission on Private Philanthropy and Public Needs. He was a member of the committee that wrote the second edition of *Standards of Accounting and Financial Reporting for Voluntary Health and Welfare Organizations* and a coauthor of the *Museum Accounting Handbook*. He served as an advisor to the Financial Accounting Standards Board in the early phases of its work on setting accounting standards for not-for-profit organizations and to the New York State Charities Registration Office, as well as an adjunct professor of accounting at Lehigh University, his alma mater. After retirement from Price Waterhouse, he was president of a not-for-profit organization, the National Aeronautics Association. He now lives in the San Juan Islands off the state of Washington.

**John H. McCarthy** is Senior Vice President for Administration and Finance at Northeastern University. Jack is also affiliated with Harvard University's Hauser Center for Nonprofit Organizations and a lecturer at the Kennedy School of Government. He served as the National Leader of PricewaterhouseCoopers' Education & Nonprofit Practice before his retirement from the firm in 2005. He was a coauthor of the sixth and seventh editions of this text. He is a coauthor of *Understanding Financial Statements: A Strategic Guide for Independent College & University Boards*, published by the Association of Governing Boards of Universities and Colleges, 2nd edition (2007), as well as several publications by PricewaterhouseCoopers including: *The Changing Role of the Audit Committee: Leading Practices for Colleges, Universities and Other*

*Not-for-Profit Educational Institutions* (2004); *A Foundation for Integrity* (a 2004 guide for codes of conduct, conflicts of interest, and executive compensation); *Meeting the Challenges of Alternative Investments* (2004); *Understanding Underwater Endowment Funds (2003);* and *Financial Reporting and Contributions: A Decision Making Guide to FASB Nos. 116– 117 (1996)* among others. He is a CPA who, for 37 years, served Price-waterhouseCoopers' education and not-for-profit clients, including many of the most prestigious institutions in the United States. He graduated from Boston College and holds an MBA from the University of Michigan Business School.

**Nancy E. Shelmon** is a senior partner of PricewaterhouseCoopers LLP. She is a frequent speaker at AICPA and state CPA conferences on financial reporting and accounting issues affecting not-for-profit organizations and is currently a member of the AICPA Not-for-Profit Expert Panel. She was chair of the planning committee for the AICPA's annual Not-for-Profit Conference for five years. She has been serving education and not-for-profit clients for over 30 years and has been involved with some of the most widely respected organizations in North America. She serves on the board of directors of the Los Angeles Urban League and Executive Service Corps of Southern California. In addition to being a CPA, she is also a Certified Fraud Examiner. She holds her accounting degree from the University of Minnesota.

# Contributors

We also want to recognize the past contributions of **Richard F. Larkin**, who was a coauthor of the fourth, fifth, and sixth editions of *Financial and Accounting Guide for Not-for-Profit Organizations*. Prior to his retirement from PricewaterhouseCoopers, he served as a technical director for the Education & Nonprofit practice. We are very grateful to Dick for his efforts on prior editions of this Guide.

The seventh edition of this Guide represents the collaborative efforts of many PricewaterhouseCoopers professionals who work with our not-for-profit and higher education clients throughout the United States. The authors wish to very gratefully acknowledge the contributions of the following PricewaterhouseCoopers partners, directors, and managers to this Guide: Emily Bernhardt, Ted Budge, Amy Cloud Barrett, Ralph DeAcetis, Diane Duncan, John Edie, Kaye Ferriter, Kevin Fordyce, Martha Garner, Elaine Garvey, Julie Henderson, Sandra Johnson, Elisabeth Lippuner, Dave Merriam, Brian Neumann, Christos Poulios, Robert Spear, Gwen Spencer, Jessica Vroman, Nancy Leparto, Lori Scott, and Frederick Wentzel, Jr. Their assistance has been invaluable.

# Contents

**Note to the Reader:** Chapters or sections not in the main bound volume, *Financial and Accounting Guide for Not-for-Profit Organizations, Seventh Edition* (978-0471-72445-2) are indicated by "(New)" after the title. Material from the main bound volume that has been updated is indicated by "(Revised)" after the title. Material new to or modified in *this* supplement is indicated by an asterisk (*) in the left margin in the contents and throughout the supplement.

# CONTENTS

CONTENTS

# Preface

This supplement updates the seventh edition of *Financial and Accounting Guide for Not-for-Profit Organizations*. This supplement includes all of the changes we have made to the seventh edition since it was published in 2005.

We have further revised several chapters in this supplement to reflect the most current information. The highlights of these changes follow:

- We have updated Appendix D, "Summary of Emerging Accounting, Tax, and Regulatory Issues in 2009," which highlights accounting, financial reporting, tax, and regulatory compliance issues, including their potential impact.

- The long-awaited mergers and acquisitions project is complete and is discussed in Chapter 7.

- A new Appendix E contains our "Perspectives on Higher Education" white paper.

- The anticipated launch of the FASB Accounting Standards Codification in the summer of 2009 is a major restructuring of U.S. accounting standards that will affect the day-to-day work of nearly every financial professional who prepares, reviews, or audits financial statements of private sector organizations. Because a significant portion of the governmental GAAP hierarchy consists of precodification FASB and AICPA standards that will cease to exist when the codification becomes effective, the impact of the codification also will be felt by the governmental sector. See Chapter 19 for more information.

- Not-for-profit organizations must begin applying FASB's new fair value measurement model to many of their nonfinancial assets and liabilities in financial statements for years ended December 31, 2008, and thereafter. The impact of the change in the way fair value is measured is enormous. Nearly one-third of the topics in this year's FASB section deal with fair value measurement issues, and GASB has also added a fair value measurement project to its research agenda; more information is found in Chapter 8.

Nancy Shelmon
Los Angeles, California
February 1, 2010

# CHAPTER ONE

# Responsibilities for Fiscal Management

§ 1.8  Conclusion  1

## § 1.8  CONCLUSION

**p. 12. Add the following as the second paragraph in *section 1.8*:**

In addition to this guidance, the treasurer is encouraged to develop networks and relationships with other not-for-profit organizations and trade associations to improve financial understanding and communication. Many professional associations and industry associations have publications, web sites, conferences, and seminars dedicated to education and enrichment for business officers in nonprofit organizations. Other web sites are dedicated to sharing public information about not-for-profit organizations. Keeping abreast of current issues and trends will only enhance the value the treasurer brings to the organization.

# PART ONE

# Key Financial Concepts

SECTION ONE

Key Financial Concepts

# CHAPTER FIVE

# Fixed Assets and Depreciation

## § 5.1 GENERAL PRINCIPLES—WORKING DEFINITIONS

**p. 51. Insert new *subsection (c)* before *section 5.2*:**

### (c) Capitalization of Fixed Assets—Change in Estimate (New)

Sometimes an organization will have occasion to consider a change in the estimated future benefits of an asset, the pattern of consumption of the benefits associated with an asset, or new information about the future benefits that are associated with an asset. Then the organization may change the depreciation or amortization associated with the asset. This change is considered a change in accounting estimate effected by a change in accounting principle, as defined by Financial Accounting Standards Board (FASB) Statement of Financial Accounting Standards (SFAS) 154, *Accounting for Changes and Error Corrections, a Replacement of APB Opinion No. 20 and FASB Statement No. 3*, and should be accounted for in the period of change if the change affects only the reporting period or in the period of change and future periods if the change affects both.

# § 5.7 IMPAIRMENT OR DISPOSAL OF LONG-LIVED ASSETS

pp. 58–59. Replace current *subsection (c)* with the following:

## (c) Consideration of Retirement Obligations

*Note:* This section is amended for the issuance of Financial Accounting Standards Board Interpretation No. 47, *Accounting for Conditional Asset Retirement Obligations* (FIN 47).

SFAS 143, *Accounting for Asset Retirement Obligations*, describes the accounting and reporting for legal obligations associated with the retirement of tangible long-lived assets and the associated retirement costs. This statement applies to all entities, including not-for-profit organizations. SFAS 143 and FIN 47 require recognition of a liability for the fair value of an asset retirement obligation or any conditional asset retirement obligation (CARO) when the organization has sufficient information to make a reasonable estimate by applying an expected present value technique. A CARO is defined in FIN 47 as: "A legal obligation to perform an asset retirement activity in which the timing and (or) method of settlement are conditional on a future event that may or may not be within the control of the entity." Uncertainty associated with the settlement date and method of settlement does not preclude recognition for the CARO as the legal obligation to perform the retirement activities exist.

The fair value of the liability for the asset retirement obligation should be recognized when incurred. When initially recognizing the liability for an asset retirement obligation, the organization should capitalize the asset retirement cost (ARC) by increasing the carrying amount of the related long-lived asset by the same amount as the liability. Thus, over the life of the long-lived asset, there is an annual charge to expense to depreciate the asset and the ARC. There is also an annual charge to expense to accrete the asset retirement obligation. When the asset retirement obligation is ultimately settled, the liability should approximate this cost.

Examples of situations where an asset obligation and ARCs might need to be recorded by a not-for-profit organization would include, among others:

- The removal of an underground fuel storage tank
- The dismantling of a cogeneration plant
- A requirement to undo modifications made to leased property
- A gift of a building with stipulation from the donor that after ten years the building is to be destroyed and the land converted into a garden
- The legal requirement to remove or abate asbestos in buildings

The calculation to estimate an asset retirement obligation is complex. For each asset retirement obligation, the entity must determine a settlement date, a settlement method, and a settlement cost using a current valuation. Then the current cost must be inflated to the estimated settlement date using a reasonable inflation rate. Finally, the inflated cost must be reported at its present value using a credit-adjusted risk-free rate of return. On an annual basis, the valuation of the asset retirement obligation must be updated and adjusted as necessary.

The five steps to evaluate asset retirement obligations for older assets, new assets, or on an ongoing basis are the same:

1. Take an inventory of long-lived assets that have asset retirement obligations.

2. Gather information from legal advisors, facilities management, and others.

3. Using the information gathered from others, measure the obligation.

4. Develop written policies and procedures to codify accounting for FIN 47/SFAS 143 transactions.

5. Develop financial reports and disclosures.

For many organizations with a fiscal year-end June 30, 2006, the effect of implementing FIN 47 was presented as a cumulative effect of a change in accounting principle in the statement of activities.

# CHAPTER SIX

# Investment Income, Gains and Losses, and Endowment Funds

## § 6.1  ACCOUNTING PRINCIPLES

### (h)  Display of Investment Income When a "Spending Formula" Is Used

**p. 67. Add the following as last paragraph in** *subsection (h):*

The National Conference of Commissioners on Uniform State Laws (NCCUSL) has approved a comprehensively revised version of UMIFA, called the Uniform Prudent Management of Institutional Funds Act, or UPMIFA. This new law, if adopted by the various state and territorial legislatures, is anticipated to have widespread implications for nonprofit organizations, including:

- Elimination of the historic dollar-value limitation on spending (the so-called "underwater funds" rule)

- Broadening the scope covered by the statute, which is intended to apply to trusts, governmental agencies, and any other type of entity dedicated to charitable purposes, as well as nonprofit organizations

- Comprehensive incorporation of modern portfolio investment standards by providing for diversification of assets, pooling of assets, total return investment, and whole portfolio management

- An endorsement of the concept of intergenerational equity via an optional provision that allows states to find that an organization spending more than 7 percent of its endowment in one year is acting imprudently

UPMIFA was approved by 300 state law commissioners on July 13, 2006, at NCCUSL's annual meeting. The act will now go to the American Bar Association for approval; after that, it will be introduced into the legislature of each jurisdiction. If signed into law, UPMIFA will replace UMIFA, which has been the standard in 48 states for the past three and one-half decades.

While UPMIFA adds only one word to UMIFA's title, the underlying change in the law is major in both structure and significance. UMIFA had gone unchanged over its entire 34-year existence. If adopted, UPMIFA will likely reshape the landscape of nonprofit fund management and investment.

Under UPMIFA, the rules governing expenditures from endowment funds could be modified to give a governing board more flexibility in making investment and expenditure decisions within the general standard of prudence, so that the board can cope with fluctuations in the value of the endowment.

The web site www.upmifa.org provides an up-to-date status of which states have passed UPMIFA as well as comparisons of the versions passed in different states.

UPMIFA eliminates the concept of "historical gift value," and relies on a "prudence" standard, which specifies that spending above 7 percent creates a rebuttable presumption of imprudence:

> The appropriation for expenditure in any year if an amount greater than seven percent of the fair market value of an endowment fund, calculated on the basis of market values determined at least quarterly and averaged over a period of not less than three years immediately preceding the year

in which the appropriation for expenditure was made, creates a rebuttable presumption of imprudence. [Section 4 (d)]

The Act also includes a process for releasing or modifying restrictions on a gift, and specifies appropriate circumstances for doing so:

If an institution determines that a restriction contained in a gift instrument on the management, investment, or purpose of an institutional fund is unlawful, impracticable, impossible to achieve, or wasteful, the institution, [60 days] after notification to the [Attorney General], may release or modify the restriction, in whole or part, if:

1) the institutional fund subject to the restriction has a total value of less than [$25,000]; 2) more than [20] years have elapsed since the fund was established; and 3) the institution uses the property in a manner the institution reasonably determines to be consistent with the charitable purposes expressed in the gift instrument. [Section 6 (d)]

In August 2008, the FASB issued Staff Position SFAS 117-1, *Endowments of Not-for-Profit Organizations: Net Asset Classification of Funds Subject to an Enacted Version of the Uniform Prudent Management of Institutional Funds Act, and Enhanced Disclosures for All Endowment Funds.* This FASB Staff Position (FSP) provides guidance concerning: (1) the disclosures that not-for-profit organizations should make with regard to their endowments, and (2) the effect of a state's adoption of the model Uniform Prudent Management of Institutional Funds Act of 2006 (UPMIFA) on the classification of net assets related to donor-restricted endowment funds of not-for-profit organizations within that state. The key provisions of the FSP are as follows.

**Expanded Disclosure Requirements for All Endowments.** FSP proposes a number of new disclosures that would be required for endowments of all not-for-profit organizations, not just endowments held in states where UPMIFA has been enacted. These include:

- A description of the governing board's interpretation of the law that underlies the net asset classification of donor–restricted endowment funds

- A description of endowment spending policies
- A description of endowment investment policies, including the organization's return objectives and risk parameters, how those objectives relate to the organization's endowment spending policies, and the strategies employed for achieving those objectives
- An endowment reconciliation by financial statement net asset class that shows cumulative investment returns in the permanently restricted net asset class that relate to the organization's interpretation of relevant law, rather than what is required by explicit donor stipulation
- The composition of an organization's endowment by net asset classification at the end of the period, in total and by type of endowment fund, showing donor–restricted endowment funds separately from board–designated endowment funds
- A reconciliation of the beginning and ending balances of the organization's endowment, in total and by net asset class, including, at a minimum, the following line items:
  - Investment return, separated into investment income and net appreciation or depreciation of investments
  - Contributions
  - Amounts appropriated for expenditure
  - Reclassifications
  - Other changes
- Disclosure of how much (if any) of additions of investment return to permanently restricted net assets in the current period are the result of the organization's interpretation of relevant law, beyond that required by explicit donor stipulations
- Planned appropriation for expenditures, if known, for the year following the most recent period for which the organization presents financial statements

The FSP provides an illustrative example of such disclosures.

**PwC Observations:** In substance, the changes brought about by UPMIFA merely provide organizations with short-term spending flexibility to deal with market declines that result in underwater situations. While the amount of assets associated with an endowment fund might fluctuate, the accountability to the donor for a permanent endowment remains unchanged.

Apart from the new disclosure requirements that apply to all organizations with endowments, the FSP may also impact net asset accounting depending on the relevant state UPMIFA law. In light of the short time frame for implementation, not-for-profit organizations should start preparing for the proposed FSP's expanded disclosure requirements as quickly as possible.

# CHAPTER SEVEN

# Affiliated Organizations, Pass-Through Transactions, and Mergers

## §7.2 DEFINITION OF THE REPORTING ENTITY

### (b) Combined Financial Statements

*p. 87. Insert the following sentence after the first sentence of the first bullet:

Sole corporate membership of one not-for-profit organization in another constitutes a controlling financial interest unless control does not rest with the sole corporate member.

*p. 87. Insert the following as a new subsection after *subsection (i)*:

**(ii) FASB Staff Position No. SOP 94-3-1 and AAG HCO-1.**  In May 2008, the FASB issued Staff Position No. SOP 94-3-1 and AAG HCO-1,

*Omnibus Changes to Consolidation and Equity Method Guidance for Not-for-Profit Organizations.*

The FASB Staff Position (FSP) made several changes to the guidance on consolidation and the equity method of accounting in AICPA Statement of Position 94-3, Reporting of Related Entities by Not-for-Profit Organizations, and the AICPA Audit and Accounting Guide, Health Care Organizations. This FSP:

a. Eliminates the temporary control exception to consolidation that currently exists for certain relationships between not-for-profit organizations, and makes two related changes:

   1. Amends the definition of majority voting interest in the board of another entity in SOP 94-3 and the health care Guide

   2. Conforms the categorization of sole corporate membership in SOP 94-3 to that in the health care Guide

b. Confirms the continued applicability to not-for-profit organizations of the guidance on consolidation of special-purpose entities in the following EITF Issues:

   1. No. 90-15, "Impact of Nonsubstantive Lessors, Residual Value Guarantees, and Other Provisions in Leasing Transactions"

   2. No. 96-21, "Implementation Issues in Accounting for Leasing Transactions Involving Special-Purpose Entities"

   3. No. 97-1, "Implementation Issues in Accounting for Leasing Transactions, Including those Involving Special-Purpose Entities"

c. Requires that not-for-profit organizations apply the guidance on the equity method of accounting in the following pronouncements to their investments in for-profit partnerships, limited liability companies (LLCs), and similar entities unless those investments are reported at fair value:

   1. AICPA Statement of Position 78-9, Accounting for Investments in Real Estate Ventures

2. EITF Issue No. 03-16, "Accounting for Investments in Limited Liability Companies"

3. FSP SOP 78-9-1, Interaction of AICPA Statement of Position 78-9 and EITF Issue No. 04-5

The FSP eliminates the exception to consolidation for related but separate not-for-profit organizations if control is likely to be temporary. Consolidation of one not-for-profit organization by another not-for-profit organization shall be required, permitted, or prohibited, depending on whether there is control, an economic interest, or both, and depending on the nature of the control, in accordance with the guidance in paragraphs 11–13 of SOP 94-3 and paragraphs 11.11–11.13 of the health care Guide, regardless of whether that control is likely to be temporary.

> 8. Sole corporate membership of one not-for-profit organization in another shall be considered a controlling financial interest unless control does not rest with the sole corporate member (for instance, if the other [membership] organization is in bankruptcy or if other legal or contractual limitations are so severe that control does not rest with the sole corporate member).
>
> 9. An organization shall be deemed to have a *majority voting interest in the board of another entity* if it has the direct or indirect ability to appoint individuals that together constitute a majority of the votes of the fully constituted board (that is, including any vacant board positions). Those individuals are not limited to the organization's own board members, employees, or officers.

SOP 94-3

| Relationship Type | Par. | Existing Guidance | Amended Guidance |
|---|---|---|---|
| Controlling financial interest through ownership of a majority voting interest | 10 | Consolidation is required unless control does not rest directly or indirectly with the majority owner (no temporary control exception). | No change, except sole corporate membership interests are now included here. |

(*continued*)

SOP 94-3 (*continued*)

| Relationship Type | Par. | Existing Guidance | Amended Guidance |
|---|---|---|---|
| Control through majority voting interest in the board of another entity (by means other than ownership), coupled with an economic interest | 11 | Consolidation is required unless control is likely to be temporary, in which case consolidation is prohibited. (Currently includes sole corporate membership interests, which the health care Guide deems a controlling financial interest.) | Consolidation is required (no temporary control exception). (This FSP also clarifies the definition of majority voting interest.) |
| Control through other means, coupled with an economic interest | 12 | Consolidation is permitted unless control is likely to be temporary, in which case consolidation is prohibited. Disclosures are required if not consolidated. | Consolidation is permitted. Disclosures are required if not consolidated (no temporary control exception). |

Health Care Guide

| Relationship Type | Par. | Existing Guidance | Amended Guidance |
|---|---|---|---|
| Controlling financial interest through ownership of a majority voting interest or sole corporate membership | 11.10 | Consolidation is required unless control does not rest directly or indirectly with the majority owner or sole corporate member (no temporary control exception). | No change. |
| Control through majority voting interest in board of another entity (by means other than ownership or sole corporate membership), coupled with an economic interest | 11.11 | Consolidation is required unless control is likely to be temporary, in which case consolidation is prohibited. | Consolidation is required (no temporary control exception). (This FSP also clarifies the definition of majority voting interest.) |

Health Care Guide (*continued*)

| Relationship Type | Par. | Existing Guidance | Amended Guidance |
|---|---|---|---|
| Control through other means, coupled with an economic interest | 11.12 | Consolidation is permitted unless control is likely to be temporary, in which case consolidation is prohibited. Disclosures are required if not consolidated. | Consolidation is permitted. Disclosures are required if not consolidated (no temporary control exception). |

*PwC Observations: The FSP clearly indicates that not-for-profit organizations should apply the SPE consolidation guidance in EITF Issues 90-15, 96-21, and 97-1. The FSP also clarifies one specific aspect of EITF 90-15, stating that in order for a lessee not to be required to consolidate an SPE lessor, the majority owner(s) of record of the lessor must be an independent third party. The FSP was silent on whether not-for-profit organizations should apply the SEC staff views expressed in EITF 90-15 (Questions 1–9) and Topic D-14, *Transactions Involving SPEs*. However, it explicitly addressed one of the issues covered by Topic D-14; that is, in order for a lessee not to be required to consolidate an SPE lessor, the majority owner(s) of record of the lessor must be an independent third party.

- Affected not-for-profits that do not wish to use the equity method might consider electing fair value measurement for these investments using the instrument-by-instrument option allowed under SFAS 159.

*p. 87. *Subsection (ii)* FASB FIN 46R. Renumber the *subsection (iii)* and replace the first sentence with the following:

In January 2003, the FASB issued Interpretation (FIN) 46, *Consolidation of Variable Interest Entities—An Interpretation of ARB No. 51*, and amended it by issuing FIN 46R in December 2003 and SFAS 167, *Amendment to FIN 46R*, in June 2009.

## §7.3 MERGERS OF NOT-FOR-PROFIT ORGANIZATIONS

### (a) SFAS 141R and 142

*p. 88. Replace the two paragraphs in this section with the following:

In June 2001, the FASB issued SFAS 141, *Business Combination*, as well as SFAS 142, *Goodwill and Other Intangible Assets*. Subsequently SFAS 141 was amended in December 2007 by SFAS 141R. If a not-for-profit organization is acquired by a for-profit organization, the transaction is included within the scope of SFAS 141R. All other transactions involving not-for-profit organizations—that is, mergers of two or more not-for-profit organizations or the acquisition of a for-profit entity by a not-for-profit organization—are excluded from the scope of SFAS 141R. These transactions were addressed by SFAS 164, *Not-for-Profit Entities: Mergers and Acquisitions*, which was issued in May 2009 (see section 7.3 below). Prior to the adoption of SFAS 164, the excluded transactions will continue to be governed by the AICPA's *Accounting Principles Bulletin* (APB) 16, *Business Combinations*.

Not-for-profit organizations are included in the scope of SFAS 142, *Goodwill and Other Intangible Assets*. However the effective date was deferred until the effective date of SFAS 164. As a result, not-for-profit organizations should continue to follow the guidance in APB 17, *Intangible Assets*, with respect to accounting for intangible assets.

### (b) FASB 164, Not-for-Profit Entities: Mergers and Acquisitions

*p. 89. Replace the material after the second paragraph with the following:

In May 2009, the FASB issued *Not-for-Profit Entities: Mergers and Acquisitions, Including an Amendment of SFAS 142*. The Statement provides guidance on accounting for both mergers of not-for-profit organizations and acquisitions by not-for-profit organizations. It also amends FASB Statement No. 142, *Goodwill and Other Intangible Assets*, to make that Statement fully applicable to not-for-profit organizations.

SFAS 164 should be applied prospectively to mergers occurring on or after December 15, 2009, and to acquisitions occurring in annual periods beginning on or after December 15, 2009. Early application is *prohibited.* The SFAS 142 amendments are effective for annual reporting periods beginning on or after December 15, 2009.

Under SFAS 164, most not-for-profit mergers and acquisitions will be accounted for under the acquisition method. However, where all of the combining organizations cede control to a new economic entity (as opposed to one organization obtaining control over other organizations), the assets and liabilities of the combining organizations would be brought into the new entity at their carryover basis, similar to pooling under APB 16.

A merger occurs when the governing bodies of all the combining entities cede control of their respective organizations to a new entity with a newly-formed governing body. The combining entities in a merger cannot obtain control of (or continue to control) the other entities, or dominate the merger transaction. A merger is accounted for using carryover basis (i.e., the carrying value of the assets and liabilities of the combined entities).

Combinations that are not mergers are acquisitions. Identification of the acquirer will require consideration of all facts and circumstances surrounding a combination, in particular, the ability of one organization to dominate the process of selecting a voting majority of the combined organization's governing board. SFAS 164 details various indicators organizations should consider when identifying an acquirer. The Board purposely provided guidance in the form of principles, rather than prescriptive criteria.

Once the acquirer is identified, the value of the acquired entities must be measured. This requires considering the fair value of (a) the identifiable assets acquired; (b) the liabilities assumed; and (c) the consideration transferred (if any).

If the fair value of identifiable assets acquired is greater than the fair value of liabilities assumed and consideration transferred, the acquirer recognizes contribution income. The contribution increases permanently restricted, temporarily restricted, and/or unrestricted net assets depending on the existence and types of donor-imposed restrictions that must be assumed.

If the fair value of liabilities assumed and consideration transferred exceeds the fair value of identifiable assets acquired, the accounting varies depending on whether the acquiree's operations are expected to be predominantly supported by contributions and investment return or, alternatively, by revenue earned in exchange transactions.

- If the acquiree will be predominantly contribution-supported, the excess is immediately expensed (as if the acquirer had made a contribution in taking on the acquired entity). This amount is reported as a separate line item in the statement of activities.

- If the acquiree's operations are expected to be predominantly supported by revenue earned in exchange transactions, the acquired net deficit represents goodwill.

As it relates to goodwill and intangible assets, the Board concluded that at the date of acquisition, the assets acquired and liabilities assumed (including goodwill, if any) should be assigned to reporting units as described in SFAS 142. In assigning assets and liabilities to reporting units, acquirers will use operating segment concepts from SFAS 131, *Disclosures about Segments of an Enterprise and Related Information.*

Additionally, the amendments to SFAS 142 require that goodwill and certain intangible assets that have indefinite useful lives will no longer be amortized. Intangible assets that have finite useful lives would continue to be amortized over their useful lives. An acquirer predominantly supported by contributions and investment returns would write off any previously recognized goodwill; all other acquirers must perform SFAS 142's transitional impairment evaluation on any preexisting goodwill.

Lastly, SFAS 164 provides not-for-profit reporting model guidance for reporting a not-for-profit's minority interest (now referred to as "noncontrolling interest") in subsidiaries. Noncontrolling interests should be reported on the balance sheet as a separate component of the appropriate net asset class.

# CHAPTER EIGHT

# Contributions, Pledges, and Noncash Contributions

## § 8.2 GIFTS-IN-KIND

### (a) Fixed Assets (Land, Buildings, and Equipment) and Supplies

**p. 109. Insert the following new paragraph before *subsection (b)*:**

The noncash contribution of physical assets must be valued under the provisions of SFAS 157 (fiscal years beginning after November 15, 2008), *Fair Value Measurements*, and an organization must look at the "highest and best use" of the physical asset and what is the most advantageous market. How the organization is planning on utilizing the physical asset is irrelevant. The perspective has to be that of a willing market participant—an unbiased, impartial, independent party who is a hypothetical buyer in the market for this physical asset—and what they would be willing to pay to acquire the physical asset based on what they would view as the most profitable use of the asset. SFAS 157 includes examples of such situations and should be referred to in order to better understand this concept.

Unless the contributed physical asset represents "other investments" that are carried at fair value by the organization on a recurring basis, the contribution is measured at fair value only at initial recognition and therefore no additional disclosures under SFAS 157 are required. However, if the organization reports alternative investments at fair value under the Audit Guide, then the disclosures under SFAS 157 for recurring measurements would be required.

## § 8.3 SUPPORT NOT CURRENTLY EXPENDABLE

**(b) Pledges (Promises to Give)**

**(iii) Discounted to Present Value**

*p. 117. Insert the following new paragraphs before *subsection (iv)*:

The AICPAS's Not-for-Profit Expert Panel developed and presented a draft white paper to the AICPA's Accounting Standards Executive Committee (AcSEC) on not-for-profit FASB Statement No. 157 issues. Specifically, the project addresses issues pertaining to

- The fair value of unconditional promises to give cash.
- Interests in perpetual trusts held by third parties.
- Split-interest agreements.

At its September 2009 meeting, AICPA's Accounting Standards Executive Committee AcSEC generally supported the conclusions in the documents it considered and approved them for posting to the AICPA.org for informal public input, subject to AcSEC Chair clearance, with an aim toward issuing the non-authoritative Issues Paper fourth quarter of 2009.

The agenda materials and highlights of the AcSEC meeting can be found at http://www.aicpa.org/Professional+Resources/Accounting +and+Auditing/Accounting+Standards/general/September+22-23 +2009+AcSEC+Agenda+Materials.htm.

**Fair Value of Unconditional Promises.** Paragraphs B4 and B5 of SFAS 157 state:

> B4. A fair value measurement, using present value, is made under conditions of uncertainty because the cash flows used are estimates rather than known amounts. In many cases, both the amount and timing of the cash flows will be uncertain. Even contractually fixed amounts, like the payments on a loan, will be uncertain if there is risk of default.
>
> B5. Risk-averse market participants generally seek compensation for bearing the uncertainty inherent in the cash flows of an asset or liability (risk premium). A fair value measurement should include a risk premium reflecting the amount market participants would demand because of the risk (uncertainty) in the cash flows. Otherwise, the measurement would not faithfully represent fair value. In some cases, determining the appropriate risk premium might be difficult. However, the degree of difficulty alone is not a sufficient basis on which to exclude a risk adjustment.

Therefore, AcSEC believes it is necessary to consider risk in fair value measurements of multi-year pledges. Such considerations of risk would include the donor's ability to pay, factors that may impact the donor's commitment to honor its promise, and the not-for-profit's historical experience with similar pledges. If the underlying asset is held in an irrevocable trust, that would serve to reduce the associated risk.

The white paper will also discuss the two different present value techniques that are described further in Appendix B of SFAS 157.

**Interests in Perpetual Trusts Held by Third Parties.** AcSEC believes that the guidance in SFAS 117 and Chapter 6 of the Not-for-Profit Audit Guide continues to be relevant and that the not-for-profit should value such an interest at fair value of the assets contributed to the trust.

**Split-Interest Agreements.** As the assets of split-interest agreements are generally recognized at fair value, the question becomes how to calculate fair value of the liability. AcSEC differentiated between those situations with fixed payments versus those situations with variable payments, and it is suggested that the reader refer to the white paper for guidance in his or her specific situation.

Paragraph 6.06 of the NFP Guide provides that "[r]eference to IRS guidelines and actuarial tables used in calculating the donor's charitable deduction for income tax purposes may be helpful in assessing the reasonableness of the method used for measuring fair value." However, AcSEC felt this was not the case:

> AcSEC believes that tables provided by the IRS or tables in planned giving software based on those IRS tables may be inappropriate for estimating fair value of liabilities under split-interest agreements with fixed payments. For example, life expectancy tables are updated annually, yet the IRS tables are only updated every 10 years. The updates to the tables issued in May 2009 were based on the 2000 census and likely will not be replaced until 2019, at which time the mortality statistics will be 19 years old. The tables updated by the May 2009 publications were based on mortality statistics from 1989–1991. Further, actuarial assumptions and the resulting actuarial tables used in IRS tables and software based on those tables may be based on the population at large, rather than the population likely to buy an annuity or enter into a split-interest agreement. AcSEC believes evidence exists that the population likely to buy an annuity or enter into a split-interest agreement has a greater life expectancy than the general population, because of the demonstrated relationship between wealth, health, and expected life. AcSEC believes that quoted market prices for fixed-payment annuities in active markets appropriately consider the estimated life of the relevant pool of annuitants.

# CHAPTER NINE

# Accounting Issues Relating to Fundraising

## §9.1 ACCOUNTING FOR GIFTS

### (e) Pass-through Gifts

**p. 147. Delete first sentence in fourth complete paragraph beginning with *"The FASB currently . . . "*.**

**p. 147. Insert as fourth complete paragraph:**

In October 2006, the FASB issued two exposure drafts related to its long-standing not-for-profit combinations project. The first exposure draft, "Not-for-Profit Organizations, Mergers, and Acquisitions," would eliminate the use of the pooling-of-interests method of accounting and would instead require the application of the acquisition method. The second exposure draft, "Not-for-Profit Organizations: Goodwill and Other Intangible Assets Acquired in a Merger or Acquisition," proposes guidance for intangible assets acquired after a merger or acquisition.

# PART TWO

# Financial Statement Presentation

# CHAPTER ELEVEN

# Accrual-Basis Financial Statements

## § 11.1  SIMPLE ACCRUAL-BASIS STATEMENTS

**p. 171. Replace with revised Exhibit 11.2:**

**EXHIBIT 11.2**

Example of a Balance Sheet for a Large International Not-for-Profit Organization

**CAMP SQUA PAN, INC.**
**BALANCE SHEET**
DECEMBER 31, 20X1 and 20X2

| ASSETS | 20X1 | 20X2 |
|---|---|---|
| Current assets: | | |
| Cash | $ 13,107 | $ 9,997 |
| U.S. treasury bills at market | 10,812 | — |
| Accounts receivable | 1,632 | 853 |
| Prepaid insurance | 2,702 | 1,804 |
| Total current assets | 28,253 | 12,654 |

**Exhibit 11.2** (*continued*)

Example of a Simple Accrual-Basis Balance Sheet

**CAMP SQUA PAN, INC.**
**BALANCE SHEET**
DECEMBER 31, 20X1 and 20X2

| ASSETS | 20X1 | 20X2 |
|---|---|---|
| Fixed assets, at cost: | | |
| Land | 13,161 | 13,161 |
| Buildings | 76,773 | 76,773 |
| Furniture | 22,198 | 23,615 |
| Automobiles | 13,456 | 14,175 |
| Canoes and other equipment | 12,025 | 12,675 |
| | 137,613) | 140,399 |
| Less: Accumulated depreciation | (71,242) | (76,629) |
| Net fixed assets | 66,371 | 63,770 |
| Total assets | $ 94,624 | $ 76,424 |
| LIABILITIES AND NET ASSETS | | |
| Current liabilities: | | |
| Accounts payable and accrued expenses | $ 4,279 | $ 3,416 |
| Camp deposits | 18,275 | 1,610 |
| Total current liabilities | 22,554 | 5,026 |
| Deferred compensation payable | 11,820 | 12,650 |
| Total liabilities | 34,374 | 17,676 |
| Unrestricted net assets: | | |
| Original YMCA contribution | 50,000 | 50,000 |
| Accumulated excess of income over expenses | 10,250 | 8,748 |
| Total net assets | 60,250 | 58,748 |
| Total liabilities and net assets | $ 94,624 | $ 76,424 |

# § 11.2 ACCRUAL-BASIS STATEMENTS—FUNDRAISING ORGANIZATION

**p. 175. Replace with revised Exhibit 11.4:**

**EXHIBIT 11.4**

Example of a Simple Accrual-Basis Balance Sheet

**UNITED FUND DRIVE OF RICHMOND HILL, INC.**
**BALANCE SHEET**

| | January 31, | |
| --- | --- | --- |
| ASSETS | 20X1 | 20X2 |
| Cash | $ 38,727 | $  59,805 |
| Pledges receivable, less allowance for uncollectible pledges of $ 31,161 in 20X1 and $ 39,192 in 20X2 | 168,516 | 229,517 |
| Total assets | $ 207,243 | $ 289,322 |
| LIABILITIES AND NET ASSETS | | |
| Allocated to agencies | $ 557,862 | $ 645,284 |
| Less payments to date | (361,536) | (389,517) |
| Net unpaid | 196,326 | 255,767 |
| Payroll taxes and accounts payable | 3,615 | 8,715 |
| Total liabilities | 199,941 | 264,482 |
| Net assets (unrestricted) | 7,302 | 24,840 |
| Total liabilities and net assets | $ 207,243 | $ 289,322 |

## § 11.3 ACCRUAL-BASIS STATEMENTS— INTERNATIONAL ORGANIZATION

**p. 176. Replace with revised Exhibit 11.5:**

### Exhibit 11.5

Example of a Simple Accrual-Basis Balance Sheet for a Typical United Fund Drive

**CHILDREN OVERSEAS INC.**
**CONSOLIDATED STATEMENT OF ACTIVITIES IN UNRESTRICTED NET ASSETS**
(IN THOUSANDS)

|  | For the Year Ended June 30, | |
|---|---|---|
|  | 20X1 | 20X2 |
| Income: | | |
| Pledges for children | $ 9,210 | $ 9,073 |
| Gifts for special purposes | 1,372 | 1,514 |
| Contributions and bequests | 450 | 661 |
| Government grants | 155 | 82 |
| Investment and miscellaneous income | 44 | 74 |
| Unrealized gain (loss) on investments | (44) | 92 |
| Total income | 11,187 | 11,496 |
| Expenses (Exhibit 11.6) | | |
| Aid and services to children | 8,649 | 8,206 |
| Supporting operations | 2,081 | 2,353 |
| Fundraising | 454 | 583 |
| Total expenses | 11,184 | 11,142 |
| Change in unrestricted net assets | 3 | 354 |
| Net assets, beginning of year | 1,449 | 1,452 |
| Net assets, end of year | $ 1,452 | $ 1,835 |

## p. 178. Replace with revised Exhibit 11.7:

**EXHIBIT 11.7**

Example of a Comparative Statement of Income, Expenses, and Changes in Net
Assets for a Large International Not-for-Profit Organization

**CHILDREN OVERSEAS INC.**
**CONSOLIDATED BALANCE SHEET**
(IN THOUSANDS)

|  | June 30, | |
| --- | --- | --- |
| **ASSETS** | 20X1 | 20X2 |
| Cash | $   563 | $   704 |
| Investments, at market | 1,066 | 1,331 |
| Accounts receivable: | | |
| Estimated unpaid pledges and gifts due from foster parents | 155 | 135 |
| Foreign government grants | 24 | 18 |
| U.S. government grants | 3 | 3 |
| Other receivables | — | 22 |
| Prepaid expenses | 73 | 35 |
| Land, building, equipment, net of accumulated for depreciation of $ 85 in 20X1 and 20X2 | 60 | 65 |
| Total assets | $ 1,944 | $ 2,313 |
| **LIABILITIES AND NET ASSETS** | | |
| Liabilities: | | |
| Accounts payable and accrued payroll taxes | $     84 | $     48 |
| Estimated statutory severance pay liability | 92 | 101 |
| Unremitted gifts for special purposes | 316 | 329 |
| Total liabilities | 492 | 478 |
| Unrestricted net assets | 1,452 | 1,835 |
| Total liabilities and net assets | $ 1,944 | $ 2,313 |

# CHAPTER TWELVE

# Multiclass Financial Statements

## § 12.2   PREPARATION OF STATEMENT OF CASH FLOWS

**p. 187. Replace with revised Exhibit 12.3:**

### EXHIBIT 12.3

Sample Performing Arts Organization Statement of Financial Activity ($000) Year Ended June 30, 20X2

|  | Unrestricted | Temporarily Restricted | Permanently Restricted | Total |
|---|---|---|---|---|
| Operating revenue |  |  |  |  |
| Ticket sales | $ 857 |  |  | $ 857 |
| Other performance fees | 128 |  |  | 128 |
| Concessions | 103 |  |  | 103 |
| Investment income | 21 | $ 2 |  | 23 |
| Gains/losses on investments | 55 |  | $ 4 | 59 |
| Net assets released from restrictions | 188 | (188) |  | — |
| Total operating revenue | 1,352 | (186) | 4 | 1,170 |
| Operating expenses: |  |  |  |  |
| Regular season productions | 815 |  |  | 815 |
| Ballet school | 201 |  |  | 201 |

**EXHIBIT 12.3**

Sample Performing Arts Organization Statement of Financial Activity ($000) Year Ended June 30, 20X2 (*continued*)

| | Unrestricted | Temporarily Restricted | Permanently Restricted | Total |
|---|---|---|---|---|
| Other production | 378 | | | 378 |
| Production administration | 497 | | | 497 |
| Management and general | 390 | | | 390 |
| Total operating expenses | 2,281 | —— | —— | 2,281 |
| Deficiency from operations | (929) | (186) | 4 | (1,111) |
| Support: | | | | |
| Annual giving | 584 | 39 | | 623 |
| Grants | 140 | 125 | | 265 |
| Endowment gifts | | | 4 | 4 |
| Governments | 200 | 30 | | 230 |
| Donated services and materials | 43 | | | 43 |
| Less: Fundraising costs | (36) | —— | —— | (36) |
| Net support | 931 | 194 | 4 | 1,129 |
| Change in net assets: | | | | |
| Unrestricted | 2 | | | 2 |
| Temporarily restricted | | 8 | | 8 |
| Permanently restricted | —— | —— | 8 | 8 |
| Total change in net assets | 2 | | 8 | 18 |
| Net Assets: | | | | |
| Beginning of year | 211 | 44 | 69 | 324 |
| End of year | $ 213 | $ 52 | $77 | $ 342 |

(Complete comparative prior year information can be presented on a separate page, or a total column for the prior year added at the right side of this page.)

## pp. 192–194. Replace with revised Exhibit 12.6:

### Exhibit 12.6

| Worksheet for Statement of Cash Flows—Direct Method | | | |
|---|---|---|---|
| | Current | Prior | [Dr. (Cr.)] Balance Sheet Changes |
| Balance Sheet [A] | | [B] | |
| Cash | $116 | $169 | $(53) |
| Short-term investments | 154 | 151 | 3 |
| Accounts receivable, net of allowance | 70 | 28 | 42 |
| Grants receivable | 28 | 6 | 22 |
| Long-term investments, at market value | 180 | 156 | 24 |
| Property and equipment, net of depreciation | 155 | 140 | 15 |
| Rent and other deposits | 4 | 9 | (5) |
| Other assets | 11 | 13 | (2) |
| Accounts payable and accrued expenses | $111 | $ 66 | (45) |
| Deferred season subscription revenue | 206 | 193 | (13) |
| Current portion of mortgage | 30 | 30 | 0 |
| Mortgage payable, 8%, due 20X3 | 29 | 59 | 30 |
| Total net assets | 342 | 324 | (18) |
| | | | 0 |

| [C] Income Statement: | Unrestricted | Temporarily Restricted | Permanently Restricted | Total |
|---|---|---|---|---|
| Operating revenue: | | | | |
| Ticket sales | $857 | | [D] | $(857) |
| Other performance fees | 128 | | | (128) |
| Concessions | 103 | | | (103) |
| Investment income | 21 | $2 | | (23) |
| Gains/losses on investments | 55 | | $4 | (59) |

Exhibit 12.6

| Worksheet for Statement of Cash Flows—Direct Method (*continued*) | | | |
| --- | --- | --- | --- |
| | **Current** | **Prior** | **[Dr. (Cr.)] Balance Sheet Changes** |
| Net assets released from restrictions | 188 | (188) | 0 |
| Operating expenses: | | | |
| Regular season productions | 815 | | 815 |
| Ballet school | 201 | | 201 |
| Other productions | 378 | | 378 |
| Production administration | 497 | | 497 |
| Management and general | 390 | | 390 |
| Total operating expenses | 2,281 | | 2,281 |
| Interest | | | |
| Support: | | | |
| Annual giving | 584 | 39 | (623) |
| Grants | 140 | 125 | (265) |
| Endowments gifts | | 4 | (4) |
| Governments | 200 | 30 | (230) |
| Donated services and materials | 43 | | (43) |
| Less: Fundraising costs | (36) | — | (36) |
| Change in net assets | 2 | 8 | 8 | 18 |
| | | | 0 |

Noncash financing and investing items (memo):

| [E] | | [G] | [H] | | [I] | | | [J] |
| --- | --- | --- | --- | --- | --- | --- | --- | --- |
| | | | | | | | [Source (Use)] | |
| **Reclassifications** | | | **Gross-up** | | **Statement of Cash Flows** | | | |
| **Within B/S or P/L** | **Between B/S & P/L** | **Subtotal** | **Purchases** | **Sales** | **Operating** | **Investing** | **Financing** | **Other** |
| | | (53) | | | | | | (53) |
| [1](3) | | 0 | | | | | | |
| | [6](42) | 0 | | | | | | |
| | [7](22) | 0 | | | | [(84) | | |
| [1]3 | [8](59) | (32) | 84 | (116) | | -[116 | | |

# MULTICLASS FINANCIAL STATEMENTS

## Exhibit 12.6

### Worksheet for Statement of Cash Flows—Direct Method (continued)

| [E] | | [G] | [H] | | [I] | | [J] | |
|---|---|---|---|---|---|---|---|---|
| Reclassifications | | | Gross-up | | [Source (Use)] Statement of Cash Flows | | | |
| Within B/S or P/L | Between B/S & P/L | Subtotal | Purchases | Sales | Operating | Investing | Financing | Other |
| | [9](10)20[10] | 25 | | | | (25) | | |
| | [11]5 | 0 | | | | | | |
| | [12](7)9[13] | 0 | | | | | | |
| | [14]45 | 0 | | | | | | |
| | [15]13 | 0 | | | | | | |
| [2]30 | | 30 | | | | | (30) | |
| [2](30) | | 0 | | | | | | |
| | [16]18 | 0 | | | | | | |
| | [15](13) | (870) | | 870 | | | | |
| | [6]42]- | (189) | | 189 | | | | |
| | ] | | | | | | | |
| | | (23) | | 23 | | | | |
| | [8]59 | 0 | | | | | | |
| -[[4](43) | [10](20)] | | | | | | | |
| [[5]36 | [11](5)]- | 2,190 | | (2,190) | | | | |
| [[3](5) | [13](9)] | | | | | | | |
| | [14](45)] | | | | | | | |
| [3]5 | | 5 | | (5) | | | | |
| | [12]7] | | | | | | | |
| | [9]10] | | | | | | | |
| | [7]22]- | (1,079) | | 1,079 | | | | |
| | | (4) | | | | 4 | | |
| | ] | | | | | | | |
| [4]43 | | 0 | | | | | | |
| [5](36) | | 0 | | | | | | |
| ___ | [16](18) | 0 | | | | | | |
| 0 | 0 | | | | (34) | +7 | +(26) | =(53) |
| [F] | | | | | | | | |
| | [9]10 | | | Equipment | | | | $10 |
| | [12]7 | | | Life insurance | | | | 7 |

## Exhibit 12.6

### Worksheet for Statement of Cash Flows—Direct Method (continued)

1. To group change in short-term investments (other than those that are cash equivalents; these are included with cash) with change in long-term investments.

2. To move change in long-term portion of mortgage to the line related to the actual payment made—that is, the current portion. (This entry is really just a formality, and need not be made.)

3. To break interest paid (requires separate disclosure) out of operating expenses. Number obtained from general ledger.

4. To offset noncash donation against the expense reflecting use of the donated item. (Note: This does not appear as part of the supplemental disclosure of noncash transactions, since it is an operating item, not financing or investing.) Number obtained from contribution records.

5. To include fundraising costs (reported as an offset against contributions) with other cash expenses.

6. To adjust performance fee revenue for change in related receivables.

7. To adjust grant revenue for change in related receivable.

8. To reclassify gain on sale of investments to the investment line.

9. To reduce contribution revenue and the change in fixed assets by the amount of donated fixed assets. (This is one of the supplemental noncash items disclosed, since it is an investing transaction.) Number obtained from contribution records.

10. To reclassify depreciation expense to the fixed assets line. Number obtained from general ledger.

11. To adjust operating expenses for the change in prepaid expenses.

12. To reduce contributions, and change in other assets, by the amount of the donated life insurance policy. Number obtained from contribution records. This is also a separate disclosure item.

13. To adjust operating expenses for the change in other assets. Note that this entry cannot be made until after entry 12 since this is really a plug to zero out the change in other assets, after reflecting the change due to the life insurance policy, which must be treated separately since it is a noncash item.

14. To adjust operating expenses by the change in payables and accruals.

15. To adjust ticket sale revenue by the amount of the change in deferred ticket revenue.

16. To offset the two changes in total net assets numbers.

These entries are illustrative only; not all will be required for every organization, and additional entries will be required for many organizations.

## pp. 196–197. Replace with revised Exhibit 12.7:

EXHIBIT 12.7

### Worksheet for Reconciliation to Operating Cash Flows

| Balance Sheet | Current | Prior | [B] | [Dr. (Cr.)]<br>[Balance Sheet<br>Changes |
|---|---|---|---|---|
| Cash | $116 | $169 | | $(53) |
| Short-term investment | 154 | | | 3 |
| Accounts receivable, net of allowance | 70 | 28 | | 42 |
| Grants receivable | 28 | 6 | | 22 |
| Long-term investments, at market value | 180 | 156 | | 24 |
| Property and equipment, net of depreciation | 155 | 140 | | 15 |
| Rent and other deposits | 4 | 9 | | (5) |
| Other assets | 11 | 13 | | (2) |
| [A] | | | | |
| Accounts payable and accrued expenses | $111 | $ 66 | | (45) |
| Deferred season subscription revenue | 206 | 193 | | (13) |
| Current portion of mortgage | 30 | 30 | | 0 |
| Mortgage payable, 8%, due 20X3 | 29 | 59 | | 30 |
| Total net assets | 342 | 324 | | (18) |
| Items to reconcile to operating cash flows: | | | | 0 |
| Gain on sales | | | | |
| Depreciation | | | | |
| Noncash contributions: | | | | |
| Equipment | | | | |
| Life insurance | | | | |
| Services and materials | | | | |
| Expense representing use of donated services and materials | | | | |
| Nonexpendable gift | | | | |
| Financing cash flow—nonexpendable gift | | | | |
| (Steps C, D not used) | | | | |

**Exhibit 12.7**

Worksheet for Reconciliation to Operating Cash Flows (*continued*)

| [E] | [F] | [G] | [H] | | [I] | | [J] |
|---|---|---|---|---|---|---|---|
| Reclassifications | | Gross-up | | | [Source (Use)] Statement of Cash Flows | | |
| Within B/S or P/L | Between B/S & P/L | Subtotal | Purchases | Sales | Operating | Financing Investing | Other |
| | | (53) | | | | | (53) |
| [1](3) | | — | | | | | |
| | | 42 | | | (42) | | |
| | | 22 | | | (22) | | |
| [1]3 | [8](59) | (32) | 84 | (116) | | 32 | |
| | [9](10)20[10] | 25 | | | | (25) | |
| | | (5) | | | 5 | | |
| | [12](7) | (9) | | | 9 | | |
| | | (45) | | | 45 | | |
| | | (13) | | | 13 | | |
| [2]30 | | 30 | | | | (30) | |
| [2](30) | | — | | | | | |
| | | (18) | | | 18 | | |
| | [8]59 | 59 | | | (59) | | |
| | [10](20) | (20) | | | 20 | | |
| | [9]10 | 10 | | | (10) | | |
| | [12]7 | 7 | | | (7) | | |
| [4](43) | | | | | | | |
| | | 0 | | | | | |
| [4](43) | | | | | | | |
| | | 4 | | | | | |
| [17]4 | | | | | (4) | | |
| [17](4) | | (4) | | | | 4 | |
| 0 | 0 | 0 | | | (34) | +(19) | =(53) |

[F] − (26)

[I]  −7

(19)

# §12.3 "CLASS" FINANCIAL STATEMENTS EXPLAINED

## p. 207. Replace with revised Exhibit 12.11:

### Exhibit 12.11

Example of a Columnar Statement of Income, Expenses, and Changes in Net Assets

THE MCLEAN COMMUNITY SERVICE CENTER STATEMENT OF INCOME, EXPENSES,
AND CHANGES IN NET ASSETS
For the Year Ended August 31, 20X1

| | Unrestricted | Temporarily Restricted | Permanently Restricted | Total |
|---|---|---|---|---|
| Income: | | | | |
| Contributions and gifts | $ 85,000 | $ 24,000 | $ 25,000 | $134,000 |
| Service fees | 110,000 | | | 110,000 |
| Investment income from endowment | 20,000 | | | 20,000 |
| Gains on sale of investments | 40,000 | | 6,000 | 46,000 |
| Other | 13,000 | | | 13,000 |
| | 268,000 | 24,000 | 31,000 | 323,000 |
| Net assets released from restrictions | 23,000 | (23,000) | | |
| Total income | 291,000 | 1,000 | 31,000 | 323,000 |
| Expenses: | | | | |
| Program services | 163,000 | | | 163,000 |
| Administration | 43,000 | | | 43,000 |
| Fundraising | 12,000 | | | 12,000 |
| Total expenses | 218,000 | | | 218,000 |
| Excess of income over expenses | 73,000 | 1,000 | 31,000 | 105,000 |
| Reclassification of unrestricted net assets to meet terms of challenge grant | (25,000) | | 25,000 | |
| Change in net assets | 48,000 | 1,000 | 56,000 | 105,000 |
| Net assets, beginning of year | 82,000 | 10,000 | 225,000 | 317,000 |
| Net assets, end of year | $130,000 | $11,000 | $281,000 | $422,000 |

# Financial Statements of Not-for-Profit Organizations—Review Points

**(b) Balance Sheet**

**(i) Net Assets.**

**p. 225. Replace first bullet with the following:**

- The amount of temporarily and/or permanently restricted net assets must equal or exceed pledges receivable (normally).

**p. 225. Replace second bullet with the following:**

- If the unrestricted net assets caption includes a subcaption for equity in fixed assets, this caption should equal (or at least approximate) the net of fixed assets minus long-term debt used to finance fixed assets.

# PART THREE

# Accounting and Reporting Guidelines

# CHAPTER THIRTEEN

# Voluntary Health and Welfare Organizations

## § 13.2  ACCOUNTING FOR CONTRIBUTIONS

### (g)  Timing of Reporting of Gifts

### (ii) Pledges.

**p. 236. Replace fourth sentence in *subsection (ii)* with the following:**

The discount is then accreted (or built up) to fair value over the period between the time the pledge is made and the time it is due to be paid.

## § 13.5 ACCOUNTING FOR ASSETS

### (a) Carrying Value of Investments

**p. 237. Replace third sentence of second paragraph with the following:**

The audit guide for *Not-for-Profit Organizations* states (in paragraph 8.11 and Appendix 6-A of Chapter 6) that these other investments should be reported in accordance with whichever one of the old audit guides was applicable to the type of organization concerned.

### (b) Fixed-Asset Accounting

### (i) Reason for Depreciation.

**p. 237. Replace *subsection (i)* with the following:**

In discussing the question of depreciation accounting, the *Not-for-Profit Organizations Audit Guide* stated:

> Paragraph 149 of FASB Concepts Statement No. 6, *Elements of Financial Statements*, describes depreciation as a "systematic and rational" process for allocating the cost of using up assets' service potential or economic benefit over the assets' useful economic lives. FASB Statement No. 93, *Recognition of Depreciation by Not-for-Profit Organizations*, requires all not-for-profit organizations to recognize depreciation for all property and equipment except land used as a building site and similar assets and collections. Depreciation should be recognized for contributed property and equipment as well as for plant and equipment acquired in exchange transactions.

## § 13.6 NET ASSETS

### (a) Appropriations

**p. 238. Replace second sentence of second paragraph with the following:**

The expense must be included in the Statement of Support, Revenue and Expenses, and Changes in Net Assets (also called the Statement of Activities).

# §13.7 FINANCIAL STATEMENTS

### p. 239. Replace *Statement 2* with the following:

2.  Statement of Support, Revenue and Expenses, and Changes in Net Assets, or Statement of Activities (Exhibit 13.2)

## (c) Reporting of Expenses

## (iii) Supporting Services.

FUNDRAISING EXPENSES

### p. 247. Replace first sentence of second paragraph with the following:

Fundraising expenses are normally recorded as an expense in the Statement of Support, Revenue and Expenses, and Changes in Net Assets at the time they are incurred.

## (e) Appreciation of Investments

### p. 253. Replace second sentence of *subsection (e)* with the following:

This means that the organization must reflect appreciation (or depreciation) on its Statement of Support, Revenue and Expenses, and Changes in Net Assets (also called the Statement of Activities).

## (g) Statement of Functional Expenses

### p. 256. Replace third sentence of *subsection (g)* with the following:

In order to arrive at the functional expense totals shown in the Statement of Support, Revenue and Expenses, and Changes in Net Assets (also called the Statement of Activities), an analysis must be prepared that shows all of the expenses going into each program category.

### p. 257. Replace with revised Exhibit 13.4:

# Exhibit 13.4

Analysis of the Various Program Expenses Showing the Natural Expense Categories Making Up Each of the Functional or Program Categories

## NATIONAL ASSOCIATION OF ENVIRONMENTALISTS STATEMENT OF FUNCTIONAL EXPENSES
### FOR THE YEAR ENDED DECEMBER 31, 20X2

| | Total All Expenses | Program Services | | | | Supporting Services | | |
| --- | --- | --- | --- | --- | --- | --- | --- | --- |
| | | National Environment Magazine | Clean-up Month Campaign | Lake Erie Project | Total Program | Management and General | Fundraising | Total Supporting |
| Salaries | $170,773 | $24,000 | $68,140 | $60,633 | $152,773 | $15,000 | $3,000 | $18,000 |
| Payroll taxes and employee benefits | 22,199 | 3,120 | 8,857 | 7,882 | 19,859 | 1,950 | 390 | 2,340 |
| Total compensation | 192,972 | 27,120 | 76,997 | 68,515 | 172,632 | 16,950 | 3,390 | 20,340 |
| Printing | 84,071 | 63,191 | 18,954 | 515 | 82,660 | 1,161 | 250 | 1,411 |
| Mailing, postage, and shipping | 14,225 | 10,754 | 1,188 | 817 | 12,759 | 411 | 1,055 | 1,466 |
| Rent | 19,000 | 3,000 | 6,800 | 5,600 | 15,400 | 3,000 | 600 | 3,600 |
| Telephone | 5,615 | 895 | 400 | 1,953 | 3,248 | 2,151 | 216 | 2,367 |
| Outside art | 14,865 | 3,165 | 11,700 | — | 14,865 | — | — | — |
| Local travel | 1,741 | — | 165 | 915 | 1,080 | 661 | — | 661 |
| Conferences and conventions | 6,328 | — | 1,895 | 2,618 | 4,513 | 1,815 | — | 1,815 |
| Depreciation | 13,596 | 2,260 | 2,309 | 5,616 | 10,185 | 3,161 | 250 | 3,411 |
| Legal and audit | 2,000 | — | — | — | — | 2,000 | — | 2,000 |
| Supplies | 31,227 | — | 1,831 | 28,516 | 30,347 | 761 | 119 | 880 |
| Miscellaneous | 6,027 | 115 | 4,378 | — | 4,493 | 1,445 | 89 | 1,534 |
| Total | $391,667 | $110,500 | $126,617 | $115,065 | $352,182 | $33,516 | $5,969 | $39,485 |

VOLUNTARY HEALTH AND WELFARE ORGANIZATIONS

# CHAPTER FOURTEEN

# Colleges and Universities

## § 14.1 AUTHORITATIVE PRONOUNCEMENTS

### (a) AICPA Audit Guide

**p. 263. Replace second sentence of** *subsection (a)* **with the following:**

Then, in 1996, the American Institute of Certified Public Accountants (AICPA) issued a new audit guide (most recently published in 2007) for all not-for-profit organizations, superseding the previous audit guides and authoritative sources that had been used by colleges and universities up to that time, namely, *Not-for-Profit Organizations*.

## § 14.2 THE PRINCIPAL FINANCIAL STATEMENTS

**p. 264. Replace** *Statement 2* **with the following:**

2. Statement of Activities (Exhibit 14.2)

## (b) Statement of Revenues, Expenses, and Changes in Net Assets

**p. 266. Change title of *section (b)* to Statement of Activities and replace first paragraph with the following:**

The Statement of Activities summarizes all of the activity of the institution for the entire period that affects a change in its net assets (net worth). Exhibit 14.2 shows the Statement of Activities for Mary and Isla College.

## § 14.3   ACCOUNTING PRINCIPLES

### (b)   Unrestricted Gifts

**p. 268. Replace paragraph in *subsection (b)* with the following:**

Additional discussion on accounting for contributions is in Chapter 9 of this book and in Chapters 5 and 6 of the AICPA *Audit Guide for Not-for-Profit Organizations*. All unrestricted gifts, donations, and bequests are recorded as unrestricted revenue in the Statement of Activities in the year received. While the board is free to designate any portions of such unrestricted gifts or bequests as "board-designated endowment" or for other designated purposes, such gifts must, nonetheless, be reported in the unrestricted class of net assets. These amounts may also then be segregated and separately identified within the unrestricted net asset class presentation on the statement of financial position in order to indicate the nature of the board designation.

### (c)   Temporarily Restricted Gifts

**p. 269. Replace paragraph in *subsection (c)* with the following:**

Gifts restricted by the donor for a particular purpose or restricted by time (i.e., the gift is due to be received in future periods) are reported in their entirety in the temporarily restricted class in the Statement of Activities, until either the purpose or the time restriction is satisfied. Note, however, that an institution may elect to recognize as "unrestricted revenues" gifts that are secured and expended for the restricted purpose in the same operating period. If an organization adopts this policy, it must be disclosed in the accounting policies footnote.

### (d) Permanently Restricted Gifts

**p. 269. Replace second sentence in *subsection (d)* with the following:**

Further discussion of the treatment of appreciation and depreciation on endowments is included in Chapter 6 of this book.

### (e) Pledges

**p. 269. Replace last sentence in *subsection (e)* with the following:**

Further discussion of accounting for pledges is in Chapters 8 and 9.

### (f) Investment Income, Gains, or Losses on Investments

**p. 269. Replace *subsection (f)* with the following:**

All investment income (dividends and interest) must be reported as revenues directly in the class of net assets appropriate to any restrictions of the revenue. All investment income must be reported as revenue in the year in which earned.

In August 2008, FASB Staff Position No. SFAS 117-1 (FSP 117-1), *Endowments of Not-for-Profit Organizations: Net Asset Classification of Funds Subject to an Enacted Version of the Uniform Prudent Management of Institutional Funds Act, and Enhanced Disclosures for All Endowment Funds* was issued. This FSP provides guidance on the net asset classification of endowment funds (both donor-restricted and board designated) for an organization that is subject to an enacted version of the Uniform Prudent Management of Institutional Funds Act of 2006 (UPMIFA). This FSP also expands the disclosures required by organizations regarding their endowment funds.

A significant classification change within FSP 117-1 is that all income not classified as permanently restricted net assets shall be recorded as temporarily restricted net assets until such funds are appropriated by the organization for expenditures.

Additional discussions regarding FSP 117-1—the accounting aspects and the disclosure requirements—are further discussed in Chapter 6. of this book.

The provisions of FSP 117-1 are effective for fiscal years ending after December 15, 2008. Earlier application is permitted provided that annual financial statements for that fiscal year have not been previously issued.

### (h) Carrying Value of Investments

**p. 270. Replace fifth sentence in *subsection (h)* with the following:**

The AICPA *Audit Guide for Not-for-Profit Organizations* states in paragraphs 8.03 and 8.35 that these other investments should be reported in accordance with whichever one of the audit guides is applicable to the type of organization concerned.

For those investments that are carried at fair value, SFAS 157 modifies how fair value is calculated—from entrance price to exit price. This is further discussed in Chapter 6 of this book, but an organization has to determine what information is available for determining the fair value (using the SFAS 157 definition), or whether management must develop a model to estimate the fair value of the investment.

SFAS 159 allows management to elect to report certain financial assets and liabilities at fair value (such as real estate investments) utilizing the SFAS 157 criteria. If fair value is elected for an individual financial asset/liability, then that election can not be changed for the life of the financial asset/liability.

SFAS 157 also increases the amount of disclosure that is required for all items recorded at fair value. The expanded disclosures could be extensive, depending on the inputs utilized by the organization.

### (j) Fixed-Asset Accounting

**p. 271. Replace third sentence in *subsection (j)* with the following:**

This is discussed further in Chapter 5 of this book and in Chapter 9 of the AICPA *Audit Guide for Not-for-Profit Organizations*.

### (l)  Tuition Revenue

**p. 271. Replace first paragraph in *subsection (l)* with the following:**

Accounting for tuition revenue is fairly straightforward: prepayments are deferred and amortized over the period of instruction; and unpaid amounts for which a student (or other payor) is contractually liable are receivables, offset by an appropriate allowance for estimated uncollectible amounts.

### (m)  Expenses

**p. 272. Replace first paragraph in *subsection (m)* with the following:**

Like all not-for-profit organizations, colleges and universities are required to report expenses on a functional basis (program, management, and fundraising) to comply with SFAS 117 and the AICPA *Audit Guide for Not-for-Profit Organizations*. Reporting by natural categories (personnel, occupancy, travel, supplies, etc.) is not required, but this information is often of interest to management and the governing board. The functional expenses may be presented either on the face of the statement of activities or in a separate schedule or footnote.

**p. 272. Add a new *section 14.4, "New Accounting Rules:"***

## § 14.4  NEW ACCOUNTING RULES (NEW)

In June 2006, the Emerging Issues Task Force (EITF) issued EITF 06–2, "Accounting for Sabbatical Leave and Other Similar Benefits Pursuant to FASB Statement No. 43."

Institutions may provide its employees with a sabbatical leave benefit under which an employee receives compensated time off. This sabbatical leave is generally provided after a specified period of service. Sabbatical leaves also generally consist of two types: (1) the employee is required to "engage in research or public service to enhance the reputation of or otherwise benefit the employer," or (2) no effort is required by the employee and the sabbatical leave is essentially a vacation.

The issue that arises is whether or not the sabbatical leave benefit should be accrued over the period in which it is earned.

If the institution requires the employee to engage in research or public service, then the sabbatical leave is not to be accrued over the vesting period, as the employee is required to expend efforts and in accordance with the matching principle, the employee is being paid during the sabbatical period in which they are conducting the research or providing public service.

On the other hand, if the employee is not required to expend any efforts on behalf of the institution, then just as with "normal" vacation policies, the amount of the sabbatical will be accrued during the vesting period.

# CHAPTER FIFTEEN

# The External Financial Statement Reporting Model for Public Colleges and Universities and Other Not-for-Profit Organizations Reporting under the GASB

## § 15.6    BASIC FINANCIAL STATEMENTS

### (a)    Statement of Net Assets

### (iii) Capital Asset Impairment.

**p. 288. Replace last paragraph before *subsection (b)* with the following:**

Impaired capital assets that will no longer be used by public colleges or universities should be reported at the lower of the carrying value or fair value. Impaired capital assets that will continue to be used by institutions should be measured using the method that best reflects their diminished service utility. Statement No. 42 does not require a write-down when the impairment of the assets is considered temporary; only permanent impairments are recognized. Impairment losses should be reported as a program expense, special item, or extraordinary item per Statement No. 34. The impairment loss to be recognized should be net of any insurance recovery associated with events or changes in circumstances resulting in impaired capital assets. Restoration or replacement of the capital asset using the insurance recovery should be reported as a separate transaction. Statement No. 42 does not permit the reversal of impairment in future years.

## § 15.7    FOOTNOTE DISCLOSURES

### (d)    Deposit and Investment Risk

**p. 297. Add the following new paragraphs in *subsection (d)*:**

Statement No. 40 also requires disclosures of deposit and investment policies related to the identified risks.

Statement No. 40 generally requires that investment disclosures be organized by investment type. The financial statements should also contain accounting policies related to the risks covered by this Statement, that is, credit risk, interest rate risk, and foreign currency risk, as relevant to the institution's deposit and investment holdings.

The Statement requires the disclosure of credit quality ratings of investments in debt securities. Obligations of the U.S. government or obligations explicitly guaranteed by the U.S. government are excluded from this requirement based on the rebuttable presumption that they do not have credit risk.

Organizations should disclose, by amount and issuer, investments in any one issuer that equal or exceed 5 percent of total investments. Again, U.S. government obligations (or those explicitly guaranteed) are excluded from this requirement, as are mutual funds, external investment pools, and pooled investments.

Statement No. 40 requires the disclosure of interest rate risk using one of the methods described in paragraph 15. In addition, investments that are considered highly sensitive to interest rate changes must be specifically disclosed.

If organizations hold deposits or investments that are exposed to foreign currency risk, the balances should be disclosed in U.S. dollars organized by denomination and investment type.

The GASB Implementation Guide Q&A is helpful to use when working through the disclosure requirements of this Standard.

**p. 297. Insert the following new *subsection (e)* before *section 15.8:***

**(e)   Termination Benefits (New)**

The GASB issued its Statement No. 47, *Termination Benefits*, in June 2005. This Statement requires governments to disclose a description of the termination benefit arrangement, the cost of the termination benefits (required in the period in which the government becomes obligated if that information is not otherwise identifiable from information displayed on the face of the financial statements), and significant methods and assumptions used to determine termination benefit liabilities, regardless of whether they are provided as a result of a voluntary or involuntary termination of employment. These requirements do not apply if the terminated benefit results in an obligation of either a defined benefit pension plan (DBPP) or a defined benefit other postemployment benefit plan (DBOPBP).

Under Statement No. 47, the government is required to:

- Segregate voluntary and involuntary, health care and non–health care related, termination benefits expense, and liabilities from all other salaries and benefits expense and liabilities.

- Record a liability and expense for termination benefits under voluntary terminations (e.g., early retirement incentives) when the offer is accepted.

- Record a liability and expense for termination benefits under involuntary terminations when a plan of termination has been approved by those with the authority to commit the government to the plan and that plan has been communicated to the employees.

- Exclude from these considerations any obligations that would be satisfied through any DBPPs or DBOPBPs.

- Disclose a description of the termination benefit arrangement and the cost of the termination benefits for the year the liability and expense are recognized.

- Disclose the change in actuarial accrued liability that is attributable to the termination benefits for any DBPPs or DBOPBPs, if any.

GASB Statement No. 47:

- Generally prescribes new reporting requirements, rather than amending previous guidance, although this Statement supersedes paragraphs 6, 7, 8b, 12, 17, and 18 of National Council on Governmental Accounting (NCGA) Interpretation 8, *Certain Pension Matters*, and amends paragraph 5 of NCGA Interpretation 6, *Notes to the Financial Statements Disclosure*; paragraph 8 of

GASB Statement No. 1, *Authoritative Status of NCGA Pronouncements and AICPA Industry Audit Guide*; paragraph 2 of GASB Statement No. 10, *Accounting and Financial Reporting for Risk Financing and Related Insurance Issues*; paragraph 2 and footnote 2 of GASB Statement No. 12, *Disclosure of Information on Postemployment Benefits Other Than Pension Benefits by State and Local Governmental Employers*; paragraphs 12 and 44 of GASB Statement No. 25, *Financial Reporting for Defined Benefit Pension Plans and Note Disclosures for Defined Contribution Plans*; paragraphs 5 and 11 of GASB Statement No. 26, *Financial Reporting for Postemployment Healthcare Plans Administered by Defined Benefit Pension Plans*; footnotes 2 and 3 and paragraphs 5, 6, and 39 of GASB Statement 27; paragraph 81 of GASB Statement No. 34, *Basic Financial Statements—and Management's Discussion and Analysis—for State and Local Governments*; paragraphs 9 and 46 of GASB Statement No. 43, *Financial Reporting for Postemployment Benefit Plans Other Than Pension Plans*; paragraphs 8 and 40 of GASB Statement 45; and paragraphs 5, 6, 9, 11, and 14 and footnote 7 of GASB Interpretation No. 6, *Recognition and Measurement of Certain Liabilities and Expenditures in Governmental Fund Financial Statements*.

- Is effective for FY 2005–2006. Depending on materiality, the cumulative effect of applying this Statement should be reported as a restatement of beginning net assets for the liability at June 30, 2005, associated with termination plans or benefits that are in effect as of June 30, 2005.

- Does not apply to any defined contribution benefit plans, 403(b) plans, or 457(b) plans.

**p. 297. Insert the following new *subsection (f)* before *section 15.8:***

### (f) Postemployment Benefits Other than Pensions (New)

In addition to pensions, many institutions provide other postemployment benefits (OPEB) as part of the total compensation offered to attract and retain the services of qualified employees. In April 2004, the GASB issued its Statement No. 43, *Financial Reporting for Postemployment Benefit Plans Other than Pension Plans*, to establish uniform financial reporting standards for OPEB plans. Statement No. 43 supersedes the interim guidance included in Statement No. 26, *Financial Reporting for Postemployment Healthcare Plans Administered by Defined Benefit Pension Plans*. The approach followed in Statement No. 43 generally is consistent with the approach adopted in Statement No. 25, *Financial Reporting for Defined Benefit Pension Plans and Note Disclosures for Defined Contribution Plans*, with modifications to reflect differences between pension plans and OPEB plans. In July 2004, the GASB issued Statement No. 45, *Accounting and Financial Reporting by Employers for Postemployment Benefits Other Than Pensions*, which establishes standards for the measurement, recognition, and display of OPEB expense/expenditures and related liabilities (assets), note disclosures, and, if applicable, RSI in the financial reports of employers.

The standards in Statement No. 43 apply for OPEB trust funds included in the financial reports of plan sponsors, as well as for standalone financial reports on OPEB plans or other parties that administer them. Statement No. 43 also provides requirements for reporting of OPEB funds of multiple-employer plans when the fund used to pay benefits or premiums and to accumulate assets is not a trust fund.

The GASB issued Statement No. 45 to address how institutions should account for and report costs and obligations related to postemployment health care and other nonpension benefits. Statement No. 45 improves the relevance and usefulness of financial reporting by (a) requiring systematic, accrual-basis measurement and recognition of OPEB cost over a period that approximates employees' years of service and (b) providing information about actuarial accrued liabilities associated with OPEB and whether and to what extent progress is being made in funding the plan. Annual OPEB cost for most institutions will be based on actuarially determined amounts that, if paid on an ongoing basis, generally would provide sufficient resources to pay benefits that come due. The disclosure requirements include information about the plan in which an employer participates, the funding policy followed, the actuarial valuation process and assumptions, and, for certain institutions, the extent to which the plan has been funded over time.

The measurement and disclosure requirements of Statement No. 43 and Statement No. 45 are related, and disclosure requirements are coordinated to avoid duplication when an OPEB plan is included as a trust or agency fund in an employer's financial report.

Statements No. 43 and 45 are effective in three phases based on an institution's total annual revenues in the first fiscal year ending after June 15, 1999:

a. Institutions with total annual revenues of $100 million or more, are required to implement Statement No. 43 for financial statement periods beginning after December 15, 2005 and Statement No. 45 for financial statement periods beginning after December 15, 2006.

b. Institutions with total annual revenues of $10 million or more but less than $100 million are required to implement Statement No. 43 for financial statement periods beginning after December 15, 2006 and Statement No. 45 for financial statement periods beginning after December 15, 2007.

c. Institutions with total annual revenues of less than $10 million are required to implement Statement No. 43 for financial statement periods beginning after December 15, 2007 and Statement No. 45 for financial statement periods beginning after December 15, 2008.

**p. 297. Insert the following new *subsection (g)* before *section 15.8:***

## (g) GASB Statement No. 50 *Pension Disclosures* (New)

GASB Statement No. 50, *Pension Disclosures—an Amendment of GASB Statement Nos. 25 and 27*, is effective for fiscal years ending June 30, 2008, and later and more closely aligns the financial reporting requirements for pensions with those for other postemployment benefits (OPEB) and, in doing so, enhances information disclosed in notes to financial statements or presented as required supplementary information (RSI) by pension plans and by employers that provide pension benefits.

This Statement amends GASB Statement No. 25 to require defined benefit pension plans and defined contribution plans to disclose in the notes to financial statements the methods and assumptions used to determine the fair value of investments, if the fair value is based on other than quoted market prices.

This Statement also amends GASB Statement No. 27 to require cost-sharing employers to include, in the note disclosure of the required contribution rates of the employer(s) in dollars and the percentage of that amount contributed for the current year and each of the two preceding years, how the contractually required contribution rate is determined (for example, by statute or by contract, or on an actuarially determined basis) or that the cost-sharing plan is financed on a pay-as-you-go basis. In addition, if a cost-sharing plan does not issue a publicly available stand-alone plan financial report prepared in accordance with the requirements of GASB Statement No. 25, as amended, and the plan is not included in the financial report of another entity, each employer in that plan should present as RSI the schedules of funding progress and employer contributions for the plan (and notes to these schedules). Each employer also should disclose that the information presented relates to the cost-sharing plan as a whole, of which the employer is one participating employer, and should provide information helpful for understanding the scale of the information presented relative to the employer.

\* p. 297. Insert the following new *subsection (h)* before *section 15.8:*

### (h)   GASB Statement No. 53 (GASB 53), *Accounting and Financial Reporting for Derivative Instruments* (New)

In June 2008, GASB Statement 53 was issued, which requires most derivative instruments to be reported at fair value on the economic resources measurement focus financial statements. The fair value of the derivative instrument is either the value of its future cash flows in today's dollars or the price it would bring if sold on an open market. As a result, reporting is more consistent and transparent to users of the financial statements, who will have access to information needed to evaluate the inherent risks that derivative instruments pose. Note disclosure, which requires summary information about a government's derivative instruments, is required.

**PwC Observation:** All derivative instruments covered in GASB 53's scope except for synthetic guaranteed investment contracts (SGICs) that are fully benefit-responsive are required to be reported at fair value. Excluded from GASB 53's scope are derivative instruments that are normal purchases and normal sales contracts, insurance contracts accounted for under Statement No. 10, *Accounting and Financial Reporting for Risk Financing and Related Insurance Issues*, certain financial guarantee contracts, certain contracts that are not exchange-traded, and loan commitments. In addition, derivative instruments reported under the current financial resources measurement focus financial statements are excluded.

Under GASB 53, the fair value of a derivative instrument as of the end of the period covered by the financial statements will be reported in the statement of net asset. Changes in fair value should be reported in the statement of activities as investment gains or losses. However, the annual changes in the fair value of an effective hedging derivative instrument should be reported as deferred inflows or deferred outflows on the statements of net assets. GASB 53 describes the methods of evaluating effective hedges.

The disclosures required by Technical Bulletin No. 2003-1, *Disclosure Requirements for Derivatives Not Reported at Fair Value on the Statement of Net Assets*, have been incorporated into GASB 53. The objectives, terms, and risks of hedging derivative instruments are required disclosures. Disclosures also include a summary of derivative instrument activity that provides an indication of the location of fair value amounts reported on the financial statements. The disclosures for investment derivative instruments are similar to the disclosures of other investments.

GASB 53 is effective for periods beginning after June 15, 2009. Earlier implementation is encouraged.

**PwC Observation:** The application of GASB 53 improves financial reporting with respect to measuring derivative instruments by allowing financial statement users to more fully understand a government's resources available to provide services. The disclosures provide a summary of the government's derivative instrument activity and the information necessary to assess the government's objectives for derivative instruments, their significant terms, and the risks associated with the derivative instruments.

*p. 297. Insert the following new *subsection (i)* before *section 15.8*:

### (i)   GASB Statement No. 54 (GASB 54), *Fund Balance Reporting and Governmental Fund Type Definitions* (New)

In February 2009, GASB Statement 54 was issued, which clarifies fund classifications for governmental reporting. This statement updates GASB 34 to ensure that classifications are consistent and comparable across funds. Funds are initially classified as spendable or non-spendable. Additionally they are broken into restricted, committed, assigned, and unassigned.

**PwC Observation:** This Statement establishes accounting and financial reporting standards for all governments that report governmental funds. It establishes criteria for classifying fund balances into specifically defined classifications and clarifies definitions for governmental fund types.

Fund balance for governmental funds should be reported in hierarchical classifications based primarily on the extent to which the government is bound to honor constraints on the specific purposes for which amounts in those funds can be spent. The non-spendable fund balance classification includes amounts that cannot be spent because they are either (a) not in spendable form or (b) legally or contractually required to be maintained intact. The "not in spendable form" criterion includes items that are not expected to be converted to cash; for example, inventories and prepaid amounts.

Fund balance should be reported as restricted when constraints placed on the use of resources are either: (a) externally imposed by creditors, grantors, contributors, or laws or regulations of other governments; or (b) imposed by law through constitutional provisions or enabling legislation. Amounts that can only be used for specific purposes pursuant to constraints imposed by formal action of the government's highest level of decision-making authority should be reported as committed fund balance. Amounts that are constrained by the government's *intent* to be used for specific purposes, but are neither restricted nor committed, should be reported as assigned fund balance. Unassigned fund balance is the residual classification for the general fund. This classification represents fund balance that has not been assigned to other funds and that has not been restricted, committed, or assigned to specific purposes within the general fund.

GASB 54 is effective for periods beginning after June 15, 2010. Earlier implementation is encouraged.

**PwC Observation:** The application of GASB 54 improves financial reporting by clarifying the classifications for government funds. It will ensure that all transactions of a similar nature are represented in the same manner on financial statements. This increased consistency will enable users to more effectively compare financial statements of different governments.

\* **p. 297. Insert the following new *subsection (j)* before *section 15.8*:**

**(j)   GASB Statement No. 55 (GASB 55), *The Hierarchy of Generally Accepted Accounting Principles for State and Local Governments* (New)**

In March 2009, GASB Statement 55 was issued in order to incorporate the hierarchy of generally accepted accounting principles (GAAP) for state and local governments into the Governmental Accounting Standards Board's (GASB) authoritative literature. The "GAAP hierarchy" consists of the sources of accounting principles used in the preparation of financial statements of state and local governmental entities that are presented in conformity with GAAP, and the framework for selecting those principles.

The current GAAP hierarchy is set forth in the American Institute of Certified Public Accountants' (AICPA) Statement on Auditing Standards No. 69, *The Meaning of Present Fairly in Conformity with Generally Accepted Accounting Principles*, rather than in the authoritative literature of the GASB.

GASB 55 is effective on its issuance, March 2009.

**PwC Observation:** By incorporating the GAAP hierarchy into GASB authoritative literature, GASB is contributing to its efforts to codify all of GAAP for state and local governments into a single source. GASB 55 will make it easier for preparers of state and local government financial statements to identify and apply all relevant guidance. The statement should not affect current practice.

\* **p. 297. Insert the following new** *subsection (k)* **before** *section 15.8*:

**(k) GASB Statement No. 56 (GASB 56),** *Codification of Accounting and Financial Reporting Guidance Contained in the AICPA Statements on Auditing Standards* **(New)**

In March 2009, GASB Statement 56 was issued in order to incorporate into the Governmental Accounting Standards Board's (GASB) authoritative literature certain accounting and financial reporting guidance newly presented in the American Institute of Certified Public Accountants' Statements (AICPA) on Auditing Standards. These accounting principles, related party transactions, going concern considerations, and subsequent events, are being incorporated from existing guidance into GASB standards.

**PwC Observation:** The accounting principles included in GASB 56's scope apply to all state and local governments.

Under GASB 56, existing guidance on the presentation of related party transactions, going concern considerations, and subsequent events are incorporated into GASB. Related party transactions are required to be disclosed, and should the transaction significantly differ in form due to the related party, the financial statement should recognize the substance over the legal form. Subsequent events may require adjustments to the financial statements while others may require disclosure in the notes. Should there be substantial doubt regarding an entity's ability to continue as a going concern, disclosure is required.

GASB 56 is effective on its issuance, March 2009.

**PwC Observation:** By incorporated certain AICPA standards into GASB authoritative literature, GASB is contributing to its efforts to codify all of GAAP for state and local governments into a single source. GASB 56 will make it easier for preparers of state and local government financial statements to identify and apply all relevant guidance. The statement should not affect current practice.

\* **p. 297. Insert the following new** *subsection (l)* **before** *section 15.8:*

**(l)  GASB Technical Bulletin No. 2008-1 (GTB 08-1),** *Determining the Annual Required Contribution Adjustment for Postemployment Benefits* **(New)**

Issued November 2008, GTB 08-1 clarifies the requirements of Statements 27, Accounting for Pensions by State and Local Governmental Employees, and 45, Accounting and Financial Reporting by Employers for Postemployment Benefits Other Than Pensions, for calculating the annual required contribution (ARC) adjustment. Specifically, this bulletin applies to situations in which the actuarial valuation separately identifies the actual amount that is included in the ARC related to the amortization of past employer contribution deficiencies or excess contributions to a pension or other postemployment benefit (OPEB) plan.

Per GTB 08-1, if the actual amount to be included in the ARC related to the amortization of past employer contribution deficiencies or excess contributions to a pension or other postemployment benefit (OPEB) plan is known, the actual amount should be used as opposed to the estimated amount derived from GASB 27 or GASB 45 for determining annual pension or OPEB cost respectively.

GTB 08-1 is effective for periods ending after December 15, 2008, or simultaneously with the initial implementation of Statement 45 for OPEB, whichever is later. Earlier application is encouraged.

**PwC Observation:** Note that GTB 08-1 relates to both GASB 27 and GASB 45.

\* **p. 297. Insert the following new** *subsection (m)* **before** *section 15.8:*

**(m)  Concept Statement No. 5,** *Service Efforts and Accomplishments Reporting* **(New)**

GASB's Concept Statement No. 5, issued November 2008, serves to amend Concept Statement No. 2, *Service Efforts and Accomplishments*

*Reporting*, to reflect developments since it was issued in 1994. The section of Concept Statement 2 on Developing Reporting Standards for SEA Information has been deleted. The sections of Concept Statement 2 on Purpose and Scope, The Elements of SEA Reporting, Limitations of SEA Information, and Enhancing the Usefulness of SEA Information are modified and presented in Concept Statement 5.

Changes to the purpose and scope sections of Concept Statement 2 to include a clarification that it is beyond the scope of the GASB to establish (a) the goals and objectives of state and local governmental services, (b) specific nonfinancial measures or indicators of service performance, or (c) standards of, or benchmarks for, service performance.

The section on the elements of SEA performance measures separates the elements of SEA reporting from related information. Elements of SEA performance measures for reporting purposes focus on the three different types of SEA performance measures—measures of service efforts, measures of service accomplishments, and measures that relate service efforts to service accomplishments. The discussion of related information that provides a context for understanding and assessing results has been expanded to include comparisons, unintended effects, the concept of demand for services, factors that influence results, and narrative information. A discussion of the initial, intermediate, and long-term nature of outcome measures also has been added. Changes to the discussion of explanatory factors shift the focus to both external and internal factors that influence results.

**PwC Observation:** Note that Concept Statement No. 5 relates to Concept Statement No. 2. The amendment serves to update provisions based upon findings by GASB and others related to service efforts and accomplishments (SEA) performance information.

## § 15.8   MANAGEMENT'S DISCUSSION AND ANALYSIS

**p. 297. Delete first sentence in *section 15.8* and replace with the following:**

Management's discussion and analysis (MD&A) was for the first time required through Statement No. 34, which asked financial managers to share with users information about the transactions, events, and conditions that are reflected in the institution's financial report and about the fiscal policies that govern its operations.

**p. 297. In second sentence, replace** *"government's"* **with** *"institution's"*.

**p. 298. Revise third bullet to read as follows:**

- An analysis of significant changes that occur in various funds

**p. 298. Add new bullet before fourth bullet:**

- An analysis of significant variances between budgeted activities and actual results of activities only in the case of the general fund (Ref. No. 34 ¶11.2)

**p. 298. Add new** *sections 15.8A* **and** *15.8B* **before** *section 15.9:*

## § 15.8A  REQUIRED SUPPLEMENTAL INFORMATION OTHER THAN MD&A (NEW)

In addition to the MD&A, Statement No. 34 requires institutions to present as Required Supplementary Information (RSI) budgetary comparison schedules for governmental funds and information about infrastructure assets reported using the modified approach. Statement No. 41, *Budgetary Comparison Schedules—Perspective Differences  An Amendment of GASB Statement No. 34*, provides a clarification on the budgetary presentation requirements for institutions whose structure of financial information for budgetary purposes differs from the fund structure defined in Statement No. 34.

Statement No. 34 requires budgetary comparison schedules for the general fund and for each major special revenue fund that has a legally adopted annual budget. The budgetary comparison schedule should present (a) the original or first complete appropriated budget; (b) the final legally authorized budgets for the reporting period; and (c) actual inflows, outflows, and balances, stated on the institution's budgetary basis. Variance between the original and final budget and between final budget and actual amounts may be reported.

Institutions that are not able to present budgetary information comparisons for the general fund and each major special revenue fund because of perspective differences are required by Statement No. 41 to present budgetary comparison schedules based on the fund, organization, or program structure that the institution uses for its legally adopted budget.

Statement No. 34 provides that infrastructure assets eligible under the modified approach are not depreciated. All expenditures made for these eligible infrastructure assets (except for additions and improvements) should be expensed in the period incurred. Additions and improvements to the eligible assets should be capitalized. In order to be eligible to the modified approach of reporting, infrastructure assets must meet certain requirements, namely: (a) the institution manages the eligible infrastructure assets using an asset management system that has the characteristics set forth in paragraph 23 of Statement No. 34; and (b) the institution documents that the eligible infrastructure assets are being preserved approximately at (or above) a condition level established and disclosed by the institution.

Paragraphs 132 and 133 of Statement No. 34 require institutions to present two schedules for all infrastructure assets eligible to the modified approach: (a) the assessed condition for at least the three most recent complete condition assessments that were performed at least every three years; and (b) the estimated annual amount. The said schedules should be accompanied by disclosures on (a) the basis for the condition measurement and the measurement scale used; (b) the condition level at which the infrastructure asset is intended to be preserved; and (c) factors that affect significantly the information reported in the schedules.

## § 15.8B  STATISTICAL SECTION (NEW)

NCGA Statement 1, *Governmental Accounting and Financial Reporting Principles*, provides guidance on the preparation of the statistical section. Statement No. 44, *Economic Condition Reporting: The Statistical Section—An Amendment of NCGA Statement 1*, amends portions of NCGA 1. The statistical section presents detailed (typically in ten-year trends) information that assists users in utilizing the basic financial statements, notes to basic financial statements, and RSI to assess the economic condition of an institution. The statistical section is a required part of a comprehensive annual financial report (CAFR), although institutions are not required to prepare a statistical section if they do not present their basic financial statements within a CAFR. The provisions of Statement No. 44 are effective for statistical sections prepared for periods beginning after June 15, 2005.

In order to clarify that the requirements are applicable to all types of state and local governmental entities that prepare a statistical section, Statement No. 44 establishes the objectives of the statistical section and the five categories of information it contains: financial trends information, revenue capacity information, debt capacity information, demographic and economic information, and operating information. The more specific requirements of this Statement should be adapted by each type of institution in order to meet their overarching objectives.

Statement No. 44 adds new information that users have identified as important and eliminates certain previous requirements. For instance, an institution's statistical section should now include trend information on governmental fund balances and principal employers. However, institutions are no longer required to present in their statistical sections information that users have identified as less useful, such as special assessment levies and collections, construction activity, and bank deposits. Additionally, statistical sections do not have to include a separate schedule of debt service ratios; the most useful information from that schedule will be presented with the changes in fund balances information.

The most significant new information added to the statistical section is the government-wide, accrual-based information required by Statement No. 34. The statistical section will include ten-year trend information about net assets and changes in net assets. The debt information presented in the statistical section will also be more comprehensive due to the inclusion of information from the government-wide financial statements and notes. Finally, Statement No. 44 further improves the understandability and usefulness of the statistical section information by requiring institutions to augment their schedules with notes regarding sources, methodologies, and assumptions, and to provide narrative explanations of (a) the objectives of statistical section information, (b) unfamiliar concepts, (c) relationships between information in the statistical section and elsewhere in the financial report, and (d) atypical trends and anomalous data that users would not otherwise understand.

# CHAPTER SIXTEEN

# Health Care Providers

## § 16.3 FINANCIAL STATEMENTS

### (c) Statement of Operations

### (ii) Extraordinary Items, Discontinued Operations, and Effect of Changes in Accounting Principle

**p. 308. Add the following new paragraph:**

After the effective date of SFAS 154 (fiscal years beginning after December 15, 2005), *Accounting Changes and Error Corrections*, voluntary changes in accounting principles will no longer be reported via a cumulative-effect adjustment to change in net assets of the period of change.

**(d)  Statement of Cash Flows**

**p. 309. Replace third major bullet with the following:**

- Equity transfers, restricted investment income for long-lived assets, and restricted contributions (including contributions restricted for purchase of long-lived assets) will need to be "transferred" to the financing category by adjusting them out of operating cash flows and increasing (or decreasing, as appropriate) the financing category by that same amount.

## § 16.4  ACCOUNTING PRINCIPLES

**(h)  Investments**

**p. 320. Add the following new *subsection (iii)*:**

**(iii) Framework for Assessing the Accounting for Alternative Investments Held by a Not-for-Profit Health Care Organization (New).**
The accounting for investments held by enterprises in all industries is often challenging due to the broad range of available investment alternatives, the variety of legal forms of investment entities, and the nature of the rights they convey to the investors. The authoritative accounting literature can be quite complex, and for some, it may be further complicated by specialized industry accounting practices.[8.1] Generally, the current accounting guidance follows a hierarchy where consolidation accounting is considered first, equity method of accounting second, and the accounting for equity securities with

---

8.1. Some industries have industry-specific accounting guidance for investments. For example, organizations within the scope of the AICPA industry audit and accounting guides *Not-for-Profit Organizations* or *Investment Companies* have the ability to mark all investments to market in certain circumstances based on those guides; employee benefit plans and SFAS 60 insurance enterprises have the ability to mark investments to market based on specialized FASB standards. A nonprofit HCO should not base its accounting for investments on specialized guidance developed for other industries unless the investments are held by a subsidiary that falls within the scope of that guidance and it is appropriate to carry those specialized industry practices forward in consolidation.

readily determinable market values and debt securities is considered third. To the extent the conditions at one of these levels are met, then subsequent analysis at the remaining lower levels in the hierarchy are not considered necessary. As an example, to the extent that an investment fails to meet the requirements for consolidation accounting, but does meet the requirements for the equity method of accounting, then consideration of the accounting for equity securities with readily determinable market values and debt securities is not needed nor permitted, and the equity method should be applied. In those instances where an investment falls through each of the methods in the hierarchy and is not covered by any other specific accounting guidance or specialized industry accounting practices, then the cost method should generally be applied.

The determination of where a particular investment falls within the accounting hierarchy requires careful analysis of the investment, particularly with respect to the rights of the investor. The following framework is designed to assist not-for-profit health care organizations (HCOs) with working through their evaluation of the hierarchy of accounting literature for investments. It is important to note that there may be investment structures that do not appear to clearly fall within the accounting hierarchy. In some instances, it may be acceptable for HCOs to apply the existing guidance applicable to a similar structure by analogy. In other instances, HCOs may find that the terms used in the accounting guidance may not be sufficiently defined to easily apply the guidance to an investment. In those instances, a reasonable interpretation of the guidance within the spirit of the overall principle may be acceptable.

1. Should the HCO's investment be accounted for using the consolidation method?

The first step in analyzing an HCO's investments or financial interests in other entities is to determine whether consolidation is required, which is generally the case if the investor has a controlling financial interest. Chapter 11 of the *AICPA Audit and Accounting Guide for Health Care Organizations* ("HCO Guide"), paragraphs 11.10 through 11.16, goes through various scenarios and provides guidance for determining whether the investor has a controlling financial interest. The primary source for the HCO Guide's conclusions is ARB No. 51, *Consolidated Financial Statements*, as amended by FASB Statement No. 94, *Consolidation of all Majority Owned Subsidiaries*. Additionally, for investments in partnerships and similar entities (such as limited liability companies that are the functional equivalent of a limited partnership), the guidance in EITF Issue No. 04-5, *Determining Whether a General Partner, or the General Partners as a Group, Controls a Limited Partnership or Similar Entity When the Limited Partners Have Certain Rights* (EITF 04-5), and FSP No. SOP 78-9-1, *Interaction of AICPA Statement of Position 78-9 and EITF Issue No. 04-5*, should be considered. The scope exception provided in FASB Interpretation No. 46 (FIN 46), *Consolidation of Variable Interest Entities*, applies to all not-for-profit entities, including HCOs subject to the HCO Guide, unless a not-for-profit entity is used by a business enterprise in a manner to circumvent the provisions of FIN 46.

2. SHOULD THE HCO'S INVESTMENT BE ACCOUNTED FOR USING THE EQUITY METHOD?

If consolidation accounting is not applicable, the next step is to determine whether the equity method of accounting is appropriate. The significant factor in making this determination is the amount of influence that the investor has over the operating and financial policies of the investee.

A. Noncontrolling investments in common stock or "in-substance" common stock (as defined by EITF Issue No. 02-14, *Whether an Investor Should Apply the Equity Method of Accounting to Investments Other than Common Stock*) of corporations and corporate joint ventures should consider the guidance in APB Opinion No. 18, *The Equity Method of Accounting for Investments in Common Stock* (APB 18), and FASB Interpretation No. 35, *Criteria for Applying the Equity Method of Accounting for Investments in Common Stock* (FIN 35), paragraph 4 (HCO Guide, Chapter 11., paragraph 17), which requires the application of the equity method when the investor has the ability to significantly influence the operating and financial policies of the investee. APB 18 indicates a presumption that in the absence of evidence to the contrary, the investor has the ability to exercise significant influence when it owns (directly or indirectly) 20 percent or more of the outstanding voting securities of the investee. FIN 35 sets forth indicators which should be considered in determining whether or not an investor is able to exercise significant influence.

**B.** Noncontrolling investments in general and limited partnerships should follow the guidance in the AICPA's Statement of Position 78-9, *Accounting for Investments in Real Estate Ventures* (SOP 78-9), paragraphs 6 through 10.

  **(i)** Noncontrolling general partnership investments follow the equity method because a general partner is presumed to have the ability to significantly influence the operating and financial policies of the investee.

  **(ii)** Noncontrolling limited partnership investments generally follow equity method of accounting unless the interest in the partnership is so minor that the limited partner may have virtually no influence over partnership operating and financial policies. If a partner has virtually no influence, then the equity method of accounting should not be used. EITF Topic No. D-46, *Accounting for Limited Partnership Investments*, discusses the SEC staff's view that generally investments of more than 3 to 5 percent are considered more than minor. However, depending on the circumstances, it is possible that this threshold (i.e., the level of ownership where an investment is so minor that the limited partner has virtually no influence) may be lower than a 3 percent investment. Therefore, each partnership's governing documents should be analyzed to determine what rights the limited partners have, and what ability the investor has to influence the investee's operating and financial policies. The facts and circumstances to consider when making this evaluation may include:

    • Whether decisions regarding changes to the partnership require a simple majority, supermajority, or unanimous vote

- The voting interest of each limited partner, that is, one vote per limited partner or votes based on investment amount/units held

- The size of the HCO's investment as compared to other limited partners

- To what extent the rights of the limited partners are participating rights or protective rights

The guidance provided in EIFT 04-5 should be considered when evaluating the level of influence held by the limited partners.

C. Noncontrolling investments in limited liability companies (LLCs) should follow the guidance in EITF Issue No. 03-16, *Accounting for Investments in Limited Liability Companies* (EITF 03-16).

Under the provisions of EITF 03-16, the application of the equity method of accounting to an LLC depends on its structure and its similarity to partnership or corporate forms of organization.

(i) An investment in an LLC that maintains a "specific ownership account" for each investor similar to a partnership capital structure should be viewed as similar to an investment in a limited partnership for purposes of determining whether a noncontrolling interest in an LLC should be accounted for using the cost equity method. The usage of specific ownership accounts is often a by-product of how the LLC is designed to be taxed. An LLC will be established with specific ownership accounts generally when the members prefer that the LLC be taxed like a partnership. An LLC will be established without specific ownership accounts (i.e., "unitized") if it elects to be treated like a corporation for tax purposes. However, only LLCs with units specifically called for in the underlying governing legal or offering documents should be considered unitized.

(ii) Investments in LLCs that do not maintain "specific ownership accounts" (e.g., the investments are unitized rather than providing ownership accounts for each investor) are to be accounted for like investments in common stock and apply the equity method as appropriate if there is evidence of substantive rights that indicate the ability of the investor to exert significant influence over the operating and financial policies of the company (e.g., where the ownership level is greater than 20 percent). See section 2A, above.

(iii) EITF 03-16 does not apply to investments in LLCs that are required to be accounted for as debt securities pursuant to paragraph 14 of FASB Statement No. 140, *Accounting for Transfers and Servicing of Financial Assets and Extinguishment of Liabilities* (SFAS 140). LLCs are sometimes formed in connection with certain securitizations. The interests in these LLCs are subject to the income and impairment recognition established by EITF Issue No. 99-20, *Recognition of Interest Income and Impairment on Purchased and Retained Beneficial Interests in Securitized Financial Assets*.

D. In EITF 03-16, some Task Force members indicated that in determining whether the equity method of accounting should be applied to investments in other entities with specific ownership account structures, it may be appropriate to analogize to the guidance in that issue. Therefore, the equity method of accounting may be applied to noncontrolling investments in other organizational forms (i.e., those other than corporations, partnerships, or LLCs discussed in 2A, 2B, and 2C above) with specific ownership account structures, unless the investment is so minor that the investor has virtually no influence. However, this accounting should be adopted as a matter of accounting policy, consistently applied to all applicable investments, and the policy disclosed in the financial statements if material. If such a policy is not elected or the investment does not have a specific ownership account structure, the guidance in APB 18 should still be considered.

### 3. SHOULD THE HCO'S INVESTMENT BE ACCOUNTED FOR USING THE GUIDANCE IN FASB STATEMENT NO. 124, *ACCOUNTING FOR CERTAIN INVESTMENTS HELD BY NOT-FOR-PROFIT ORGANIZATIONS* (SFAS 124)?

If the HCO's investment does not follow the consolidation or equity methods of accounting or the specific guidance addressed above, the next step in analyzing the accounting treatment is to review the scope provisions of SFAS 124 (HCO Guide, Chapter 4). That Statement applies to noncontrolling investments in equity securities with readily determinable fair values that are not accounted for under the equity method and all investments in debt securities. Investments within the scope of SFAS 124 should be recognized at fair value and subsequently marked to market each period. Investment return (including unrealized and realized gains and losses) not restricted by donors or by law shall be classified as changes in unrestricted net assets in accordance with the HCO Guide, Chapter 4. All debt and equity securities should be evaluated for other-than-temporary impairment.

**A.** Does the HCO investment meet the definition of a *debt* or *equity security?*

SFAS 124 defines a *security*, *equity security*, and *debt security* as:

### Security
A share, participation, or other interest in property or in an enterprise of the issuer or an obligation of the issuer that (a) either is represented by an instrument issued in bearer or registered form or, if not represented by an instrument, is registered in books maintained to record transfers by or on behalf of the issuer, (b) is of a type commonly dealt in on securities exchanges or markets or, when represented by an instrument, is commonly recognized in any area in which it is issued or dealt in as a medium for investment, and (c) either is one of a class or series or by its terms is divisible into a class or series of shares, participations, interests, or obligations.

### Equity security
Any security representing an ownership interest in an enterprise (for example, common, preferred, or other capital stock) or the right to acquire (for example, warrants, rights, and call options) or dispose of (for example, put

options) an ownership interest in an enterprise at fixed or determinable prices. However, the term does not include convertible debt or preferred stock that by its terms either must be redeemed by the issuing enterprise or is redeemable at the option of the investor.

## Debt security

Any security representing a creditor relationship with an enterprise. It also includes (a) preferred stock that by its terms either must be redeemed by the issuing enterprise or is redeemable at the option of the investor and (b) a collateralized mortgage obligation (CMO) (or other instrument) that is issued in equity form but is required to be accounted for as a nonequity instrument regardless of how that instrument is classified (that is, whether equity or debt) in the issuer's statement of financial position. However, it excludes option contracts, financial futures contracts, forward contracts, and lease contracts.

- Thus, the term *debt security* includes, among other items, U.S. Treasury securities, U.S. government agency securities, municipal securities, corporate bonds, convertible debt, commercial paper, all securitized debt instruments, such as CMOs and real estate mortgage investment conduits (REMICs), and interest-only and principal-only strips.

- Trade accounts receivable arising from sales on credit by industrial or commercial enterprises and loans receivable arising from consumer, commercial, and real estate lending activities of financial institutions are examples of receivables that do not meet the definition of *security*; thus, those receivables are not debt securities (unless they have been securitized, in which case they would meet the definition).

B.  As noted above, preferred stock that is redeemable by the issuing enterprise or at the option of the investor is included within the definition of debt securities regardless of whether it has a readily determinable fair value. However, common stock or residual equity of an entity, even if it has redemption features, is not considered a debt security and is within the scope of SFAS 124 only if it meets the definition of an equity security with a readily determinable fair value.

C.  If it is determined that the investment meets the definition of an equity security described in A above, does the investment have a readily determinable fair value as defined by SFAS 124?

SFAS 124 defines *readily determinable fair value* in paragraph 3:

a. The fair value of an equity security is readily determinable if sales prices or bid-and-asked quotations are currently available on a securities exchange registered with the Securities and Exchange Commission (SEC) or in the over-the-counter market, provided that those prices or quotations for the over-the-counter market are publicly reported by the National Association of Securities Dealers Automated Quotations systems or by the National Quotation Bureau. Restricted stock does not meet that definition.

b. The fair value of an equity security traded only in a foreign market is readily determinable if that foreign market is of a breadth and scope comparable to one of the U.S. markets referred to above.

c. The fair value of an investment in a mutual fund is readily determinable if the fair value per share (unit) is determined and published and is the basis for current transactions.

When analyzing the applicability of SFAS 124 for each HCO investment, the actual nature of the investments underlying the actual form of the initial investment should not be used as a basis for determining the overall accounting treatment of the investment. During its deliberations of SFAS 124, the Board considered many of the same concerns that were examined for business enterprises in FASB Statement No. 115, *Accounting for Certain Investments in Debt and Equity Securities* (SFAS 115). The FASB Staff Implementation Guide to SFAS 115 within question 5 addresses this issue in relation to an investment within a limited partnership that meets the definition of an equity security but does not have a readily determinable fair value, however substantially all of the partnership's assets consist of investments that have a readily determinable fair value. The FASB staff asked whether in that scenario it would be appropriate to "look through" the form of the investment to determine the applicability of SFAS 115. The response provided was that a "look through" was inappropriate and in the scenario described, SFAS 115 would not apply to that investment.

With respect to the application of the guidance in paragraph 3c of SFAS 124 to mutual funds, the words *mutual fund*, *published*, and *basis for current transactions* have not been specifically defined or clarified further in accounting literature and are therefore subject to interpretation by clients.

The term *mutual fund* is the popular name for an open-end management investment company as defined in the Investment Company Act of 1940 (the 1940 Act). Mutual funds registered with the SEC under the 1940 Act are the most common form of investment companies. Investors typically purchase mutual fund shares from the fund itself (or through a broker for the fund), not from a secondary market such as the NYSE or NASDAQ. The price investors pay for the mutual fund shares is the fund's per-share net asset value (NAV). Mutual fund shares are redeemable; investors sell the shares back to the fund at their approximate NAV, less applicable fees, and have normal settlement provisions. Mutual funds generally sell and redeem their shares on a continuous (i.e., daily) basis. Larger mutual fund NAVs are published daily in the popular press such as the *Wall Street Journal*, but NAVs for less active or small mutual funds are readily available from brokers. The mutual funds described above would typically be accounted for under the guidance provided by SFAS 124, as they meet the requirement of paragraphs 3(c).

There are other investment funds that are very similar to the funds described above, but are not mutual funds registered under the 1940 Act. Some HCOs may conclude that paragraph 3(c) is limited to only registered mutual funds that allow daily purchases and redemptions by investors and have NAV's that are published in the press each day. Therefore, they believe that nonregistered investment funds are not within the scope of SFAS 124 regardless of the similarities to registered funds. Other HCOs may believe that a broader policy permits each investment to be analyzed to determine whether it represents a pooled investment that has a fair value per share or unit that is determined and published and is the basis for current transactions. In the absence of further guidance, usually either view is acceptable provided that it is applied consistently to all investments and if material, the policy is disclosed in the financial statements. However with respect to the broader policy, it should be limited to those professionally managed investments that (1) pool the capital of investors to invest in stocks (equity securities), bonds (debt securities), options, futures, currencies, or money market securities for current income, capital appreciation, or both consistent with the investment objectives of the fund; (2) have an NAV provided to the investor periodically, but no less frequently than at each month end; and (3) the month-end NAV is the price paid or received by investors purchasing or selling investments at month end. A fund that withholds or holds back a certain percentage of the sale proceeds would generally be inconsistent with having a readily determinable fair value if the withholding/holdback is significant (e.g., greater than 10 percent) or is held for significant periods (e.g., greater than one month). Other terms, such as a notice period that restricts the frequency of transacting fund sales, should be carefully analyzed to determine if they conflict with an assertion that the investment fund has a published fair value that is the basis for current transactions.

4. IF CONSOLIDATION ACCOUNTING, THE EQUITY METHOD OF ACCOUNTING, AND THE ACCOUNTING GUIDANCE IN SFAS 124 DO NOT APPLY TO THE HCO'S INVESTMENT, WHAT ACCOUNTING MODEL SHOULD BE USED?

### A. Real estate, oil/gas interests, and other investments not deemed to be "financial instruments"

The definition of "financial instrument" is found in FASB Statement No. 107, *Disclosures about Fair Value of Financial Instruments*. Paragraph 4.02 of the HCO Guide states that investments not deemed to be financial instruments, such as real estate or oil/gas interests, are to be accounted for at amortized cost and are subject to the impairment provisions consistent with FASB Statement No. 144, *Accounting for the Impairment or Disposal of Long-Lived Assets*.

### B. Undivided interests

If the HCO's investment legally represents an undivided interest in each underlying asset and is proportionately liable for its share of any liability, then the investor may account for its pro rata share of the assets, liabilities, revenues, and expenses of the investment. However, if control of the investment entity resides with the investors collectively, similar to a limited partnership, then the investment should follow the equity method of accounting. HCOs should refer to the guidance provided in paragraph 11 of SOP 78-9 and EITF Issue No. 00-01, *Investor Balance Sheet and Income Statement Display under the Equity Method for investments in Certain Partnerships and Other Ventures.*

C. **Investments included within the scope of SFAS 140**

As provided by paragraph 14 of SFAS 140, interest-only strips, retained interests in securitizations, loans, other receivables, or other financial assets within the scope of SFAS 140 that can contractually be prepaid or otherwise settled in such a way that the holder would not recover substantially all of its recorded investment shall be subsequently measured like investments in debt securities classified as available for sale or trading under SFAS 124.

D. **Common/commingled/collective trusts**

Some pooled investment vehicles are organized as trusts. The trust instrument/trust deed is the legal document under which the trust is formed (similar to articles of incorporation). The trust instrument provides that the beneficial ownership of the trust is divided into interests that are allocated to the beneficiaries. The rights of the beneficial interest holders are defined in the trust deed. The beneficial interest may be structured similar to a separate ownership account in a partnership, on a unitized basis similar to a share in a corporation, or on some other basis. An investment trust may be classified for federal income tax purposes as a partnership, corporation, or trust, depending on its structure.

Investments in non–publicly traded common/commingled/ collective trusts that are not within the scope of SFAS 140 as discussed above should follow the hierarchy outlined in this framework. Consistent with the guidance in section 2D above, some clients may adopt a policy to apply the guidance in EITF 03-16 to other organizational forms by analogy. Accordingly, to the extent a noncontrolled trust is considered to have a separate ownership account structure the equity method may be applied, unless the trust investment is so minor that the investor has virtually no influence over the trust's operating and financial policies. Likewise, consistent with the guidance in section 3B above, some clients may adopt a broader policy for applying the mutual fund guidance in SFAS 124. Accordingly, to the extent a trust is not required to apply consolidation accounting or the equity method of accounting and meets the criteria outlined in section 3B, the guidance in SFAS 124 may be applied. Absent meeting one of these levels in the hierarchy, the cost method should be applied as stated in section 4G below.

E. **Investments in pools sponsored by other HCOs**

Some HCOs may pool their funds for investment purposes. Those investments may be formal arrangements with separate legal structures, such as investment partnerships or investment trusts, or may be structured without the formation of a separate legal entity. In determining the accounting for these investments, it is important that the HCO carefully analyze the nature of the investment structure, which may necessitate the involvement of legal counsel. If the structure of the investment falls within the accounting hierarchy described above, this framework should be applied.

F. **Insurance subsidiaries**

FASB Statement No. 60, *Accounting and Reporting by Insurance Companies* (SFAS 60), establishes specialized industry accounting and reporting standards for insurance companies. If a not-for-profit HCO conducts insurance activities in a separate subsidiary that are within the scope of SFAS 60, that subsidiary should account for all investments in debt securities and investments in equity securities that have readily determinable fair values in accordance with SFAS 124. For entities that are within the scope of SFAS 60, investments in equity securities that are not addressed by SFAS 115 or SFAS 124 because they do not have "readily determinable fair values" as defined by those Statements shall be nevertheless reported at fair value in accordance with paragraph 46 of SFAS 60.

## G. Cost method of accounting

If it is determined that SFAS 124 or any other alternative described above is not appropriate, then the HCO should account for the investment at cost, following the guidance in paragraph 6 of APB 18. Dividends received that are distributed from net accumulated earnings of the investee since the date of acquisition by the investor would be recognized as income. Dividends received in excess of earnings subsequent to the date of investment are considered return of investment and recorded as reductions of cost of the investment. If a series of operating losses of an investee or other factors indicate that a decrease in value of the investment has occurred which is other than temporary then an impairment loss should be recognized and the cost basis of the investment written down to its fair value. Consideration should be given to the requirements of FSP No. SFAS 124-1, *The Meaning of "Other-than-Temporary Impairment" and Its Application to Certain Investments*.

## (k) Malpractice Contingencies

**p. 324. Replace first sentence of second paragraph with the following:**

As indicated above, a key determinant of the amount of malpractice losses to be accrued by health care providers is the degree of risk the provider has transferred to an independent third-party insurer versus the risk of loss the organization has retained.

## (l) Related Organizations

## (ii) Business Combinations.

**p. 327. Replace second sentence of first full paragraph with the following:**

An acceptable practice for reporting such business combinations is to report the assets, liabilities, and net asset balances of the combined entities as of the beginning of the year and disclose the information that would be required to be disclosed for a pooling-of-interests under APB 16, *Business Combinations*.

# CHAPTER SEVENTEEN

# Accounting Standards for Other Not-for-Profit Organizations

## § 17.1  ACCOUNTING PRINCIPLES

### (b)  Fund Accounting

p. 344. In third line, replace *GAP* with *GAAP*.

### (e)  Donated Services

p. 345. In first line, replace *on* with *in*.

# CHAPTER EIGHTEEN

# Special Accounting Issues for Specific Organizations

## § 18.7  PRIVATE FOUNDATIONS

### (b)  Distinction between Principal and Income

**p. 368. Replace fifth sentence with the following:**

In the absence of legal restrictions, these two amounts *should* be combined and reported simply as net assets.

# CHAPTER NINETEEN

# The Financial Accounting Standards Board and Future Trends in Not-for-Profit Accounting

## § 19.2  TRENDS IN NOT-FOR-PROFIT ACCOUNTING

**(b)  Reporting Certain Assets at Current Value**

**p. 381. Modify first sentence in *section 19.2(b)* to read as follows:**

Recent years have seen a trend in accounting for all entities (not just not-for-profit organizations) toward more reporting of assets at current fair value (market value when determinable, and best estimates of fair value when market values are not available), rather than just historical cost.

### (j) Federal Reporting Requirements

**p. 385. Add the following new *subsection (iii):***

**(iii) Recent Developments (New).** In 2005, the U.S. Senate Finance Committee issued a draft document entitled "Exempt Status Reforms." This document would establish federal Sarbanes-Oxley–type regulations and other rules for not-for-profit organizations. The Senate Finance Committee encouraged the not-for-profit industry to review this draft document and to offer thoughts and comments. The organization leading the industry response is the Independent Sector (www.independentsector.org). Not-for-profit organizations are encouraged to monitor the developments regarding this matter.

**p. 385. Add the following new *subsection (k)* before *section 19.3:***

### (k) State Regulations (New)

In response to a call for additional Sarbanes-Oxley–type regulations for not-for-profit organizations, some states have passed legislation establishing such rules and regulations. Many of the states that have enacted such legislation have it available on their specific state attorney general's web site.

## § 19.3 NEW FASB STATEMENTS OF FINANCIAL ACCOUNTING STANDARDS THAT AFFECT NOT-FOR-PROFIT ORGANIZATIONS

**p. 385. Modify first sentence to read as follows:**

The FASB has issued many new standards since April 2002:

**p. 388. Insert the following at the end of** *section 19.3:*

- SFAS 151, *Inventory Costs—An Amendment of ARB No. 43,* Chapter 4, was issued in November 2004. It clarifies the accounting for abnormal amounts of idle facility expense, freight, handling costs, and wasted material (spoilage). It may impact organizations with some inventory, such as a university bookstore. However, it is not likely to have a significant impact on not-for-profit organizations.

- SFAS 152, *Accounting for Real Estate Time-Sharing Transactions,* was issued December 2004. It is not likely to affect not-for-profit organizations.

- SFAS 153, *Exchanges of Nonmonetary Assets,* was issued December 2004. It is not likely to affect not-for-profit organizations.

- SFAS 154, *Accounting Changes and Error Corrections—a Replacement of APB No. 20 and SFAS No. 3,* was issued May 2005.

- SFAS 155, *Accounting for Certain Hybrid Financial Instruments,* was issued in February 2006. This Statement amends FASB Statements No. 133, *Accounting for Derivative Instruments and Hedging Activities,* and No. 140, *Accounting for Transfers and Servicing of Financial Assets and Extinguishments of Liabilities.* This Statement resolves issues addressed in Statement 133 Implementation Issue No. D1, "Application of Statement 133 to Beneficial Interests in Securitized Financial Assets."

**PwC Observation:** If an organization has hybrid financial instruments, the benefit of adopting SFAS 155 is simplification—in many instances, valuing the embedded derivative separately from its host contract is more complicated than measuring the entire hybrid instrument at fair value. For example, certain forms of split-interest agreements can have derivatives embedded in the obligation to other beneficiaries. A not-for-profit organization can avoid having to bifurcate (i.e., separately account for) the derivative by electing the fair value option for the hybrid instrument (i.e., by electing to carry the obligation to other beneficiaries at fair value). In this case, fair value measurement could be achieved simply by using a current discount rate in a present value–based calculation of the obligation.

- SFAS 156, *Accounting for Servicing Financial Assets*, was issued March 2006. It is not likely to affect not-for-profit organizations.
- SFAS 157, *Fair Value Measurements*, was issued September 2006. We discuss SFAS 157 and the anticipated impact in our Summary of Emerging Issues for Not-for-Profit Organizations in 2008 in Appendix D in greater detail
- SFAS 158, *Employers' Accounting for Defined Benefit Pension and Other Postretirement Plans—An amendment of FASB Statements No. 87, 88, 106, and 132(R)*, was issued September 2006. We briefly discuss SFAS 158 and the anticipated impact in our Summary of Emerging Issues for Colleges and Universities in 2006, included in Appendix D.
- SFAS No. 159, *The Fair Value Option for Financial Assets and Financial Liabilities*, which was issued in February 2007, extended the availability of the fair value option to a wide range of financial instruments—both assets and liabilities. An organization may irrevocably elect to apply the fair value option to eligible financial assets and liabilities acquired or issued subsequent to adoption of the standard. The election is also available when a previously recognized asset or liability is subject to a "remeasurement event" as defined in paragraph 8 of SFAS 159. SFAS 159 generally permits organizations to apply the fair value option on an instrument-by-instrument basis, with some exceptions. The table on the next page provides examples of financial assets and liabilities that are or are not eligible for the fair value measurement election under SFAS 159.

Under both SFAS 159 and SFAS 155, not-for-profit health care organizations report unrealized gains and losses on items for which the fair value option has been elected within the performance indicator or as a part of discontinued operations, as appropriate. For all other not-for-profit organizations, the unrealized gains and losses are reported as changes in net assets or discontinued operations, as appropriate. If the organization reports an intermediate measure of operations, it may report the gains and losses either within or outside that measure.

- SFAS 161, *Disclosures about Derivative Instruments and Hedging Activities*, was issued in March 2008, amends and expands the disclosure requirements in FASB Statement No. 133 (SFAS 133), *Accounting for Derivative Instruments and Hedging Activities*, and related literature. Those disclosures had been criticized for not being transparent enough to allow financial statement users to assess a reporting entity's overall risk from derivatives from both a quantitative and qualitative perspective. SFAS 161's requirements are aimed at providing users of financial statements with an enhanced understanding of how and why an entity uses derivative instruments; how derivative instruments and related hedged items are accounted for under SFAS 133 and its related interpretations; and how derivative instruments affect an entity's financial position, results of operations/changes in net assets, and cash flows. SFAS 161 also amends SOP 02-2, *Accounting for Derivative Instruments and Hedging Activities by Not-for-Profit Health Care Organizations, and Clarification of the Performance Indicator*, to require the disclosure of where and in what financial statement captions derivative gains and losses are displayed. SFAS 161 focuses only on disclosures; it does not change any of SFAS 133's accounting or financial statement presentation guidance.

Among other things, SFAS 161 requires that organizations provide disclosure in a tabular format of the Balance Sheet captions in which derivatives are reported, and the fair value amounts of derivative instruments are reported in those captions. Similar disclosures are required for the location and amounts of gains and losses reported in the statement of activities/statement of operations.

The latter requires separate categories for derivatives designated and qualifying as fair value hedges, those designated and qualifying as cash flow hedges (for health care organizations), those not designated or not qualifying as hedging instruments, and other categories, if applicable. Within each of the categories, separate line items should further categorize derivatives by purpose (i.e., the item being hedged or the exposure created). For not-for-profit organizations, the disclosure requirements are tailored to SFAS 117's not-for-profit reporting model.

- FSP SFAS 117-a, *Endowments of Not-for-Profit Organizations: Net Asset Classification of Funds Subject to an Enacted Version of the Uniform Prudent Management of Institutional Funds Act, and Enhanced Disclosures*, was issued in August 2008 and provides guidance concerning: (1) the disclosures that not-for-profit organizations should make with regard to their endowments, and (2) the effect of a state's adoption of the model Uniform Prudent Management of Institutional Funds Act of 2006 (UPMIFA) on the classification of net assets related to donor-restricted endowment funds of not-for-profit organizations within that state.

The FSP proposes a number of new disclosures that would be required for endowments of all not-for-profit organizations, not just endowments held in states where UPMIFA has been enacted. These include:

- A description of the governing board's interpretation of the law that underlies the net asset classification of donor-restricted endowment funds
- A description of endowment spending policies
- A description of endowment investment policies, including the organization's return objectives and risk parameters, how those objectives relate to the organization's endowment spending policies, and the strategies employed for achieving those objectives

- An endowment reconciliation by financial statement net asset class that shows cumulative investment returns in the permanently restricted net asset class that relate to the organization's interpretation of relevant law, rather than what is required by explicit donor stipulation

- The composition of an organization's endowment by net asset classification at the end of the period, in total and by type of endowment fund, showing donor-restricted endowment funds separately from board-designated endowment funds

- A reconciliation of the beginning and ending balances of the organization's endowment, in total and by net asset class, including, at a minimum, the following line items:

  ○ Investment return, separated into investment income and net appreciation or depreciation of investments

  ○ Contributions

  ○ Amounts appropriated for expenditure

  ○ Reclassifications

  ○ Other changes

- Disclosure of how much (if any) of additions of investment return to permanently restricted net assets in the current period are the result of the organization's interpretation of relevant law, beyond that required by explicit donor stipulations

- Planned appropriation for expenditures, if known, for the year following the most recent period for which the organization presents financial statements

The FSP provides an illustrative example of such disclosures.

**Impact of UPMIFA on Permanently Restricted Net Assets.** UPMIFA is a modernization of the Uniform Management of Institutional Funds Act of 1972 (UMIFA), the model act on which most states have based their laws governing the investment and management of donor-restricted endowment funds. A number of states have already

replaced UMIFA with UPMIFA. Among other changes, UPMIFA prescribes new guidelines for expenditure of endowment funds in the
absence of explicit donor restrictions. UMIFA allowed only for the
spending of the net appreciation on endowment investments

Readers should refer to Appendix D as well as the FASB's web site
for the latest discussion of each of these new statements as well as
exposure drafts of other statements.

## §19.4   OTHER FASB PRONOUNCEMENTS AND PROJECTS

\* Appendix D contains the latest summary of other proposed statements by FASB as well as other groups.

**p. 390. Insert the following new** *subsection (c)* **after** *subsection (b):*

### (c)   FIN 47 (New)

The FASB published its Interpretation No. 47, *Accounting for Conditional Asset Retirement Obligations—An Interpretation of FASB Statement
No. 143*, in March 2005. We briefly discuss FIN 47 and the anticipated
impact in our *Summary of Emerging Issues for Not-for-Profit Organizations in 2007,* included in Appendix D.

**p. 390. Renumber** *subsection (c), EITF Issues 01-8, Determining
Whether an Arrangement Is a Lease,* **as** *subsection (d).*

**p. 391. Add the following new** *subsections (e)* **and** *(f):*

### (e)   EITF Issue 05-6, Determining the Amortization Period
### for Leasehold Improvement (New)

At its June 15–16, 2005, meeting, an EITF Task Force reached a consensus regarding the amortization period for leasehold improvements.
We briefly discuss EITF Issue 05-6 in our *Summary of Emerging Issues
for Not-for-Profit Organizations in 2007,* included in Appendix D.

**(f)  EITF Issue 06-2, Accounting for Sabbatical Leave and Other Similar Benefits Pursuant to FASB Statement No. 43, *Accounting for Compensated Absences* (New)**

At its March, April, and June 2006 meetings, an EITF Task Force discussed the accounting for sabbatical leave and ultimately reached a consensus. We briefly discuss EITF Issue 06-2 in our *Summary of Emerging Issues for Not-for-Profit Organizations in 2007*, included in Appendix D.

**p. 391. Renumber** *subsection (d) Pension Plans* **as** *subsection (g).*

**(g)  Pension Plans**

**p. 391. Add the following as the last sentence:**

Refer also to the discussion of SFAS No. 158 in section 19.3 above.

# PART FOUR

# Controlling the Not-for-Profit Organization

# CHAPTER TWENTY-FOUR

# Effective Internal Accounting Control for Not-for-Profit Organizations

## § 24.1  INTRODUCTION TO INTERNAL ACCOUNTING CONTROL

p. 458. Add new *subsection (f):*

**(f)  New Thresholds for Internal Control Weaknesses (New)**

In May 2006, the Auditing Standards Board issued Statement of Auditing Standards No. 112, *Communicating Internal Control Related Matters Identified in an Audit*. This Statement, which was amended by SAS 115, will be effective for fiscal years ending on or after December 15, 2009:

- Defines the terms *significant deficiency* and *material weakness*, incorporating the definitions already in use for public companies and prescribed by the Public Company Accounting Oversight Board (PCAOB)

- Provides guidance on evaluating the severity of control deficiencies identified in an audit of financial statements
- Requires the auditor to communicate, in writing, to management and those charged with governance (e.g., board of trustees), significant deficiencies and material weaknesses identified in an audit

While this new standard does not change audit procedures, it does change the process for evaluating deficiencies that come to our attention and brings the thresholds for reporting control deficiencies in line with the thresholds required for public organizations. As these revised thresholds effectively lower the bar, it is expected that the reporting of significant deficiencies and material weaknesses will become increasingly common. There is a possibility that items not previously identified as control deficiencies could elevate to a significant deficiency or material weakness. Common areas of weakness include controls in place over the financial statement closing process, information technology (IT) controls over significant systems, segregation of duties, complex spreadsheets, and consideration of the use of third-party service providers.

For entities that receive federal funding, any identified material weaknesses in internal controls would be specified in the Report of Independent Auditors on Internal Control over Financial Reporting and on Compliance and Other Matters Based on an Audit of Financial Statements Performed in Accordance with Government Auditing Standards, which is part of the A-133 report that is filed with the Federal Audit Clearinghouse. Additionally, material weaknesses could negatively impact future debt covenants, as well as public perception of management's ability to oversee the operations of an organization.

*p. 458. Add new *subsection (g):*

### (g) SAS 114 Communications (New)

Statement on Auditing Standards No. 114, *The Auditor's Communications with Those Charged with Governance* (SAS 114), replaces SAS No.

61, *Communication with Audit Committees* (SAS 61), for audits of the financial statements of non-public companies for periods beginning on or after December 15, 2006 (i.e., for calendar year 2007 audits of non-public companies). SAS 114 has no effect on auditor communications for audits of public companies conducted in accordance with Public Company Accounting Oversight Board (PCAOB) standards. For those public company audits conducted in accordance with PCAOB standards, SAS 61 continues to apply.

SAS 114 introduces several new requirements for audits of private company financial statements. For example, the auditor should communicate with those charged with governance an overview of the planned scope and timing of the audit, but without compromising the effectiveness of the audit. The auditor also should communicate representations the auditor is requesting from management. In addition, SAS 114 requires the auditor to evaluate whether the two-way communication between the auditor and those charged with governance has been adequate for the purpose of the audit in terms of assessing the risk of material misstatement and obtaining sufficient evidence.

SAS 114 requires that specific items be communicated, many of which were already in SAS 61, but some of the disclosures are new (Note: paragraph references are to the SAS):

1. The auditor should communicate with those charged with governance:

   a. The auditor's responsibilities under generally accepted auditing standards (see paragraphs 26 through 28);

   b. An overview of the planned scope and timing of the audit (see paragraphs 29 through 33); and

   c. Significant findings from the audit (see paragraphs 34 through 44).

2. The auditor should communicate with those charged with governance the auditor's responsibilities under generally accepted auditing standards, including that:

**a.** The auditor is responsible for forming and expressing an opinion about whether the financial statements that have been prepared by management with the oversight of those charged with governance are presented fairly, in all material respects, in conformity with generally accepted accounting principles.

**b.** The audit of the financial statements does not relieve management or those charged with governance of their responsibilities.

3. The auditor may also communicate that:

**a.** The auditor is responsible for performing the audit in accordance with generally accepted auditing standards and that the audit is designed to obtain reasonable, rather than absolute, assurance about whether the financial statements are free of material misstatement.

**b.** An audit of financial statements includes consideration of internal control over financial reporting as a basis for designing audit procedures that are appropriate in the circumstances, but not for the purpose of expressing an opinion on the effectiveness of the entity's internal control over financial reporting.

**c.** The auditor is responsible for communicating significant matters related to the financial statement audit that are, in the auditor's professional judgment, relevant to the responsibilities of those charged with governance in overseeing the financial reporting process. Generally accepted auditing standards do not require the auditor to design procedures for the purpose of identifying other matters to communicate with those charged with governance.

**d.** When applicable, the auditor is also responsible for communicating particular matters required by laws or regulations, by agreement with the entity or by additional requirements applicable to the engagement.

# § 24.3 BASIC INTERNAL ACCOUNTING CONTROL SYSTEM

## (b) Disbursement of Cash

**p. 467. Add the following bullet points:**

- Are wire transfers initiated and approved by different individuals? (An approver may be an individual outside of the business office.)

- Is the bank account for incoming wire transfers prohibited (per agreement with the bank) from sending outgoing wire transfers? (This is so that the pertinent information on the account can be distributed to applicable parties without concern of fraudulent outgoing wire transfers.)

- Are wire transfers subject to reviews and controls consistent with writing checks?

## (e) Accounts Payable

**p. 471. Add the following bullet point:**

- Are tax ID numbers and addresses of employees compared to those of accounts payable vendors, in an attempt to identify potentially fraudulent/fictitious businesses?

## (g) Fixed Assets

**p. 472. Add the following bullet point:**

- Is equipment purchased with federal funds easily identifiable to ensure it is not utilized for unallowable activities?

**p. 473. Add new *subsection (i)*:**

## (i) Compensation and Expenses (New)

### 1. Executive Compensation

Executive compensation continues to be a primary focus of the IRS, the media, donors, and others. As evidence of this, the IRS has included a new section in the 2005 Form 990 for organizations to disclose compensation currently paid to former officers and has expanded the disclosure for compensation paid by related organizations.

Leading practices for institutions to consider are:

- Develop a formal process to set executive compensation.

- Obtain and review comparable data—the compensation that other individuals in similar positions in similar organizations receive—to document whether compensation is reasonable.

- Consider all forms of compensation and benefits, including expenses (see below).

- Approve executive compensation at the board level and document the approval in the board minutes. A board member who has a conflict of interest should abstain from the vote. The board may delegate its responsibility to a separate compensation committee, but if it does so, the full board must gain an understanding of the compensation committee decisions, approve the decisions, and document the approval in their meeting minutes. Contemporaneous documentation frequently is overlooked but is essential for an institution to establish a rebuttable presumption of reasonableness in order to reduce the risk of intermediate sanctions.

- Report compensation completely and accurately on Form 990. The audit committee or the external auditors—preferably both—should review the most important disclosures on Form 990.

- Report compensation completely and accurately on the recipient's Form W-2.

**Author's observation:** Establishing a compensation committee to set compensation levels for senior executives is a best practice.

## 2. Expense Reporting

Similar to compensation, the IRS and the media are focused on situations where employees are being reimbursed for personal expenditures and these amounts are not reported as compensation. Therefore, it is essential that organizations make certain that their expense-reporting procedures are adequate and are followed by both employees and officers.

Expense reports should be submitted on a timely basis, and they should include adequate documentation in order to satisfy the rules. Receipts must be provided together with the name of the individual(s) involved and the business purpose for the expenditures.

Institutions also should establish appropriate policies regarding the approval and sign-off of expense reports submitted by senior management. For example, the CFO might sign off as to the completeness of the president's expense report and that it is in compliance with institutional policies. Trustees should periodically review the overall level of expenses incurred by the senior management for reasonableness. Such actions protect both the organization and senior management.

**Author's Observation:** Institutions must establish adequate policies and procedures for reimbursing and documenting business expenses. They also should be aware that some "expenses" may constitute additional compensation. Institutions must identify and appropriately report additional compensation received by key employees through the reimbursement of non-business-related expenses. Additional compensation that is not considered when establishing a rebuttable presumption of reasonableness may result in an automatic excess benefit transaction under intermediate sanctions. Therefore, we recommend that the board consider all forms of compensation, including the reimbursement of personal expenses, when considering whether key employees are receiving reasonable compensation.

## § 24.4 SPECIFIC NONPROFIT INTERNAL ACCOUNTING CONTROLS

### (g) Endowments and Investment Income

**p. 481. Add the following bullet points:**

- Does management have procedures in place to determine the carrying value of hard-to-value investments?

- Are custodian agreements reviewed to determine whether the custodian is permitted to lend out the organization's securities?

# CHAPTER TWENTY-FIVE

# Independent Audits

## § 25.2  BENEFITS OF AN INDEPENDENT AUDIT

**p. 489. Insert the following new item:**

5.  Open communications between the auditors and those charged
with governance

**p. 490. Insert the following new *subsection (e)* before *section 25.3:***

**(e)  Open Communications between the Auditors and Those
Charged with Governance (New)**

Under Statement of Auditing Standards No. 114, *The Auditor's Communication with Those Charged with Governance* (SAS 114), the auditor has certain communication responsibilities with the audit committee, or the group within the client charged with governance.

Matters that should be communicated by the auditors should include:

- The auditor's responsibilities under generally accepted auditing standards.

- The financial statements are presented fairly, in all material respects, in conformity with generally accepted accounting principles.

- The audit does not relieve management or those charged with governance with their responsibilities.

- Audit is to be performed in accordance with generally accepted auditing standards.

- Audit is designed to obtain reasonable, not absolute, assurance about whether the financial statements are free of material misstatement.

- Internal controls are considered in planning the audit, but not for the purpose of opining on the effectiveness of the organization's internal controls over financial reporting.

- An overview of the planned scope and timing of the audit.

- How the auditor will address the significant risk of material misstatement.

- The auditor's approach with regard to internal controls.

- Factors considered in determining materiality.

- Extent of reliance on internal audit (if applicable).

- Significant findings from the audit.

- Auditor's views about the qualitative aspects of the organization's significant accounting practices and accounting policies.

- Significant difficult, if any, encountered during the audit.

- Adjustments recorded by management as a result of the audit.

- Adjustments proposed by the auditors and not recorded by management.

- Disagreements with management, if any.

- Representations being requested from management by the auditors (draft of the management representation letter).

- Management's consultation with other auditors.

- Significant written communications with management.
- Any issues discussed with management prior to the auditors being retained.

## § 25.5  AUDIT COMMITTEES

**p. 494. Insert at end of section:**

In order to assist audit committees in fulfilling their responsibilities, a subcommittee of the AICPA's Not-for-Profit Expert Panel developed a series of tools that are available free for download at the AICPA's web site: www.aicpa.org/Audcommctr/toolkitsnpo/homepage.htm.

### *Administrative Tools*

- Audit Committee Charter Matrix
- Financial Expertise
- Sample RFP for CPA Services
- Independence and Related Issues
- Peer Review of CPA Firms
- Evaluating the Auditor's Engagement Letter
- Hiring the Chief Audit Executive
- Hiring External Experts

### *Audit Process Tools*

- Internal Control
- Fraud and the Audit Committee
- Whistleblower Tracking Report
- Conducting an Audit Committee Executive Session
- Issues Report from Management
- Discussions with the Independent Auditors

## *Performance Evaluation and Other Tools*

- Evaluating the Independent Auditors
- Evaluating the Internal Audit Team
- Conducting an Audit Committee Self-Evaluation
- Single Audits—Circular No. A-133
- Unique Transactions and Financial Relationships
- Resources for Audit Committees

# CHAPTER TWENTY-SIX

# Investments

## §26.1  VALUING INVESTMENTS

### (b)  Alternative Investments

**p. 513. Add the following paragraph at the end of** *subsection (b):*

In July 2005, the American Institute of Certified Public Accountants (AICPA) issued Auditing Interpretations 9328, *Auditing Fair Value Measurements and Disclosures*, and 9332, *Auditing Derivative Instruments, Hedging Activities, and Investments in Securities*. In both of the Interpretations, the AICPA references AU Section 328, paragraph .04, which states:

> Management is responsible for making the fair value measurements and disclosures included in the financial statements. As part of fulfilling its responsibility, management needs to establish an accounting and financial reporting process for determining the fair value measurements and disclosures, select appropriate valuation methods, identify and adequately support any significant assumptions used, prepare the valuation, and ensure that the presentation and disclosure of the fair value measurements are in accordance with GAAP.

This paragraph reiterates that management ultimately has the responsibility to assign a value to *all* of its investments, including the hard-to-value investments. This requirement may cause management to meet with investees and gain an understanding of their processes, judgments, and methodologies.

Due to the increased risk of misstatement inherent with these investments, the Audit Issues Task Force of the Auditing Standards Board established the Alternative Investments Task Force. The Task Force was charged with providing additional guidance to auditors of investor entities as to how the auditor may obtain sufficient appropriate audit evidence in order to conclude that the financial statements are free of material misstatement. As a result, the Alternative Investments Task Force has developed and issued a practice aid for auditors, "Alternative Investments—Audit Considerations." The Task Force believes that this nonauthoritative practice aid will assist auditors in auditing alternative investments. The practice aid includes guidance on:

1. General considerations pertaining to auditing alternative investments

2. Addressing management's financial statement existence assertion

3. Addressing management's financial statement valuation assertion

4. Management representations

5. Disclosure of certain significant risks and uncertainties

6. Reporting

The practice aid also includes the following appendixes:

- Appendix 1: Example Confirmation for Alternative Investments
- Appendix 2: Illustrative Examples of Due Diligence, Ongoing Monitoring, and Financial Reporting Controls

The practice aid can be ordered at the AICPA's web site (www .aicpa.org).

*p. 513. Add the following paragraphs after *section (b)* as a new *section (c):*

### (c)   SFAS 157 (New)

SFAS 157, *Fair Value Measurements*, establishes a single definition of fair value and a framework for measuring fair value in generally accepted accounting principles (GAAP) that result in increased consistency and comparability in fair value measurements. SFAS 157 also expands disclosures about fair value measurements, thereby improving the quality of information provided to users of financial statements. SFAS 157 does not require any new fair value measurements, but applies whenever a fair value measure is required in financial reporting, therefore SFAS 157 applies when measuring fair value under SFAS 124, SFAS 133, and alternative investments (under AAG-NPO). See Appendix D [pages 172–174 of this Supplement] for further discussion.

In September 2009, the FASB issued Accounting Standards Updates (ASU) No. 2009-12, *Investments in Certain Entities That Calculate Net Asset Value per Share (or Its Equivalent)*, to provide a practical expedient in estimating fair value for certain alternative investments under SFAS 157. The ASU is effective for the first annual or interim reporting period ending after December 15, 2009, with early application permitted. Organizations that elect to early adopt the provisions are not required to early adopt the disclosure requirements.

Prior to the issuance of ASU 2009-12 there was significant debate about how to estimate the fair value of certain alternative investments, such as hedge funds, private equity funds, and venture capital funds. Specifically, many alternative investments have terms and conditions that restrict redemption that could arguably impact their valuation under the SFAS 157 measurement model.

The ASU states that a not-for-profit organization is allowed to estimate the fair value of certain alternative investments using net asset value (NAV) without further adjustment if NAV is calculated consistently with the guidance in ASC 946, *Financial Services—Investment Companies* (formerly the AICPA Audit and Accounting Guide, *Investment Companies*), as of the reporting entity's measurement date.

The ASU also requires significant disclosures for all not-for-profit organizations, not just for those for which a reporting entity has elected to use the practical expedient.

In October 2008, the FASB issued FSP 157-3, *Determining the Fair Value of a Financial Asset When the Market for That Asset Is Not Active.*

This FASB Staff Position (FSP) clarifies the application of FASB Statement No. 157, *Fair Value Measurements,* in a market that is not active and provides an example to illustrate key considerations in determining the fair value of a financial asset when the market for that financial asset is not active. Statement 157 was issued in September 2006 and is effective for financial assets and financial liabilities for financial statements issued for fiscal years beginning after November 15, 2007, and interim periods within those fiscal years.

This FSP applies to financial assets within the scope of accounting pronouncements that require or permit fair value measurements in accordance with Statement 157.

This FSP clarifies the application of Statement 157 in a market that is not active and provides an example to illustrate key considerations in determining the fair value of a financial asset when the market for that financial asset is not active.

All FASB statements are available at www.fasb.org.

See also Appendix D, which includes further discussion of SFAS 157 and SFAS 159.

## § 26.5 PROFESSIONAL INVESTMENT ADVICE

### (c) Selecting an Investment Advisor

p. 523. Add the following paragraphs at the end of *subsection (c):*

Management should also consider whether its money managers obtain a "SAS 70 report" (a report issued by the money manager's [or any other outside service provider's] external auditors in accordance with Statement of Auditing Standard No. 70, *Service Organizations*). A Type 2 SAS 70 report will provide the not-for-profit organization with information on the money manager's internal controls and the results of the auditor's testing of those controls. This SAS 70 report will allow the organization to evaluate the money manager at a more detailed level. Additionally, the SAS 70 report will document the "user controls," or those controls/procedures that the service provider is expecting the organization to undertake as part of its internal control structure. A positive SAS 70 report should provide the organization with additional comfort over the information received from the money manager. A negative SAS 70 report, or no SAS 70 report, could cause the organization to reconsider its decision to engage this particular service provider.

It should be noted that there is also a Type 1 SAS 70 report. A Type 1 report only documents the controls in place at the service provider, but the external auditor has not tested these controls; thus no assurance is provided with regard to whether the controls are functioning as designed or not.

# PART FIVE

# Principal Federal Tax and Compliance Requirements

# CHAPTER TWENTY-SEVEN

# E-Business for Not-for-Profit Organizations: How Can Not-for-Profits Manage the Risks to Maximize E-Business Opportunities?

## § 27.5   WHERE ARE WE TODAY?

**p. 536. Replace first sentence with the following:**

The growth of the Internet has been nothing short of phenomenal. For example, experts estimate that there are over 2.7 billion web pages today; this number is growing at rate of approximately 5 million new pages a day. According to a January 4, 2006, article on the Computer Industry Almanac web site (www.c-i-a.com/), there are 197.8 million Internet users in the United States. China is second with 119.5 million web surfers. Japan is third, with 86.3 million Internet users. (For more Internet statistics, see Exhibit 27.2.)

## §27.8 HOW ARE ACADEMIC INSTITUTIONS USING E-BUSINESS?

### (c) E-Learning

**p. 558. Replace last sentence in carryover paragraph with the following:**

Winning full accreditation, which is the final step in the three-step process, usually takes two to five years, but in the meantime, candidate status should give the university more legitimacy and help its enrollment grow (see www.wgu.edu).

# APPENDIX 27-A

# What E-Business Models Exist?

## (b) B2B Business Model

### p. 561. Replace fourth paragraph with the following:

Recently there has been a lot of focus on the B2B space as new B2B models have emerged. For example, some companies use a third party that creates business-to-business online auctions for buyers who are seeking industrial parts, raw materials, commodities, and other services.

## (d) C2B Business Model

### p. 562. Replace first paragraph with the following:

There are two primary forms of C2B, which is the customer-to-business model. This first involves consumer demand aggregation. Under this model, consumers who want to buy new televisions, for example, band together to leverage their bulk purchasing power.

# CHAPTER TWENTY-EIGHT

# Principal Tax Requirements

## § 28.2  CHARITABLE ORGANIZATIONS

### (c)  Intermediate Sanctions

**p. 570. Insert following second complete paragraph:**

In the past, organizations were not required to make Form 990-T, *Exempt Organization Business Income Tax Return,* available for public inspection. However, legislation passed as part of the Pension Protection Act of 2006 requires that organizations make their Form 990-T available to the public upon request. This provision is effective for organizations filing Form 990-T on or after August 17, 2006. The Technical Corrections Act of 2007 (H.R. 4195) expands on the requirement that the organization alone is responsible for making the Form 990-T available for public inspection. The legislation also requires the Secretary of the Treasury (IRS) to make the Form 990-T available to the public. This change will likely result in the Form 990-T being available on the Internet through Guidestar and other sites.

## § 28.3  TAX STATUS OF CHARITABLE ORGANIZATIONS: PUBLIC CHARITY OR PRIVATE FOUNDATION

### (a)  Public Charities

**p. 572. At the end of fourth paragraph, insert the following sentence:**

The Pension Protection Act of 2006 introduced significant new restrictions on the activities of supporting organizations and are summarized in Section 28.12.

**p. 572. Replace last sentence of the second to last paragraph with the following two sentences:**

For organizations filing a 2007 Form 990 or earlier, Schedule A calculates public support over an aggregate four-year period and the calculations are performed utilizing the cash method of accounting. For organizations filing a 2008 Form 990 or later, Schedule A calculates public support over an aggregate five-year period and the calculations are henceforth performed utilizing the organization's method of accounting (i.e., an accrual basis organization will complete its support schedule utilizing the accrual method of accounting).

**p. 573. Replace second sentence of second to last paragraph of *subsection (a)* with the following two sentences:**

For 2007 and earlier years, Schedule A includes a schedule for certain organizations to complete regarding the support they received for the four years prior to the taxable year. For 2008 and later years, Schedule A includes a schedule for certain organizations to complete regarding the support they received in the current year in addition to the four prior years (five years total).

**p. 573. Delete third sentence of last paragraph of *subsection (a)* that currently reads as:**

Also, keep in mind that this mechanical test is applied over a rolling four-year period.

**(b)   Private Foundations**

**p. 573. Add the following paragraph before *section 28.4:***

The Pension Protection Act of 2006 doubled the excise tax for the following violations of certain private foundation rules: Self-dealing (IRC § 4941), Failure to Distribute Income (IRC § 4942), Excess Business Holdings (IRC § 4943), Jeopardy Investments (IRC § 4944), and Taxable Expenditures (IRC § 4945). The increased excise tax percentages are effective for taxable years beginning after August 17, 2006.

# § 28.4 OTHER CONCERNS FOR CHARITIES

## (a) Unrelated Business Income

### (ii) Exceptions and Modifications.

**p. 575. Replace last paragraph with the following:**

In addition, items that are generally excluded from unrelated business income are passive investment income such as dividends, interest, royalties, rents from real property, and gains on the sale of property. While excluded from unrelated business income, private foundations must still pay an excise tax on these items of passive income. However, rents that are based on a percentage of the net income of the property are considered unrelated and, thus, taxable. Also, income (passive investment income and rent) from assets acquired by incurring debt (debt-financed property) and rent from personal property may be considered unrelated business income in whole or in part.[10]

### (viii) Tax Rates on Unrelated Business Income.

**p. 578. Insert as second complete paragraph in *subsection (viii):***

A majority of states also impose a tax on unrelated business income (UBI). Therefore, it is important for tax-exempt organizations to determine whether the state in which they operate imposes a tax on UBI. Organizations should also consider whether the organization engages in activities in other states either directly or through investments in limited partnerships. As a partner invested in a limited partnership, a tax-exempt organization is subject to a tax on its federal UBI that is generated through a partnership investment. The organization may also be subject to state UBI tax obligations.

## (c) Lobbying and Political Activity

**p. 580. Add the following sentence to the last bullet:**

Based on experience gathered from investigations during the 2004 election cycle, the IRS issued a fact sheet (FS-2006-17) that provides examples of the types of activities identified as violations and gives guidance for ongoing compliance.

## (d) Charitable Contributions

### (i) Contribution Disclosures.

**p. 580. Insert as second complete paragraph in** *subsection (i):*

For contributions made after July 25, 2006, the Pension Protection Act of 2006 amended the requirements necessary to claim a charitable contribution deduction for façade easements with respect to property in a registered historic district. The provision disallows a deduction with respect to a structure or land merely because it is located within a historic district, but continues to allow a deduction with respect to buildings. Façade easements must provide that all portions of the building's exterior (not just the front) remain unchanged, in a manner consistent with the historical character of the exterior. Taxpayers will also have to obtain an appraisal of the qualified real property interest to attach to their returns, along with a written agreement between the donors and the donee organization certifying that the donee organization is (a) a qualified public charity with a charitable purpose of environmental or historic preservation or protection and (b) that the donee organization has the resources and the commitment to manage and enforce the easement restrictions. Effective August 17, 2006, the charitable deduction is reduced if a rehabilitation credit has been claimed with respect to the donated property. For contributions made after February 13, 2007, donors claiming a deduction in excess of $10,000 must pay a filing fee of $500 to the IRS.

### (ii) Contribution Acknowledgments.

**p. 581. Insert as second complete paragraph in** *subsection (ii):*

For tax years beginning after August 17, 2006, the Pension Protection Act of 2006 revises the substantiation requirements for charitable deductions of monetary contributions. The revised record-keeping requirements apply to all monetary contributions, regardless of the amount, and require that the donor maintain either a bank record, such as a cancelled check, or a written communication from the charity showing the name of the charity and the date and amount of the contribution.

### (iii) Solicitation Disclosures.

**p. 581. Insert the following paragraph at the end of *subsection (iii)*:**

The Pension Protection Act of 2006 amended the requirements for charitable contribution deductions of clothing and household items for contributions made after August 16, 2006. The new law specified that no deduction is allowed for clothing and household items that are not in good used condition or better. Donors who contribute a single item of clothing or a household item worth more than $500 will be required to file a qualified appraisal of the donated property with the donor's return. The Secretary of the Department of Treasury has the authority to deny by regulation a deduction for any item with minimal monetary value.

### (e)  Corporate Responsibility and Disclosure

**p. 585. Replace item 5 with the following:**

5. Transactions with significant book-tax differences (Notice 2006-6 removed this item from the list of categories of reportable transactions, and such transactions are no longer required to be disclosed on returns filed with due dates [including extensions] after January 5, 2006.)

**p. 585. Insert the following new paragraph before *section 28.5*:**

The Tax Increase Prevention and Reconciliation Act (TIPRA) added new IRC § 4965 to the code. This section establishes new excise taxes and disclosure rules for virtually every type of exempt organization that enters into a "prohibited tax shelter transaction." Managers of affected tax-exempt organizations can also be subject to these new excise taxes. In Notice 2006-65, the IRS requested comments on these new rules and plans to issue guidance as part of its Implementing Guidelines in 2007. There is considerable uncertainty around these rules and how organizations must comply. This new law is effective for tax years ending after May 17, 2006. Consultation with a tax specialist is recommended.

# §28.5 PRIVATE FOUNDATIONS

### (a) Excise Tax on Investment Income

**p. 585. Insert as second complete paragraph in *subsection (a)*:**

For tax years beginning after August 17, 2006, the Pension Protection Act of 2006 amended the definition of capital gains included in net investment income as originally defined in the Tax Reform Act of 1969. Generally, capital gains will now include all capital gains and losses of a private foundation, whereas the old definition included only capital gains and losses from the disposition of property used for the production of interest, dividends, rents, and royalties. An exception to the new definition of *capital gains* is gains from the sale of charitable use property used for exempt purposes for at least one year and exchanged for like-kind property following rules similar to those used in § 1031 exchanges. Under the rules of § 1031, a qualified intermediary must be involved in the exchange to properly defer the recognition of capital gains on such exchanges.

### (b) Distribution of Income

**p. 586. After third sentence of first paragraph, insert the following sentence:**

Effective for tax years beginning after August 17, 2006, the initial excise tax increases from 15 to 30 percent of the amount that remains undistributed at the end of the year following the current taxable year.

**p. 586. Replace second paragraph with the following:**

The minimum investment return is 5 percent of the average fair market value of all the foundation's assets that are not used in directly carrying out the organization's exempt purpose. Cash equal to 1.5 percent of the total foundation's assets is deemed to be used in carrying out the exempt purpose (with additional amounts above 1.5 percent allowed based on facts and circumstances) and is deducted for this calculation. This means that if a foundation has marketable securities and cash with a market value of $1 million, it must make minimum qualifying distributions of 5 percent of $985,000 ($1 million less 1.5 percent of $1 million), or $49,250, regardless of its actual income. If, for example, actual investment income were only $30,000, the foundation would still have to make qualifying distributions of $49,250.

**p. 588. Replace first paragraph with the following:**

Thus, the distributable amount is $48,250. Qualifying distributions were $70,000, which exceeds the distributable amount by $21,750, and the requirement has been met. This excess distribution can be carried over for five years to meet the requirements of a year in which there is a deficiency. Where there is such a carryover, the order of application of the amounts distributed would be (1) current year, (2) carryover from earliest year, (3) carryover from next earliest year, and so forth.

**(c) Excess Business Holdings**

**p. 588. Insert as second complete paragraph in *subsection (c)*:**

The Pension Protection Act of 2006 makes the excess business holdings rules applicable to type III supporting organizations (that are not functionally integrated) as defined in IRC § 509(a)(3)(B)(iii) and donor advised funds newly defined by the same law in IRC § 4966(d)(2).

**p. 588. At end of last paragraph in *subsection (c)*, insert the following sentence:**

Effective for tax years beginning after August 17, 2006, the initial excise tax increases from 5 percent to 10 percent of the value of the excess holdings.

**(d)   Prohibited Transactions**

**(iii) Prohibited Expenditures.**

**p. 589. Insert after the third sentence in *subsection (iii)*:**

Due to tax code amendments in the Pension Protection Act of 2006, foundations must now also exercise expenditure responsibility (or control) over grants made to any type III supporting organization that is not functionally integrated, even though such an organization is recognized as a public charity by the IRS.

## § 28.8   REGISTRATION AND REPORTING

**(a)   Initial Registration**

**p. 596. Replace third paragraph of *subsection (a)* with the following paragraph:**

Previously, an organization that anticipated it would meet one of the public support tests was given an advance-determination letter. This determination letter allowed the organization up to 60 months to meet the public support test without being classified as a private foundation. If, at the end of the 60 months, or the advance determination period, the organization failed to meet the support test, it would be characterized as a private foundation retroactive to the date operations began. On September 8, 2008, the IRS issued temporary regulations that eliminated the advance-ruling process and an organization that is reasonably expected to meet its public support tests will initially be classified as a public charity without any retroactive private foundation ramifications if the public support test is not met after its first five years of operations. In addition, an organization that was in its advance-ruling period at the time the September 2008 temporary regulations were issued can treat its original advance-ruling determination letter as its final IRS determination letter.

**p. 596. Insert the following as fourth complete paragraph:**

Effective August 17, 2006, the Pension Protection Act of 2006 now requires that each organization intending to maintain donor-advised funds must give notice that it intends to do so when submitting Form 1023. Such notice must also describe how the organization will maintain such funds. Section 28.11 of this chapter discusses new legislative provisions affecting donor-advised funds.

## (b) Annual Return—Public Charities

**p. 596. Insert after the first paragraph in** *subsection (b):*

Effective for tax years ending after August 17, 2006, the Pension Protection Act of 2006 requires every supporting organization defined in IRC § 509(a)(3) to file an annual return regardless of its size. In addition, the new law requires organizations with gross receipts of normally less that $25,000 to furnish to the Secretary of the Treasury, in electronic form, the legal name of the organization, its mailing address, identification number, the name and address of its principal officer, and evidence of its continuing basis for exemption.

**p. 596. Insert after the second paragraph in** *subsection (b):*

Some large exempt organizations are now required to file Form 990 electronically. For fiscal years ending on or after December 31, 2005, the electronic filing requirement applies to organizations with $100 million or more in total assets ($10 million for fiscal years ending on or after December 31, 2006) if the organization also files at least 250 federal returns in a calendar year. In determining whether the 250-return threshold is met, organizations should count all income, excise, employment tax, and information returns, including all Forms W-2 and 1099.

## (c) Annual Returns for Private Foundation

**p. 597. Insert as second complete paragraph in** *subsection (c):*

Some private foundations are now required to file Form 990-PF electronically. For fiscal years ending on or after December 31, 2006, all private foundations are required to file Form 990-PF electronically regardless of the private foundation's asset size if the private foundation files at least 250 federal returns in a calendar year. In determining whether the 250 returns threshold is met, private foundations should count all income, excise, employment tax, and information returns, including all Forms W-2 and 1099.

## (d) Return Inspection

**p. 597. Insert after the third sentence of the first paragraph:**

With the signing of the Pension Protection Act of 2006, all the public inspection requirements noted above now apply to any Form 990-T filed after August 17, 2006.

The Technical Corrections Act of 2007 (H.R. 4195) expands on the requirement that the organization alone is responsible for making the Form 990-T available for public inspection. The legislation also requires the Secretary of the Treasury (IRS) to make the Form 990-T available to the public. This change will likely result in Form 990-T's being available on the Internet through Guidestar and other sites.

**p. 597. Replace the second paragraph with the following:**

The final regulations provide that an organization is not required to comply with requests for copies if the organization has made Form 990 widely available. An organization may satisfy the requirement of making its Form 990 "widely available" if the form is posted on a World Wide Web page established and maintained by another entity where similar documents of other tax-exempt organizations are also available (e.g., www.guidestar.org). A Form 990 will be considered "widely available" if the World Wide Web page clearly informs the reader that the document is available and provides instructions for downloading, the document is posted in a format that exactly reproduces the image of the return as it was originally filed (except for information permitted by statute to be withheld), and an individual with access to the Internet can access, download, view, and print the document without special computer hardware or software and without paying a fee. Treas. Reg. § 301.6104(d)-2(b)(2)(i).

## § 28.9 FEDERAL INFORMATION AND TAX RETURN FILING REQUIREMENTS

**p. 598. Insert at the end of the second paragraph:**

While organizations must now make the Form 990-T available to the public upon request, these forms are not presently on the Internet. However, the Technical Corrections Act of 2007 (H.R. 4195), expands on the requirement that the organization alone is responsible for making the Form 990-T available for public inspection. The legislation also requires the secretary of the Treasury (IRS) to make the Form 990-T available to the public. This change will likely result in the Form 990-T being available on the Internet through Guidestar and other sites.

**p. 598. Insert as third complete paragraph:**

Some large exempt organizations and private foundations are now required to file Form 990 and Form 990-PF electronically. For fiscal years ending on or after December 31, 2005, the electronic filing requirement applies to Form 990 filers with $100 million or more in total assets ($10 million for fiscal years ending on or after December 31, 2006) if the organization also files at least 250 federal returns in a calendar year. For fiscal years ending on or after December 31, 2006, all private foundations are required to file Form 990-PF electronically regardless of the private foundation's asset size if the private foundation files at least 250 federal returns in a calendar year. In determining whether the 250-return threshold is met, organizations should count all income, excise, employment tax, and information returns, including all Forms W-2 and 1099.

**(a)    Form 990: Return of Organization Exempt from Income Tax**

**(i) Who Must File.**

**p. 598. Replace the fourth bullet with the following bullet:**

- Organizations with average annual gross receipts normally $25,000 or less (except all private foundations and supporting organizations no matter how small)

■  135  ■

## *(ii) Filing a Complete Form 990.

**p. 599. Replace penultimate paragraph with the following paragraph:**

Beginning with the 2008 tax years, the IRS has completely redesigned the Form 990. The new design now consists of a "core" form for all Form 990 filers to complete, along with numerous other schedules required to be completed if applicable to the filing organization (e.g., hospitals are required to complete Schedule H). Significant amounts of additional information are now required for such areas as governance, compensation, related organizations, tax-exempt bonds, and activities outside the United States. Helpful instructions and Frequently Asked Questions about many aspects of the revised form can be found by visiting the IRS web site's Charities & Non-Profits page at www.irs.gov/charities.

**p. 599. Before last paragraph, insert new paragraph:**

The Pension Protection Act of 2006 requires that Form 990 be changed to include several new reporting requirements related to donor-advised funds. For tax years beginning after August 17, 2006, an organization's Form 990 must now include: (1) the total number of donor-advised funds it is managing; (2) the aggregate total assets held in its donor-advised funds; and (3) the aggregate contributions made to and distributions from its donor-advised funds. In light of these new reporting requirements, organizations sponsoring donor-advised funds should track and maintain their records to ensure complete Form 990s can be filed in future years.

## § 28.10 STATE INFORMATION AND TAX REPORTING ISSUES

**p. 615. Insert as last paragraph before *subsection (a)*:**

A majority of states also impose a tax on unrelated business income (UBI). Therefore, it is important for tax-exempt organizations to determine whether the state in which they operate imposes a tax on UBI. Organizations should also consider whether the organization engages in activities in other states either directly or through investments in limited partnerships. As a partner invested in a limited partnership, a tax-exempt organization is subject to a tax on its federal UBI that is generated through a partnership investment. The organization may also be subject to state UBI tax obligations.

**p. 616. Insert the following new *sections 28.11* and *28.12:***

## § 28.11 DONOR-ADVISED FUNDS (NEW)

As explained in the relevant legislative history, some charitable organizations, including community foundations, establish accounts to which donors may contribute and thereafter provide nonbinding advice or recommendations with regard to distributions from the fund or the investment of assets in the fund. These accounts are popularly referred to as donor-advised funds. In recent years, a number of financial institutions have formed charitable corporations for the purpose of offering donor-advised funds. Significantly, some established charities have begun operating donor-advised funds in addition to their primary activities. The IRS has recognized both of these types of funds as being included within the exemption for § 501(c)(3) charitable organizations. Prior to the Pension Protection Act of 2006, the term *donor-advised fund* was not defined in statutes or regulations.

### (a) Definition of Donor-Advised Fund

The Pension Protection Act of 2006 added a new code section to the Internal Revenue Code (IRC), which defines donor-advised funds. In general, IRC § 4966(d)(2) defines a donor-advised fund as a fund or account:

1. That is separately identified by reference to contributions of a donor or donors
2. That is owned and controlled by a sponsoring organization
3. With respect to which a donor (or any person appointed or designated by such donor) has, or reasonably expects to have, advisory privileges with respect to the distribution or investment of

amounts held in such fund or account, by reason of the donor's status as a donor.

## (b) Excise Taxes and Penalties

The IRC currently imposes excise taxes on excess benefit transactions between disqualified persons and charitable organizations (other than private foundations) or social welfare organizations. Additionally, the Code imposes excise taxes on private foundations and their disqualified persons in a variety of situations: self-dealing between a disqualified person and a private foundation; failure to distribute income by private nonoperating foundations; excess business holdings; investments that jeopardize the foundation's charitable purpose; and taxable expenditures.

The Pension Protection Act of 2006 immediately subjects donor advised funds to IRC § 4958 [see section 28.2 (c)] relating to excess benefit transactions and applies the private foundation IRC § 4943 [see section 28.5(c)] relating to excess business holdings to donor-advised funds for taxable years beginning after August 17, 2006. In addition, two new excise tax sections specific to donor-advised funds were added to the Code. They are IRC § 4966, relating to taxable distributions, and IRC § 4967, relating to prohibited benefits. The excise tax imposed under IRC § 4967 is effective for taxable years beginning after August 17, 2006, and will not apply if the tax under IRC § 4958 has been imposed.

The new donor-advised fund excise taxes that can be imposed on donors, donor advisors, related persons, sponsoring organizations, and fund managers are substantial. For taxable expenditures made by a donor-advised fund, IRC § 4966 imposes a tax equal to 20 percent of the taxable expenditure on the sponsoring organization and a 5 percent tax on any fund manager who agreed to make the distribution knowing that it was a taxable distribution. For prohibited benefits received by a donor, donor advisor, or related person from a donor-advised fund, IRC § 4967 imposes a tax equal to 125 percent of the prohibited benefit on the donor, donor advisor, or related person and a 10 percent tax on any fund manager who agreed to make a distribution from a donor-advised fund, knowing that such distribution would confer a prohibited benefit to the donor, donor advisor, or related person.

### (c) Return Reporting Requirements

New information return disclosure requirements were enacted with the Pension Protection Act of 2006. For annual returns filed for tax years beginning after August 17, 2006, a sponsoring organization's return must now include: (1) the total number of donor-advised funds it is managing; (2) the aggregate total assets held in its donor-advised funds; and (3) the aggregate contributions made to and distributions made from its donor-advised funds.

In addition, new applications for exempt status submitted on Form 1023 after August 17, 2006, by sponsoring organizations that intend to maintain donor-advised funds must give notice that they intend to do so. Such notice must also describe how the sponsoring organization will maintain such funds.

Given that this disclosure of donor-advised fund information on a sponsoring organization's annual return will be subject to public inspection, each existing sponsoring organization should immediately begin to track and maintain its records so that the required donor-advised fund data and information on future annual returns can be reported.

### (d) Substantiation of Sponsoring Organization Control

A donor making an allowable charitable contribution to a donor-advised fund must now obtain contemporaneous written acknowledgment from the sponsoring organization affirmatively stating that the sponsoring organization has exclusive legal control over the contributed assets. Such written acknowledgment is similar to the current acknowledgment requirement from an organization for contributions received of $250 or more—IRC § 170(f)(8).

Each sponsoring organization should incorporate this new provision into its current written gift acknowledgment procedures to help it and its donors meet this written substantiation requirement.

## § 28.12  NEW RESTRICTIONS ON SUPPORTING ORGANIZATIONS (NEW)

The Pension Protection Act of 2006 amended the tax code to provide multiple reforms and new restrictions to supporting organizations defined under § 509(a)(3). The main changes are as follows.

### (a)  Restrictions Applicable to All Supporting Organizations

The following rules apply to type I, type II, and type III supporting organizations:

1. *Expanded definition of disqualified person.* Any person who is a disqualified person with respect to any type of supporting organization will now also be a disqualified person with respect to its supported organization(s)—effective August 17, 2006.

2. *No payments to contributors.* Grants, loans, compensation, or similar payments (including reimbursement of expenses) may not be made to a supporting organization's substantial contributors or to members of their family or businesses they control—effective July 25, 2006. If such a payment is made, the entire payment will be considered an automatic excess benefit transaction and taxed accordingly.

3. *No loans to any disqualified person.* Loans are not permitted to any disqualified person, including foundation managers (officers, directors, trustees of the supporting organization)—effective July 25, 2006.

4. *More information required on Form 990.* The Form 990 for each supporting organization must now list all supported organizations and indicate what type of supporting organization (I, II, or III) the filer is. The filer must also certify that it is not controlled directly or indirectly by disqualified persons (other than those who are disqualified solely by being an organization manager)—effective for Forms 990 filed after August 17, 2006.

## (b) Restrictions Applicable Only to Types I and II Supporting Organizations

The following rule applies to types I and III supporting organizations: A charity will not be able to qualify as a type I or type III supporting organization if it accepts a gift from a person who directly or indirectly controls one of its supported organizations—effective August 17, 2006.

## *(c) Restrictions Applicable Only to Type III Supporting Organizations

The new law creates two different versions of type III supporting organizations—those that are "functionally integrated" and those that are not. A functionally integrated type III supporting organization is one "which is not required to make payments to supported organizations due to the activities of the [type III] organization related to performing the functions of, or carrying out the purposes of, such supported organizations." No type III supporting organizations may support a foreign organization. The following rules apply to type III supporting organizations that are not functionally integrated:

1. *Minimum payout.* The secretary of the Treasury is directed to adopt regulations that create a minimum annual charitable distribution (or payout) requirement for type III supporting organizations (other than those that are functionally integrated) to be based on a percentage of either income or assets—effective August 17, 2006.

2. *Excess business holdings.* The IRC § 4943 private foundation rules limiting the degree of ownership of any business enterprise are now applied to type III supporting organizations that are not functionally integrated (effective for tax years beginning after August 17, 2006).

On August 3, 2007, the Department of the Treasury issued a Notice of Advance Rule-Making (REG-155929-06) requesting public comment on rules it intends to propose as regulations. This Notice included a description of: (1) criteria for determining whether type III supporting organization is functionally integrated and adding two additional tests that must be met; (2) the payout requirement for nonfunctionally integrated supporting organizations; (3) modified requirements for type III supporting organizations organized as trusts; and (4) requirements regarding the type of information a type III supporting organization must provide to its supported organizations. It is expected that Treasury will publish proposed regulations on these issues in 2009.

On September 24, 2009, the Department of the Treasury issued a Notice of Proposed Rulemaking (74 Fed. Reg. 48672) that provides detailed information defining type III supporting organizations that are both functionally integrated and not functionally integrated. These proposed regulations focus particularly on the Integral Part Test that is significantly different for a functionally integrated supporting organization compared to a supporting organization that is not functionally integrated. It is expected that these proposed regulations—with possible adjustments depending on comments from the public—will become final sometime in 2010.

# CHAPTER TWENTY-NINE

# Audits of Federally Funded Programs

## § 29.1 BASIC REQUIREMENTS

### (a) Historical Context

*p. 618. Add the following as the last paragraph in *subsection (a):*

**OMB A-133 Compliance Supplement.** The 2009 Compliance Supplement was issued in March 2009. In August 2009, the Office of Management Budget (OMB) issued the long-anticipated addendum to the March 2009 *Compliance Supplement* titled, *Compliance Supplement Addendum #1* (the Addendum).

**The Compliance Supplement Addendum.** Because of the limited time between the enactment of the Recovery Act and the issuance of the March 2009 Compliance Supplement, OMB was not able to fully incorporate needed Recovery Act guidance. At that time, OMB was only able to include Appendix VII, Other OMB Circular A-133 Advisories in the Supplement that provided some initial guidance and informed auditors to be on the lookout for future addendum to the Supplement relating to the Recovery Act. The Addendum contains new guidance on Recovery Act Expenditures and is effective for audits of fiscal years beginning after June 30, 2008, when an organization has expended Recovery Act funds. It should be used in conjunction with other Parts and Appendices of the *Compliance Supplement* in determining the appropriate audit procedures to support the auditor's opinion on compliance for each major program with expenditures of Recovery Act awards. The guidance in Part 5, *Clusters of Programs*, of the Addendum includes information on how Recovery Act programs are to be clustered which will impact the determination of what is considered a major program.

**Matrix of Compliance Requirements Updated.** The Addendum includes an updated Part 2, *Matrix of Compliance Requirements*, to show new Recovery Act programs, new clusters, and preexisting programs that now have Recovery Act funds associated with them under a preexisting CFDA number. All of these additions are identified by bold lettering, and the types of compliance requirements applicable to them are identified.

**Guidance Added for Certain Types of Compliance Requirements.** The Addendum also adds new guidance to Part 3, *Compliance Requirements*, for the following types of compliance requirements. You should refer to Part 3 for the full description of this new guidance (changed areas are noted with bold lettering).

1. **Activities Allowed or Unallowed:** Identifies a new cross-cutting unallowable activity for all Recovery Act funded awards.

2. **Davis-Bacon Act:** Identifies the Recovery Act and related OMB implementing guidance as another source of requirements for Davis-Bacon compliance.

3. **Procurement and Suspension and Debarment:** Adds guidance on the Buy-American provisions of the Recovery Act, an additional Recovery Act–related audit objective, and related suggested audit procedures.

4. **Reporting:** Clarifies that the reporting requirements imposed by Section 1512 of the Recovery Act are not applicable for audit periods with ending dates in June, July, and August of 2009 and that an additional Addendum will be issued by September 30, 2009 (the first reporting period for reports required by Section 1512) identifying compliance requirements, audit objectives, and suggested audit procedures for reports required by Section 1512. See the section of this Alert titled *OMB Issues Reporting Guidance*, for information on recently issued implementing guidance issued by OMB to assist entities that have to report under Section 1512.

5. **Subrecipient Monitoring:** Adds a new pass-through entity responsibility to identify to first-tier subrecipients the requirement to register in the Central Contractor Registration and a new suggested audit procedure relating to the requirement that pass-through entities separately identify to each subrecipient certain information at the time of the subaward and disbursement of Recovery Act funds.

6. **Special Tests and Provisions:** Adds new special tests and provisions that apply to all programs with Recovery Act expenditures (as well as new audit objectives and suggested audit procedures) relating to requirements for separate accountability for Recovery Act funding; presentation matters relating to the Schedule of Expenditures of Federal Awards (SEFA) and the Data Collection Form (DCF); and requirements for recipients to separately identify (and document) to each subrecipient at the time of a subaward (a) federal award and CFDA numbers, and (b) the amount of Recovery Act funds, as well as requiring subrecipients to meet the SEFA and DCF presentation requirements described above. Auditors should consider these special tests and provisions along with Part 4, *Agency Program Requirements*, guidance (or

Part 7, *Guidance for Programs Not Included*, for any programs not included in the *Compliance Supplement*) for each program with Recovery Act expenditures.

**New Program Sections Added to Part 4.** A number of new Recovery Act programs or revised program sections were added to the *Compliance Supplement* through the Addendum. These program sections include new Recovery Act programs, new or modified clusters, as well as existing programs that now have Recovery Act funds and related new compliance requirements associated with them under a preexisting CFDA number. Changes made to existing programs or clusters for Recovery Act implications are highlighted in bold lettering in each Part 4 program section.

**New General Guidance for Internal Control Added to Part 6.** Auditors should specifically focus on the revised Part 6, *Internal Control*, to emphasize several points relating to internal control test work related to each major program funded with Recovery Act funds.

1. The effects of the Recovery Act on single audits will increase as calendar year 2009 progresses and Recovery Act expenditures increase.

2. Auditors are encouraged to promptly inform auditee management and those charged with governance, *during the audit engagement*, of identified control deficiencies related to Recovery Act funding that are, or are likely to be, significant deficiencies or material weaknesses. The idea behind this is for auditees to have the opportunity to begin focusing on correcting such deficiencies as soon as possible to help ensure proper accountability and transparency of Recovery Act funds. The form of this interim communication is up to the auditor's judgment. However, keep in mind that regardless of how such an interim communication might be made, auditors still must communicate such matters via the normal reporting process (that is, in the schedule of

findings and questioned costs and the single audit reporting on internal control over compliance) at the end of the audit.

3. When gaining an understanding of internal control over Activities Allowed or Unallowed/Allowable Costs and Cost Principles and Eligibility, the auditor should consider the entity's internal control environment and internal control established to address the risks arising from Recovery Act funding (e.g., rapid growth of a program, new and/or increased activities, changes in regulatory environment, or new personnel).

4. When considering the likelihood and magnitude of control deficiencies, auditors should consider not only the volume of activity exposed to the deficiency in the current period, but also the volume of activity expected in the future.

**Special Tests and Provisions—R1: Separate Accountability for ARRA Funding.** Recipients must:

1. Maintain records that identify adequately the source and application of ARRA awards.

2. Separately identify to each subrecipient, and document at the time of the sub-award and disbursement of funds, the federal award number, CFDA number, and the amount of ARRA funds.

3. Provide identification of ARRA awards in their SEFA and DCF and require their subrecipients to provide similar identification in their SEFA and DCF.

**OMB Issues Reporting Guidance.** In June 2009, OMB issued a document titled *Implementing Guidance for the Reports on Use of Funds Pursuant to the American Recovery and Reinvestment Act of 2009*. The new guidance supplements the reporting guidance described in Section 1512 of the Recovery Act for recipients of grants, loans, and other forms of assistance, and goes into great detail about the reporting for both prime recipients and subrecipients.

## § 29.3 RESPONSIBILITIES OF THE RECEIVING ORGANIZATION

### (a) Compliance with Laws, Regulations, and Other Matters

**p. 624. Modify the last sentence in the discussion of compliance requirement B, "Allowable Costs/Cost Principles":**

Costs must be net of all applicable credits and must be documented in accordance with federal requirements, specifically in accordance with OMB Circulars A-21, *Cost Principles for Educational Institutions;* A-87, *Cost Principles for State, Local, and Indian Tribal Governments;* A-110, *Uniform Administrative Requirements for Grants and Other Agreements with Institutions of Higher Education, Hospitals, and Other Non-Profit Organizations;* and A-122, *Cost Principles for Non-Profit Organizations,* as applicable.

**p. 625. Modify the last sentence in the discussion of compliance requirement I, "Procurement and Suspension and Debarment":**

A listing of these companies can be found on the Excluded Parties List System, which can be accessed on the Internet at www.epls.gov.

## § 29.4 WHAT TO EXPECT FROM THE AUDIT

### (a) How Is It Different from a Financial Statement Audit?

**p. 628. Modify the last paragraph at the end of *subsection (a)* to read as follows:**

In 2003, the Government Accountability Office (GAO) issued several revisions to the Government Auditing Standards (GAS—the "Yellow Book") to strengthen and streamline these auditing standards and provide for consistent application of GAS to the various types of audits such as financial, performance, and attestation. The 2003 revisions include significantly expanded standards as they relate to performance of audit and nonaudit services.

In 2007, the GAO further revised the Yellow Book to reflect the changing audit environment in which greater transparency and accountability are expected from auditors and organizations. The 2007 revisions, which are part of the GAO's overall objective, "supporting the Congress and the nation in facing the challenges of a rapidly changing world while addressing the nation's large and growing long-term fiscal imbalance," were comprehensive. Changes include the following:

- Clarified language to distinguish between auditor requirements and guidance/explanatory material.

- Heightened emphasis on ethical principles, devoting an entire chapter to such principles.

- Clarified and streamlined the discussion of nonaudit services and added guidance on required actions if an independence impairment is identified after issuance of an audit report.

- Stressed the role of professional judgment and emphasized the role of competence in performing an audit and reporting the findings and conclusions.

- Incorporated the revised continuing professional education (CPE) requirements, issued by GAO in April 2005, and clarified the CPE requirement includes internal specialists who perform as a member of the audit team.

- Discusses clarifications and changes related to an audit organization's quality control.

- Defined those charged with governance consistent with SAS No. 114, *The Auditor's Communication with Those Charged with Governance*.

- Clarified reporting requirements for internal control deficiencies, fraud, illegal acts, violations of provisions of contracts or grant agreements, and abuse.

- Adopted recent developments in auditing standards, including SAS No. 103, *Audit Documentation*, and SAS No. 112, *Communication of Internal Control Related Matters Noted in an Audit*. The adoption of SAS 112 replaces the terms *reportable condition* and *material weakness* with the terms *significant deficiency* and *material weakness* as those terms are defined in SAS 112.

- Added requirements for reporting on the restatement of previously issued financial statements.

- Expanded discussion of the use of "matter of emphasis" paragraphs in auditor reports to encourage communication of significant concerns, uncertainties, or other unusual or catastrophic events that could have a significant impact on the financial condition or operations of a government entity or program for financial audits.

- Expanded and updated performance auditing standards.

- Added an appendix to provide supplemental guidance to assist auditors in the implementation of generally accepted government auditing standards (GAGAS) to assist auditors in their work.

Visit the GAO web site for up-to-date information concerning GAS at www.gao.gov.

## (c)  What Does an Organization Do If the Auditor Finds Something?

**p. 630. Add at the end of** *subsection (c):*

Organizations receiving federal funds should be cognizant of Statement of Auditing Standards No. 112, *Communicating Internal Control Related Matters Identified in an Audit,* which is discussed in Chapter 24. Although SAS 112 does not address federal award audits directly, the new process of evaluating deficiencies in accordance with the Standard is expected to be applied to these audits as well. This is expected to have the effect of "lowering the bar" with regard to which deficiencies are deemed to be either significant deficiencies or material weaknesses, which would be appropriate for the auditor to include in the *Report of Independent Auditors on Internal Control over Financial Reporting and on Compliance and Other Matters Based on an Audit of Financial Statements Performed in Accordance with Government Audit Standards.*

Deficiencies that are noted in this report could cast management in a negative light and could also lead funding sources to question costs.

As noted above, the GAO issued a revised "Yellow Book" that includes the same definitions for significant deficiencies and material weaknesses as are in the SAS. In addition, the OMB issued a Federal Register Notice in June 2007, which replaces references in OMB Circular A-133 to "reportable condition" and "material weakness" with the terms *significant deficiency* and *material weakness* as those terms are defined in SAS 112 and the Yellow Book.

**p. 630. Add new** *subsection (d)* **before** *section 29.5:*

### (d) Filing the Data Collection Form (New)

On August 22, 2008, the Federal Audit Clearinghouse (FAC) implemented a new submission process for Data Collection Forms (DCFs) and related Single Audit reporting packages via the new Internet Data Entry System (IDES). The DCF itself was edited to include minor changes, which are detailed below. The most significant change is that the submission process is now fully electronic, which will require additional coordination between engagement leaders and our clients.

The new submission process is effective for fiscal periods ending in 2008 or later and the IDES system will be used to accomplish the following tasks:

- Enter a Form SF-SAC data online.
- Check Form SF-SAC data for errors using the "Check Data" feature.
- Upload a PDF copy of the Single Audit reporting package.
- Certify Form SF-SAC electronically using a signature code provided by the IDES.
- Submit complete certified Form SF-SAC and Single Audit reporting package to the Federal Audit Clearinghouse electronically.

**(i) New Online Submission Process.** The most significant change incorporated into the DCF submission process is the requirement that the DCF and Single Audit reporting packages be submitted online. The FAC will no longer accept any paper submissions. The new submission process requires the DCF be submitted online using the IDES. Further, after the DCF passes all edits, an electronic PDF containing the reporting package must be attached.

To use the system, both the client and the auditor will need to utilize their email accounts to obtain certification codes and will also need the ability to upload a PDF file to the IDES. In order to complete the upload, cookies[3.1] must be enabled to allow for proper data transfer between the computer and the IDES. Instructions on how to enable cookies are provided in the detailed IDES instructions.

The process for submission of the DCF and Single Audit reporting packages for fiscal periods ending on or after January 1, 2008, are as follows:

| STEP | CLIENT RESPONSIBILITY | AUDITOR RESPONSIBILITY |
|---|---|---|
| 1. Create an online report ID and password using the IDES Introductory Page at the FAC web site: http://harvester.census.gov/fac/collect/ddeindex.html or link to the site from the FAC home page: http://harvester.census.gov/fac. | Client should start this process and communicate report ID and password to PwC once created. | N/A |
| 2. As part of the form creation process e-mail addresses will need to be entered for the auditor and auditee certifying officials. These officials should include the audit partner on the | Client should start this process. | The auditor should communicate the certifying audit partner to the client. |

---

3.1. Cookies are parcels of text sent by a *server* to a *web client* (usually a *browser*) and then sent back unchanged by the client each time it accesses that server. Cookies are used for *authenticating*, session tracking, and maintaining specific information about users.

| STEP | CLIENT RESPONSIBILITY | AUDITOR RESPONSIBILITY |
| --- | --- | --- |
| engagement and the client contact who typically signs the DCF. Additional e-mails can be entered if other users should be notified of actions taken on this particular submission. These e-mails will be used in Step 6. | | |
| 3. Complete the DCF—this part of the process is unchanged. | Client completes Part I (except Item 7) and typically lists the federal awards expended in Part III. | Auditor completes Part I, Item 7; Part II; and Part III (except client typically lists the federal awards expended). Please note, however, that in some instances the client completes the full DCF and the auditors review it, which is still acceptable. |
| 4. Check all inputs using the Check Data feature, as done previously. | This can be completed by either the auditor or the client. | This can be completed by either the auditor or the client. |
| 5. Complete component checklist: Locate and open the Single Audit reporting package to be uploaded and find the page numbers as they appear in the PDF version that correspond to the various components in the checklist. | This can be completed by either the auditor or the client. | This can be completed by either the auditor or the client. |
| 6. Upload the Single Audit reporting package. | N/A | The auditor should upload the final published A-133 report to ensure the final version is appropriately |

(*continued*)

| Step | Client Responsibility | Auditor Responsibility |
|---|---|---|
| | | attached. This version must be in a PDF format that can be opened, read, and edited.[3.2,3.3] |
| 7. Certify the submission. The SF-SAC form will need to be certified by both the client and the auditor. This process replaces the manual signatures completed previously. | • Click the "Certify Form SF-SAC" button from the Main Menu. <br> • Click the "Send Emails" button. The system will send an e-mail to the certifying officials containing instructions to certify the form. <br> • The clients' certifying official will need to log into the submission using the Report ID and password. <br> • They will click the "Certify Form SF-SAC" button from the Main Menu. <br> • The client will click the "Auditee Certification" button. <br> • Client will review the Form SF-SAC and the reporting package for accuracy. | • The certifying audit partner will need to log into the submission using the Report ID and password. <br> • They will click the "Certify Form SF-SAC" button from the Main Menu. <br> • The certifying audit partner will click the "Auditor Certification" button. <br> • The certifying audit partner will review the Form SF-SAC and the reporting package for accuracy. <br> • The certifying audit partner will review Certification Statements. <br> • The certifying audit partner will enter their name and title. <br> • The certifying audit |

3.2. The only purpose of editing would be for the FAC to attach a revised version of the report to the original if a revised report were to be issued in the future for any type of correction to the original report. At the request of the AICPA GAQC executive committee, the Clearinghouse is looking into an alternative to needing an editable PDF file. Further alerts on this topic are expected in late 2008 or early 2009.

3.3. Please note that since only one PDF can be uploaded, the clients' Corrective Action Plan should be included with the A-133 report. This practice is common (and preferred), but those who send in separate responses will need to include their Corrective Action Plan with the Single Audit reporting package.

| STEP | CLIENT RESPONSIBILITY | AUDITOR RESPONSIBILITY |
|---|---|---|
| | • Client will review their respective Certification Statements.<br>• The client will enter their name and title.<br>• Client will enter a unique signature code provided in the e-mail sent to them.<br>• If the auditee agrees to the certification statement, then he/she should click the "Agree to Auditee Certification Statement" button to complete their certification of the Form SF-SAC. | partner will enter a unique signature code provided in the e-mail sent to them.<br>• If the certifying audit partner agrees to the certification statement, then he/she should click the "Agree to Auditor Certification Statement" button to complete their certification of the Form SF-SAC. |
| 8. If information presented is not correct and either the auditee or the auditor does not certify the information, please see the instructions to the right. Once changes have been made, the certification process will need to be run again. | If the auditee does not agree to the certification statement, then he/she should click the "Reject Auditee Certification Statement" button to dispute the contents of the Form SF-SAC or the reporting package and contact the auditor to discuss making changes. | If the auditor does not agree to the certification statement, then he/she should click the "Reject Auditor Certification Statement" button to dispute the contents of the Form SF-SAC or the reporting package and contact the auditee to discuss making changes. |
| 9. Click "Submit." After both the auditor and auditee certifying officials have certified the Form SFSAC, the checklist will show that both the auditor and auditee certifying officials have certified the Form SF-SAC. An e-mail will be mailed to all representative e-mail addresses as confirmation of the submission. | Either party can perform this step. | Either party can perform this step. |

For additional step-by-step details, please see the link to the full instructions in the "Additional Information" section below. If the form cannot be completed in one session, you may exit the online form and reenter at another time. In order to revisit the online form, you must use your report ID and password.

**(ii) Other Items to Note.**

- *Passwords.* Passwords to access the DCF are much more complex than previously required and must contain at least 12 non-blank characters, which include:
  - English uppercase characters (A . . . Z)
  - English lowercase characters (a . . . z)
  - Base 10 digits (0 . . . 9)
  - Non-alphanumeric special characters (!, $, #, %)
  - Six of the characters must only occur once in the password
- *Special characters.* A useful method in creating a password to meet these criteria is to insert the special character(s) in place of the letters they resemble. The following examples were provided by the FAC for guidance:
  - MYcompany2%08
  - $anDiegoCharger$#1
  - myFir$tName08
- *Submissions for years ending in 2007 or prior.* The previous version of the DCF will be used for audit periods ending in 2004, 2005, 2006, and 2007 and can be accessed on the FAC web site by clicking on the DCF options link. The final form must be printed, signed, and mailed with the Single Audit reporting package in hardcopy format, as completed previously.
- *Revisions of previous submissions.* Please refer to the links related to the IDE Instruction Booklet and 2008 Single Audit Submission Questions and Answers attached below for additional details.

The electronic submission is new and while relatively straightfor-ward and self-explanatory, still has the potential to be challenging from a coordination standpoint, especially during the first year of use.

**(iii) Changes to the DCF Form.** The 2008–2010 version of the DCF remains largely unchanged. Two items of particular note are as follows:

1. *Change in terminology.* The term *reportable condition* has been changed to *significant deficiency* in Part II, Items 3 and 4, and Part III, Items 4 and 5 to be consistent with changes made in 2007 to OMB Circular A-133, *Audits of States, Local Governments, and Non-Profit Organizations.*

2. *Secondary auditor information may be entered.* The primary auditor may choose to enter contact information for secondary audit or-ganizations used in conducting the audit work. For instance, for some organizations DCAA performs some of the R&D cluster compliance work. It is recommended that, if applicable, second-ary auditor information be entered in order to document the di-vision of responsibility between the lead auditor and the secondary auditor.

**(iv) Additional Information.**

- Federal Audit Clearinghouse web site: **http://harvester.census .gov/fac/index.html?submit=Return+to+FAC+Home+Page**
- Internet Data Entry System: **http://harvester.census.gov/fac/ collect/ddeindex.html**
- IDE Instruction Booklet: **http://harvester.census.gov/fac/ collect08/main_instruct.pdf**
- 2008 Single Audit Submission Questions and Answers: **http:// harvester.census.gov/fac/2008SAQA.htm**

# Accounting and Disclosure Guide for Not-for-Profit Organizations (Revised)

In recent years, it has been challenging for not-for-profit organizations to keep up with all of the changes to technical literature and the resulting disclosure requirements. Rather than trying to complete annual updates to the disclosure checklist contained in the original hard volume of this related Wiley book, we would encourage people to utilize the checklist available through the AICPA.

## NOT-FOR-PROFIT ENTITIES: CHECKLISTS AND ILLUSTRATIVE FINANCIAL STATEMENTS

Updated as of May 31, 2009, these checklists help you prepare financial statements for not-for-profit entities and assist you in determining the adequacy of disclosures in the financial statements you're auditing.

From the AICPA web site, located at www.aicpa.org:

> The checklists have been updated to reflect authoritative pronouncements and interpretations issued as of May 31, 2009, including the following:
>
> SFAS No. 165, Subsequent Events
>
> SFAS No. 164, Not-for-Profit Entities: Mergers and Acquisitions— Including an amendment of FASB Statement No. 142
>
> Multiple new FSPs related to fair value measurements and impairments
>
> SSARS No. 17, Omnibus Statement on Standards for Accounting and Review Services—2008

Not–for–profit healthcare, higher education, and
other not–for–profit and governmental organizations

# Emerging issues*

Summary of emerging accounting,
tax and regulatory issues in 2009

*connectedthinking

PRICEWATERHOUSECOOPERS ⓡ

# Table of contents

# Executive summary

PricewaterhouseCoopers (PwC) is pleased to bring you this year's edition of our *Summary of Emerging Issues*. The accounting, financial reporting, tax and regulatory compliance issues described in this summary have been specifically tailored to concentrate on areas of interest to not-for-profit organizations and governmental business-type activities (BTAs). Once again, we have divided the summary into six areas: FASB, AICPA, GASB, Other Accounting Issues, Regulatory, and Tax.

"Change" is the watchword that best describes the accounting and financial developments in this year's *Summary of Emerging Issues*. Not-for-profits and governments face major changes in the year ahead.

- With the upcoming launch of the MSRB's "EMMA" system in the summer of 2009, investors and other interested parties will have unprecedented access to the audited financial statements, material event notices, and other continuing disclosure documents filed by not-for-profit and governmental municipal bond issuers.

- The anticipated launch of the FASB Accounting Standards Codification™ in the summer of 2009 is a major restructuring of US accounting standards that will affect the day-to-day work of nearly every financial professional who prepares, reviews, or audits financial statements of private sector organizations. Because a significant portion of the governmental GAAP hierarchy consists of pre-Codification FASB and AICPA standards that will cease to exist when the Codification becomes effective, the impact of the Codification also will be felt by the governmental sector.

- Not-for-profit organizations must begin applying FASB's new fair value measurement model to many of their assets and liabilities in financial statements for years ended December 31, 2008 and thereafter. The impact of the change in the way fair value is measured is enormous. Nearly one-third of the topics in this year's FASB section deal with fair value measurement issues, and GASB has also added a fair value measurement project to its research agenda.

- The advent of IFRS in the United States elevates concerns among not-for-profits and governmental BTAs related to comparability of financial reporting. Preparers, auditors and financial statement users currently struggle with interpreting measurement differences in financial statements prepared under standards issued by FASB and GASB, who increasingly appear to be taking different paths on recognition and measurement guidance for similar transactions. IFRS would interject yet a third set of standards.

Regulatory changes are also possible in the municipal securities market, a primary source of capital for many not-for-profit and governmental organizations. The events of the credit crisis demonstrated that the municipal market has become inextricably intertwined with the US financial system as a whole. The extent of that interrelationship became apparent when defaults in subprime mortgages caused the value of collateralized mortgage obligations to drop, which resulted in ratings downgrades for a number of municipal bond insurers, which ultimately led to a liquidity crisis in the municipal bond market. A massive wave of municipal refinancings ensued, along with a renewed call by the Securities and Exchange Commission for Congress to give it more direct regulatory oversight of municipal issuers and conduit borrowers.

With respect to regulatory compliance issues, the adoption of the American Recovery and Reinvestment Act of 2008 brings the promise of new award funding opportunities, but with significant monitoring, oversight, and reporting requirements that go well beyond what currently exists. The Higher Education Opportunity Act brings with it numerous changes to student financial aid regulations, but implementing regulations have not been finalized. Other matters, including conflict of interest, communication of internal control matters and more, are further described in the Regulatory Issues section of the *Summary of Emerging Issues*.

With respect to tax issues, the redesigned Form 990 represents a tremendous change for tax-exempt organizations. There will be expanded reporting in many areas, including compensation and new reporting around governance, charity care, tax-exempt bonds, and foreign activities. The IRS has continued to use compliance questionnaires that further focus on specific issues in the tax-exempt organization world that it believes may be troublesome. Further guidance has been provided regarding both Section 403(b) plans and the exemption from FICA for medical residents, and there is continued legislative attention placed on tax-exempt organizations.

Contributors to this year's *Summary of Emerging Issues* include: John Mattie, Bob Valletta, Gwen Spencer, Ralph DeAcetis, Kaye Ferriter, Martha Garner, Tom Gaudrault, Brian Huggins, Steve Luber, Dave Merriam, Jocelyn Bishop, Erin Couture, and Jeff Thomas.

Note that we have excerpted some text in this summary from FASB's and GASB's Web sites as well as from other internal sources. The information in this edition generally is current through March 15, 2009; however, many of the projects and proposals are subject to change. The latest source of these issues can be found on the following Web sites:

- AICPA (http://www.aicpa.org/)
- FASB (http://www.fasb.org/)
- GAO (http://www.gao.gov)
- IRS (http://www.irs.gov)
- OMB (http://www.whitehouse.gov/omb)
- GASB (http://www.gasb.org/)
- SEC Municipal Securities (http://www.sec.gov/info/municipal.shtml)
- EMMA (http://www.emma.msrb.org)

If you have questions about any of the issues in this summary, contact your PricewaterhouseCoopers' engagement team.

# APPENDIX D

The table below presents a snapshot of upcoming effective dates for selected pronouncements, interpretations, and consensuses recently issued by FASB (note: references to specific pronouncements, interpretations or consensuses (i.e., FAS, FIN, EITF, etc.) will not be appropriate as of the effective date of the Codification, currently expected to be July 1, 2009).

## FASB pronouncements and activities

| | | Page | Year-end | | | | |
| | | | Mar 31, 2009 | Jun 30, 2009 | Sep 30, 2009 | Dec 31, 2009 | 2010 & Beyond |
|---|---|---|---|---|---|---|---|
| FASB Codification | July 1, 2009 | 1 | | | • | • | • |
| FAS 16X | Periods beginning after 12/15/09 | 2 | | | | | • |
| FAS 162 | November 13, 2008 | 5 | • | • | • | • | • |
| FAS 161 | Periods beginning after 11/15/08 | 5 | | | | • | • |
| FAS 159 | Periods beginning after 11/15/2007 | 8 | • | • | • | • | • |
| FAS 158 | Periods ending after 12/15/08 | 9 | • | • | • | • | • |
| FAS 157 | Periods beginning after 11/15/2007 | 9 | • | • | • | • | • |
| FSP FIN 48-3 | Periods beginning after 12/15/08 | 12 | | | | • | • |
| FSP FAS 132(R)-1 | Periods ending after 12/15/09 | 12 | | | | | • |
| FSP 157-3 | October 10, 2008 | 13 | • | • | • | • | • |
| FSP FAS 117-1 | Years ending after 12/15/08 | 13 | • | • | • | • | • |
| FSP SOP 94-3-1 | Periods beginning after 6/15/08 | 16 | | | | | • |
| EITF 08-5 | Periods beginning after 12/15/08 | 17 | | | | • | • |
| EITF 07-1 | Periods beginning after 12/15/08 | 18 | | | | • | • |
| EITF 06-10/06-4 | Periods beginning after 12/15/07 | 18 | • | • | • | • | • |
| **Exposure drafts** | | | | | | | |
| Subsequent events | Periods ending after 6/15/09 | 20 | | • | • | • | • |
| Going concern | Periods ending after 6/15/09 | 20 | | • | • | • | • |
| FSP FAS 157-c | Periods that include date of issuance | 22 | • | • | • | • | • |
| FSP FAS 144-d | Periods beginning after 12/15/09 | 22 | | | | | • |
| FSP FAS 107-b | Periods ending after 3/15/09 | 23 | • | • | • | • | • |

# I. FASB pronouncements and activities

The following section highlights selected FASB pronouncements and activities that are already effective (or will be effective in the near future), along with our observations as to how they will impact not-for-profit organizations. We also include several recent Emerging Issues Task Force (EITF) issues and exposure drafts that may impact those organizations.

## FASB Accounting Standards Codification™

Private-sector GAAP (generally accepted accounting principles) is a proliferation of thousands of standards established by a variety of standard setters—FASB, the AICPA, and the EITF, among others—over the last 50-plus years. As such, the standards lack a consistent and logical structure. Additionally, there has been an explosive increase in the volume of financial reporting guidance over the past 20 years, which has compounded the difficulties encountered by preparers and auditors in applying and interpreting GAAP.

In response to concerns that the current structure of GAAP is unwieldy, difficult to understand, and difficult to use; several years ago FASB launched a project to codify and simplify authoritative private-sector GAAP. In contrast to the current multi-tiered GAAP hierarchy, this "Codification" was envisioned as integrating all accounting standards currently within levels (A) through (D) of the GAAP hierarchy into one central, topically organized, electronically searchable site. The GAAP hierarchy would be flattened, and all information within the Codification would be considered level A (authoritative) GAAP. (All other accounting literature not included in the Codification will become nonauthoritative.)

FASB is expected to formally approve the FASB Accounting Standards Codification™ as the single source of authoritative US GAAP effective July 1, 2009. Once that occurs, most of the individual standards used to populate the Codification will be superseded.

*PwC observation: The Codification does not change GAAP; instead it reorganizes the thousands of GAAP pronouncements into roughly 90 accounting topics, and displays all topics using a consistent structure. Like other sectors, not-for-profit organizations are expected to benefit from these efforts to simplify and improve GAAP.*

## Using the Codification

The Codification represents a major change in how accounting literature will be accessed. Its content is arranged within Topics, Subtopics, Sections, and Subsections. Topics reside in four main areas:

- Presentation—topics relating to financial statement presentation matters (e.g., statement of activities, balance sheet)

- Financial Statement Accounts (Assets, Liabilities, Equity, Revenue and Expenses)—topics related to specific financial statement accounts (e.g., revenue recognition, contributions, receivables)

- Broad Transactions—transaction-oriented topics (e.g., business combinations, derivatives)

- Industries—accounting that is unique to an industry (e.g., not-for-profit organizations, healthcare organizations)

To find information on the GAAP requirements for the Statement of Activities of a not-for-profit organization, for example, one could start with either the "Presentation" or "Industries" Topic. Moving down through the topics and subtopics, any of the following paths would retrieve that guidance:

**Start: Presentation**

205—Presentation of Financial Statements
958—Not-for-Profit Organizations

**Start: Presentation**

225—Income Statement
958—Not-for-Profit Organizations

**Start: Industry**

958—Not-for-Profit Organizations
205—Presentation of Financial Statements

The Codification's home page (http://asc.fasb.org/home) provides general information about how to use the online research system. An online tutorial is available. Recently the AICPA issued a Financial Reporting Alert, FASB Codification Developments—2008, to help accountants understand the structure of the Codification's research system and, using case studies, understand how to navigate the system by providing step-by-step illustrations of how to navigate it.

A basic view of the Codification can be accessed free of charge. A subscription service will offer a more sophisticated version which provides high level search and retrieval functions.

*PwC observation: The Codification has an indirect impact on governmental enterprises because a significant portion of the level (A) guidance in the governmental GAAP hierarchy consists of FASB standards that have been made applicable to governmental business-type organizations. GASB is exploring various options for preserving that important component of the governmental GAAP hierarchy (see page 47).*

Final pronouncements, staff positions, interpretations, and EITF consensuses

**FASB Statement No. 16X, *Not-for-Profit Entities: Mergers and Acquisitions* (expected Spring 2009)**

FASB's ten-year-long project to provide guidance on accounting for not-for-profit mergers and acquisitions is expected to come to fruition in Spring 2009 with the issuance of this standard, which represents the not-for-profit analog of FASB Statements No. 141(R), *Business Combinations* (FAS 141(R)) and No. 160, *Noncontrolling Interests in Consolidated Financial Statements* (FAS 160). This standard's scope will include combinations of two or more not-for-profit organizations and transactions in which a not-for-profit organization acquires a for-profit organization. (An acquisition of a not-for-profit organization by a for-profit company is within the scope of FAS 141(R).)

FASB employed a "differences-based" approach to this project, in that it assumed that the general framework for business combinations set forth in FAS 141(R) generally would apply; any departures would need to be justified by specific differences in the nature of not-for-profit combination transactions. The key difference identified in the nature of the transactions is that a business combination is presumed to be a bargained exchange—a transaction in which each party sacrifices and receives commensurate value—whereas not-for-profit combinations often are motivated by reasons that consider mission in addition to financial considerations. Many not-for-profit mergers do not involve any exchange of consideration other than the assumption of the acquiree's liabilities. Thus, unlike business combinations, there may be some transactions with no exchange price paid to provide evidence of the acquired not-for-profit organization's fair value. Also, if consideration is involved, it may not represent the fair value of the acquiree.

Summary of emerging accounting, tax and regulatory issues in 2009
PricewaterhouseCoopers

Based on those differences, the major differences between this standard and FAS 141(R) are:

- FAS 141(R) requires an acquiree to be designated for every transaction. In FAS 16X, the Board permits some combinations to be accounted for as mergers using the carryover basis (i.e., "pooling-type" accounting).

*PwC observation: The original exposure draft required that an acquirer be designated for every transaction, similar to the requirement in FAS 141(R). Based on comments received during the exposure period, FASB reconsidered that decision for situations where both of the combining organizations cede control to a new economic entity.*

- In an acquisition, the fair value of an acquiree would be based on the fair values of its individual assets and liabilities, rather than on its "enterprise value."

- No goodwill would be recognized in acquisitions of organizations predominantly supported by contributions (including investment return from endowments). In acquisitions of not-for-profit organizations that are more "business-like" in nature, goodwill would be recognized only in limited circumstances, and in some cases will represent the acquisition of a net deficit.

The standard will require not-for-profit organizations to distinguish transactions that are a combination from those that are not (e.g., joint ventures, asset acquisitions, transactions between entities under common control). A combination will be defined as a merger of not-for-profit entities or an event that results in initial inclusion of a not-for-profit or business organization in a not-for-profit parent's consolidated financial statements (i.e., an acquisition). Ceding control to a new entity is the sole definitive criterion for identifying a merger, and an entity obtaining control over another entity is the sole definitive criterion for an acquisition.

A merger would occur when the governing bodies of all the combining entities cede control of their respective organizations to a new entity with a newly-formed governing body. Unlike an acquisition, in a merger none of the combining entities obtain control of (or continues to control) the other entities, or dominates the merger transaction. A merger would be accounted for by combining the assets and liabilities of the combining entities as of the merger date at their carryover basis, adjusted as necessary to conform the respective accounting policies (the "carryover method"). Operations of the new entity are reported from the merger date forward. In developing the guidance on applying the carryover method, the Board used as a starting point the guidance in APB Opinion No. 16, *Business Combinations* (APB 16) on applying the pooling method. Except for the guidance on reporting operations of the new entity from the merger date forward and related presentation and disclosure issues, the carryover method guidance is consistent with APB 16's guidance on applying the pooling method. Disclosures required for a merger are a hybrid of the disclosures that will be required for acquisitions and the disclosures currently required by APB 16 for poolings (as appropriate).

*PwC observation: The requirement to measure operations from the merger date forward will be a significant change from current practice. APB 16 requires the combined entity that resulted from a pooling to report combined operations retroactively (in essence, as if the combining entities had always been one organization). FAS 16X's requirement will be consistent with the Board's view that in a merger, a new entity (which would have no previous operations) has emerged from the formerly separate organizations.*

Combinations that are not mergers are acquisitions. If no one of the combining entities clearly acquired the others, identification of the acquirer will require consideration of all facts and circumstances surrounding a combination—in particular, the ability of one organization to dominate the process of selecting a voting majority of the combined organization's governing board. The standard details various indicators organizations should consider when identifying an acquirer. FASB purposely provided guidance in the form of principles, rather than prescriptive criteria.

 166

Once the acquirer has been identified, the next step would be to measure what was acquired. In doing so, the acquirer considers: a) the fair values of the identifiable assets acquired (excluding some exceptions such as unrecognized collections and conditional promises to give), b) the fair values of liabilities assumed, and c) the fair value of consideration transferred (if any).

*PwC observation: This measurement method represents a significant departure from FAS 141(R). The standard will not require the acquiree's fair value to be determined based on an "enterprise value" for the acquired organization as a whole. Rather, the acquiree will be valued based on the sum of the fair values of its individual assets acquired and liabilities assumed, plus consideration (if any). A primary reason for this difference was due to anticipated difficulties in applying the "market participant" concepts of FASB Statement No. 157, "Fair Value Measurements," in estimating enterprise values for transactions involving a change in control without an exchange of consideration. Because not-for-profit organizations are not routinely bought and sold in bargained exchange transactions, there may be no readily available evidence of the "enterprise" fair value of an acquired not-for-profit organization.*

If the fair value of identifiable assets acquired is greater than the fair value of liabilities assumed and consideration transferred (if any), the acquiring organization would recognize *contribution income*. The contribution would increase permanently restricted, temporarily restricted, and/or unrestricted net assets, depending on the types of donor-imposed restrictions assumed by the acquiring entity. If the acquirer is a health care organization, any unrestricted portion of the contribution would be presented within the performance indicator. (This is a change from the exposure draft, which required the contribution to be reported below the performance indicator.)

*PwC observation: We expect most transactions in which a not-for-profit organization is acquired without an exchange of consideration to result in contribution income. This will be the bulk of the transactions that previously were reported as poolings.*

If the fair value of liabilities assumed and consideration transferred exceeds the fair value of identifiable assets acquired, the accounting will differ depending on whether the acquiree's operations are expected to be predominantly supported by contributions or alternatively, by revenues earned in exchange transactions. For acquirees that will be predominantly contribution-supported, the excess is immediately expensed (as if the acquirer made a contribution in taking on the acquired entity) and reported as a separate line item in the statement of activities (e.g., "excess of liabilities assumed over assets acquired in acquisition"). (If the acquirer is a health care organization, the expense is reported above the performance indicator.) If the acquiree's operations are expected to be predominantly supported by revenues earned in exchange transactions (e.g., a hospital acquires another hospital), the excess represents *goodwill*.

*PwC observation: Unless the transaction is a fair-value exchange, we anticipate that goodwill would rarely be recognized, given that the revaluation to fair value of the acquiree's long-lived assets (i.e., buildings, property and equipment) would likely result in significant increases to the asset side of the equation.*

At the date of the acquisition, the assets acquired and liabilities assumed (including goodwill, if any) would be assigned to reporting units as described in FASB Statement No. 142, *Goodwill and Other Intangible Assets* (FAS 142). Goodwill and other intangible assets acquired in the combination would be subsequently accounted for in accordance with FAS 142. Goodwill and certain intangible assets that have indefinite useful lives would not be amortized. Intangible assets that have finite useful lives would be amortized over their useful lives, but without the constraint of an arbitrary ceiling of 40 years previously applied under APB Opinion No. 17, *Intangible Assets*. An acquirer that is predominantly supported by contributions and investment return would write-off any previously recognized goodwill; all other acquirers must perform FAS 142's transitional impairment evaluation on any pre-existing goodwill.

*PwC observation: In assigning assets and liabilities to reporting units, acquirers will use "operating segment" concepts from FASB Statement No. 131, "Disclosures about Segments of an Enterprise and Related Information," (FAS. 131). Because not–for–profit organizations were explicitly excluded from the scope of FAS 131, financial statement preparers may not be familiar with its complex requirements. Further, we believe that few not–for–profit organizations (with the possible exception of some larger hospital systems) regularly review their financial information on the basis of operating segments. Therefore, we expect that the exercise of assigning goodwill to reporting units using FAS 131 concepts (which have proved difficult for for–profit organizations to apply in practice) will prove challenging.*

The guidance in FAS 160 was tailored to the not–for–profit reporting model to provide guidance for the reporting of nonprofits' minority interests (now referred to as "noncontrolling interests") in subsidiaries. Noncontrolling interests would be reported in the balance sheet as a separate component of the appropriate net asset class.

The standard would be applied prospectively to transactions for which the merger date is on or after December 15, 2009 and for acquisitions for which the acquisition date is on or after the beginning of the first annual period beginning on or after December 15, 2009. Earlier application would be prohibited.

## FASB Statement No. 162, *The Hierarchy of Generally Accepted Accounting Principles* (May 2008)

In the United States, generally accepted accounting principles—the body of authoritative accounting principles used in the preparation of financial statements—is referred to as a "hierarchy" because the various standards it contains (FASB, AICPA, EITF, etc.) have varying levels of authoritativeness. Prior to issuance of FAS 162, the GAAP hierarchy for private sector organizations resided in auditing literature.[1] This had come under criticism, as the guidance was directed solely to auditors, rather than to preparers of financial statements. The current hierarchy has

four levels of "authoritativeness" ranging from most authoritative (level A) to least authoritative (level D).

FAS 162 moves the existing multi-tiered hierarchy from the auditing literature to accounting literature with certain minor modifications that FASB does not expect will result in changes to current practice. FAS 162 became effective on November 13, 2008 (the effective date of the change to the auditing literature).

In December 2008, FASB added a project to its agenda to amend FAS 162 to allow FASB's Codification (see page 1) to become the single source of authoritative US GAAP effective July 1, 2009 (effectively superseding FAS 162). In contrast to the current multi-tiered GAAP hierarchy, the Codification collapses the hierarchy and gives all accounting principles within it equal authoritative status.

*PwC observation: The auditing literature established three separate US GAAP hierarchies: one for the private sector, one for state and local governments, and one for federal governmental entities. Issuance of FAS 162 only affects the private sector hierarchy; the GAAP hierarchies for state and local governmental entities and federal governmental entities will remain in SAS 69 pending similar action by GASB and FASAB (see page 42).*

## FASB Statement No. 161, *Disclosures about Derivative Instruments and Hedging Activities* (March 2008)

FAS 161 amends and expands the disclosure requirements in FASB Statement No. 133, *Accounting for Derivative Instruments and Hedging Activities* (FAS 133), and related literature. Those disclosures had been criticized for not being transparent enough to allow financial statement users to assess a reporting entity's overall risk from derivatives from both a quantitative and qualitative perspective. FAS 161's requirements are aimed at providing users of financial statements with an enhanced understanding of how and why an entity usesderivative instruments; how derivative instruments and related hedged items are accounted for under FAS 133 and its related interpretations; and how

---

[1] AICPA Statement on Auditing Standards No. 69, *The Meaning of Present Fairly in Conformity With Generally Accepted Accounting Principles* (SAS 69).

derivative instruments affect an entity's financial position, results of operations/changes in net assets, and cash flows. FAS 161 also amends SOP 02-2, *Accounting for Derivative Instruments and Hedging Activities by Not-for-Profit Health Care Organizations, and Clarification of the Performance Indicator*, to require the disclosure of where and in what financial statement captions derivative gains and losses are displayed. FAS 161 focuses only on disclosures; it does not change any of FAS 133's accounting or financial statement presentation guidance.

Among other things, FAS 161 requires that organizations provide disclosure in a tabular format of the balance sheet captions in which derivatives are reported and the fair value amounts of derivative instruments reported in those captions. Similar disclosures are required for the location and amounts of gains and losses reported in the statement of activities/statement of operations. The latter requires separate categories for derivatives designated and qualifying as fair value hedges, those designated and qualifying as cash flow hedges (for health care organizations), those not designated or not qualifying as hedging instruments, and other categories if applicable. Within each of the categories, separate line items should further categorize derivatives by purpose (i.e., the item being hedged or the exposure created). For not-for-profit organizations, the disclosure requirements are tailored to the FASB Statement No. 117, *Financial Statements of Not-for-Profit Organizations* (FAS 117) not-for-profit reporting model.

Simplified examples of certain of the tabular disclosures are provided below for a hypothetical not-for-profit organization whose only derivatives are interest rate swaps tied to debt. Table 1 illustrates the balance sheet tabular disclosure requirements. With respect to the tabular disclosures of gains and losses reported in the statement of activities/statement of operations, Table 2 illustrates the disclosures for non-hedging derivatives. (For a not-for-profit health care organization, the disclosure should indicate the amount of gain (loss) recognized in the performance indicator, rather than in

changes in net assets.) The disclosure must also provide information about derivatives that are designated as fair value hedges and, for a not-for-profit health care organization, for derivatives designated as cash flow hedges. Table 3 illustrates the tabular cash flow hedging disclosures for a not-for-profit health care organization. Not-for-profit organizations also are required to indicate which class or classes of net assets (unrestricted, temporarily restricted, or permanently restricted) are affected by derivative usage.

Derivatives often contain features (e.g., material adverse change clauses (MAC) or payment acceleration clauses) that could result in an immediate payment to a counterparty on an agreement that is in a liability position. For example, a MAC clause could provide the counterparty with the right to terminate the derivative agreement before maturity if specified events occur, such as a downgrade of the entity's credit rating below a certain threshold. Another common feature is a collateral posting provision which, if triggered, would require the organization to post cash, investments, or other assets as collateral against its liability. FAS 161 requires quantitative disclosures about the potential cash outflows that would be required upon the occurrence of such events to provide increased visibility into the potential impact such features could have on an organization's liquidity. Disclosures related to the volume of derivatives activity must be provided. Additionally, the qualitative disclosures currently encouraged in paragraph 44 of FAS 133 have been clarified to focus on an entity's market risks and strategies to manage those risks.

FAS 161 is effective for interim or annual periods beginning after November 15, 2008, and should be applied on a prospective basis (that is, it does not require comparative information for periods presented prior to the adoption date), with early application encouraged.

Summary of emerging accounting, tax and regulatory issues in 2009
PricewaterhouseCoopers

*PwC observation: Recent market events and the prevalent use of interest rate swaps by hospitals, universities, and other not-for-profit organizations in connection with variable-rate debt issuances, highlight the importance of these new disclosures. Many swaps that previously were effectively hedging organizations' interest rate risk have now swung into unfavorable positions, resulting in liabilities that can run to hundreds of millions of dollars. As a result, many organizations are being required to post collateral with swap counterparties, and/or are facing swap termination payments. Because of the size of those numbers, they can have a significant impact on an organizations' liquidity. In some cases, this could lead a borrower to violate financial covenants/technical default under the bond indenture or related documents like bank liquidity agreements. The new disclosures provide increased visibility into such contingencies.*

**Table 1**
*Fair Values of Derivative Instruments*

| As of December 31 | Derivatives Reported as Assets | | | | Derivatives Reported as Liabilities | | | |
|---|---|---|---|---|---|---|---|---|
| | 2009 | | 2008 | | 2009 | | 2008 | |
| | Bal. Sheet Caption | Fair Value | Bal. Sheet Caption | Fair Value | Bal. Sheet Caption | Fair Value | Bal. Sheet Caption | Fair Value |
| Interest rate swaps designated as hedging instruments under FAS 133 | Other Assets | XX,XXX | Other Assets | XX,XXX | Other Liab. | XX,XXX | Other Liab. | XX,XXX |
| Interest rate swaps not designated as hedging instruments under FAS 133 | Other Assets | XX,XXX | Other Assets | XX,XXX | Other Liab. | XX,XXX | Other Liab | XX,XXX |
| Total Derivatives | | XX,XXX | | XX,XXX | | XX,XXX | | XX,XXX |

**Table 2**
*Derivatives not designated as hedging instruments under FAS 133:*

| Classification of derivative gain (loss) in Statement of Activities | Amount of gain (loss) recognized in change in unrestricted net assets | |
|---|---|---|
| | 2009 | 2008 |
| Interest rate swaps: | | |
| Nonoperating revenue | XX,XXX | XX,XXX |

**Table 3**
*Derivatives in FAS 133 Cash Flow Hedging Relationships:*

| Classification of derivative gain (loss) in Statement of Operations | Amount of gain (loss) recognized in the PI (ineffective portion) | | Classification of gain (loss) reclassified from below to above PI | Amount of gain (loss) reclassified from below to above the PI (effective portion) | | Amount of gain (loss) recognized outside the PI (effective portion) | |
|---|---|---|---|---|---|---|---|
| | 2009 | 2008 | | 2009 | 2008 | 2009 | 2008 |
| Interest rate swaps: | | | Interest income (expense) | | | | |
| Nonoperating revenue | XX,XXX | XX,XXX | | XX,XXX | XX,XXX | XX,XXX | XX,XXX |

**FASB Statement No. 159, *The Fair Value Option for Financial Assets and Financial Liabilities* (February 2007)**

Prior to issuance of FAS 159, only a limited range of financial assets and liabilities could be measured at fair value in financial statements on a recurring basis. Now, FAS 159 provides organizations with the option to measure many of their financial assets and liabilities at fair value, if desired. This "fair value option" represents a significant step in the evolution of financial reporting because it considerably expands an organization's ability to select the measurement attribute it uses for certain assets and liabilities, and, in many cases, offers an opportunity to simplify the accounting for these assets and liabilities.

*PwC observation: The PwC publication "Fair Value Option Considerations—A Guide for Not-for-Profit Organizations" discusses the pros and cons of making fair value option elections with respect to a number of accounts typically found in the financial statements of not-for-profit organizations.*

At the initial effective date of FAS 159, organizations could consider whether to elect the fair value option for existing financial instruments held at the beginning of their financial reporting period. Although that window of opportunity has passed, an organization can continue to make fair value option elections for eligible financial assets and liabilities newly acquired or issued. The election is also available when a previously recognized asset or liability is subject to a "remeasurement event" as defined in paragraph 8 of FAS 159. FAS 159 generally permits organizations to apply the fair value option on an instrument–by–instrument basis, with some exceptions. The table below provides examples of financial assets and liabilities that are (or are not eligible) for the fair value measurement election.

Not–for–profit healthcare organizations report unrealized gains and losses on items for which the fair value option has been elected within the performance indicator or as a part of discontinued operations, as appropriate. For all other not–for–profit organizations, the unrealized gains and losses are reported as changes in net assets or discontinued operations, as appropriate. If the organization also reports an intermediate measure of operations, it may report the gains and losses either within or outside that measure.

*PwC observation: Subsequent to FAS 159's initial effective date, in general, the fair value option can only be elected for newly issued or acquired instruments. It cannot be elected retroactively for financial instruments that existed at the effective date (i.e., beginning of the fiscal year that begins after November 15, 2007).*

**Assets and liabilities eligible/ineligible for the Fair Value Option**

| Eligible | Not Eligible |
| --- | --- |
| • Investments accounted for under the equity method | • Investments in consolidated subsidiaries |
| • Investments carried at cost | • Employer benefit–related obligations and assets |
| • Multi–year promises to give | |
| • Split interest agreements without embedded derivatives | • Financial assets and financial liabilities recognized pursuant to leases |
| • Beneficial interests in trusts | |
| • Debt | |

Summary of emerging accounting, tax and regulatory issues in 2009
PricewaterhouseCoopers

## FASB Statement No. 158, *Employers' Accounting for Defined Benefit Pension and Other Postretirement Plans* (September 2006)

FAS 158 represented a landmark revision of FASB's suite of standards related to pension and post-employment benefits.[2] While its requirements related to reporting the funded status of plans on the balance sheet are already effective, organizations that have not yet adopted its measurement date provisions must do so in their financial statements for fiscal years ended after December 15, 2008.

FAS 158 eliminated an employer's ability to choose a measurement date up to three months prior to year-end for measuring the funded status of their plans. Now, employers are required to measure plan assets and benefit obligations as of the balance sheet date. The standard provides two alternatives for transitioning to the new measurement date.

- **Alternative one** (the "two-measurement" approach) requires an employer to measure plan assets and obligations as of the earlier measurement date, and to use that measurement to compute net benefit expense for the period between that date and the corresponding fiscal year-end, and then perform a second measurement of plan assets and obligations as of the beginning of the fiscal year for which the new measurement date is adopted. For example, an employer with a December 31 year-end which historically had performed its annual measurements on September 30 would have performed its first measurement on September 30, 2007, and performed a second measurement on December 31, 2007 to determine pension expense for its 2008 fiscal year. The first measurement would have covered the period between September 30, 2007 and December 31, 2007 (referred to as the "transition period"). The net benefit expense for the transition period would be reported as an adjustment to net assets at the beginning of the fiscal year for which the new measurement date is adopted (January 1, 2008 in this example), as would changes in the fair value of plan assets and the benefit obligations, such as for prior service costs and for gains and losses, (e.g., due to a change

in discount rates at year-end) that occur during the transition period.

- **Alternative two** (the "one-measurement" or "15-month" approach) requires the use of the existing early measurement date to compute net benefit expense for the period between the early measurement date in the prior year and the end of the fiscal year for which the new measurement date is adopted. Continuing with our previous example, this alternative allows the employer to report the net benefit expense for the transition period as an adjustment to either beginning or ending net assets in the year in which the new measurement date is adopted (calendar 2008). Changes in the fair value of plan assets and changes in the benefit obligations for prior service costs and gains and losses are recorded below the performance indicator (for not-for-profit healthcare organizations) or against the same line item or items within changes in unrestricted net assets (apart from expenses) as the initial adjustment for the adoption of FAS 158 for all other not-for-profit organizations.

*PwC observation: An employer must select one of these alternatives and apply it consistently. An employer may not select alternative one for some plans and alternative two for others.*

## FASB Statement No. 157, *Fair Value Measurements* (September 2006)

FAS 157 addresses how organizations should measure fair value when GAAP requires use of fair value measurement for recognition or disclosure purposes. Previously, different FASB standards contained various definitions of fair value. FAS 157 replaces these various definitions with a common definition of fair value to be used throughout GAAP. FASB believes that the new standard will make the measurement of fair value more consistent and comparable, and will improve disclosures about those measures.

*PwC observation: FAS 157 does not impose fair value measurement on any assets or liabilities; it simply provides the definition of fair value for use in standards where fair value measurement is required.*

---

[2] Statements No. 87, *Employers' Accounting for Pensions;* No. 88, *Employers' Accounting for Settlements and Curtailments of Defined Benefit Pension Plans and for Termination Benefits;* No. 106, *Employers' Accounting for Postretirement Benefits Other Than Pensions;* and No. 132(R), *Employers' Disclosures about Pensions and Other Postretirement Benefits.*

FAS 157 defines fair value as "the price that would be received to sell an asset or paid to transfer a liability in an orderly transaction between market participants at the measurement date." This definition of fair value retains the exchange–price notion contained (either explicitly or implicitly) in many earlier GAAP definitions of fair value. However, FAS 157 clarifies that the basis for a fair value measure is the price at which an organization would sell or otherwise dispose of its assets or pay to settle a liability (i.e., an exit price), not the market price at which an organization acquires its assets or assumes a liability (i.e., an entry price). The exit price concept is based on current expectations about the future inflows associated with the asset and the future outflows associated with the liability from the perspective of market participants. Under FAS 157, a fair value measure should reflect all of the assumptions that market participants would use in pricing the asset

or liability, including, for example, an adjustment for risk inherent in a particular valuation technique used to measure fair value.

FAS 157 emphasizes that fair value is a market-based measurement, not an entity-specific measurement. The valuation techniques used for measuring the fair value of the asset or liability have not changed, but in the FAS 157 framework they are applied from a market participant's perspective, rather than from the reporting entity's perspective. FAS 157 also prioritizes the quality of the data inputs used in these valuation techniques by establishing a three-level "fair value hierarchy" that gives the highest priority to quoted prices in active markets (level 1) and the lowest priority to entity-specific estimates based on internal data (level 3).

*PwC observation: FAS 157 introduces a number of new concepts, such as "exit price," "principal or most advantageous market," "highest and best use," "in-use" and "in–exchange" valuation premises, and the perspectives of "market participants." These concepts can be particularly challenging to apply to nonexchange transactions such as contributions. The PwC publication "Impact of FAS 157 on Contribution Accounting—A Guide for Not-for-Profit Organizations" provides commentary specific to those issues along with practical examples.*

FAS 157 requires extensive disclosures to provide information about: (1) the extent to which organizations measure assets and liabilities at fair value, (2) the methods and assumptions used to measure fair value, and (3) the effect of fair value measures on net assets. The disclosure requirements vary depending on whether the fair value measurement occurs once or on an ongoing basis, as well as on the level in the fair value hierarchy within which the measurement falls. Extensive quantitative (tabular) disclosures are required for assets and liabilities that are measured at fair value on a recurring basis (i.e., when fair value is the measurement attribute both initially and subsequent to initial measurement). This includes marketable securities, alternative investment portfolios carried at fair value under the option provided by the AICPA

**Some of the areas where FAS 157 will impact fair value measurements:**

- Contributions (FAS 116)
- Beneficial interests in trusts (FAS 136)
- Split–interest agreements (FAS 116, FAS 136)
- Investments in trading and available–for–sale securities (FAS 124)
- Alternative/other investments (AAG–NPO)
- Asset retirement obligations (FIN 47)*
- Impairments of long–lived assets (FAS 144)*
- Exit and disposal activities (FAS 146)*
- Assets in pensions and other postretirement benefit plans (FAS 87, FAS 106)
- Derivatives, primarily interest rate swaps (FAS 133)
- Long–term debt disclosures (FAS 107)

*Deferred for one year

Audit and Accounting Guide Not-for-Profit Organizations, derivatives, and beneficial interests in trusts held by third parties. If the recurring fair value measurement is based on level 3 inputs, disclosure requirements are even more extensive.

For nonrecurring fair value measurements, disclosures are required only in the period when the fair value measurement takes place subsequent to initial measurement. Three examples that incorporate non-recurring fair value measurements include asset retirement obligations, impairments of long-lived assets, and costs associated with exit or disposal activities. Qualitative (narrative) disclosures about the valuation techniques used to measure fair value are also required. Where practicable, the fair value information disclosed under FAS 157 should be combined and disclosed together with fair value information disclosed under other pronouncements, including FASB Statement No. 107, *Disclosures about Fair Value of Financial Instruments*, (FAS 107) (for example, in a single fair value footnote). Items that are only initially recognized at fair value need only comply with pre-existing disclosure requirements.

FAS 157 has a dual implementation date based upon the type of asset or liability and whether fair value measurement is one-time or recurring. For all financial assets and liabilities, and for nonfinancial assets and liabilities measured at fair value on a recurring basis, the standard must be applied for financial statements issued for periods beginning after November 15, 2007. For nonfinancial assets and liabilities that are measured at fair value on a nonrecurring basis, the effective date is delayed by one year (i.e., periods beginning after November 15, 2008). These include asset retirement obligations, impairments of long-lived assets, and liabilities for exit and disposal activities.

*PwC observation: PwC's "Guide to Fair Value Measurements" publication includes significant discussion on the interaction between FAS 157 and the standards governing assets and liabilities that were impacted by the deferral.*

A number of FAS 157-related pronouncements or projects are discussed elsewhere in this publication, including:

- FSP FAS 157-3, *Determining the Fair Value of a Financial Asset When the Market for That Asset Is Not Active* (see page 13)

- EITF 08-5, *Issuer's Accounting for Liabilities Measured at Fair Value with a Third-Party Credit Enhancement* (see page 17)

- Proposed FSP FAS 157-c, *Measuring Liabilities Under FASB Statement No. 157* (see page 22)

- Proposed FSP FAS 107-b/APB 28-a, *Interim Disclosures about Fair Value of Financial Instruments* (see page 23)

- An AICPA draft issues paper, FASB Statement No. 157 Valuation Considerations for Interests in Alternative Investments (see page 28)

- New FASB short-term agenda projects intended to improve the application guidance used to determine fair values and disclosure of fair value estimates (see page 23)

The "Valuation Resource Group" (VRG) is an advisory group created to provide the FASB staff with information on implementation issues surrounding fair value measurements used for financial statement reporting purposes and the alternative viewpoints associated with those implementation issues. A summary of the VRG's discussions (and the FASB staff's related observations) is available on FASB's Web site at http://fasb.org/project/valuation_resource_group.shtml.

*PwC observation: In order to effectively implement FAS 157, organizations should prepare an inventory of existing assets and liabilities that may be impacted by it. A list of potential areas of impact for not–for–profit organizations is highlighted in the chart. Next, organizations should perform an analysis to determine how fair value is currently measured, compared to how it will need to be measured using the new FAS 157 concepts. This "gap analysis" will help determine what additional information will be needed, what policies need to be documented or added, and what process changes will be required upon and after adoption.*

# APPENDIX D

**FASB Staff Position FIN 48–3,** *Effective Date of FIN 48 for Certain Nonpublic Enterprises* **(December 2008)**

**FASB Interpretation No. 48,** *Accounting for Uncertainty in Income Taxes* **(June 2006)**

FIN 48 prescribes a comprehensive model for how organizations (including not–for–profit organizations) should recognize, measure, present and disclose uncertain tax positions that they have taken (or expect to take) on a tax return. (FIN 48's provisions are discussed in detail in the "Tax Issues" section of this document.) FIN 48 was effective for fiscal years beginning after December 15, 2006. In February 2008, FASB deferred for one year the effective date for "certain nonpublic enterprises"; in December 2008, FSP No. FIN 48-3 provided an additional one-year deferral. *Note that the additional one-year deferral is not available to not–for–profit organizations that meet the definition of a "public enterprise" in FASB Statement No. 109, "Accounting for Income Taxes." "Public enterprises" includes not–for–profit organizations which have issued tax–exempt bonds that trade in a public market.* "Public enterprise" not-for-profits should already be incorporating FIN 48 in their financial statements.

*PwC observation: Tax-exempt bonds are traded in the over-the-counter markets. Generally, tax–exempt bonds issued in negotiated sales or competitive bids are deemed to trade in a public market; tax–exempt bonds issued in private placements do not.*

The additional one-year deferral is available to nonpublic entities that have not yet issued a full set of annual financial statements incorporating the requirements of FIN 48. For those entities, FIN 48 will become effective for fiscal years beginning after December 15, 2008 (i.e., calendar year 2009 and thereafter).

FASB plans to issue additional application guidance for certain organizations (see page 25).

**FASB Staff Position No. FAS 132(R)–1,** *Employers' Disclosures about Postretirement Benefit Plan Assets* **(December 2008)**

This FSP was issued to improve financial statement disclosures related to benefit plan assets reported in the sponsor's financial statements. FASB was concerned about a lack of transparency surrounding the types of assets held in postretirement benefit plans and the potential concentrations of credit risk in plan asset portfolios that are not currently disclosed. Further, FAS 157 disclosures are not required for pension and other postretirement benefit plan assets in a sponsor's financial statements. Thus, FASB determined that improvements to disclosures about assets held in an employer's defined benefit pension or other postretirement benefit plan reported under FAS 132(R) were necessary. The enhanced disclosure requirements are similar in certain respects to FAS 157's disclosure requirements for assets.

The FSP amends FAS 132(R) to require the following additional disclosures:

- The fair value of each major category of plan assets (based on the types of assets held in the plan) as of each annual reporting date for which a balance sheet is presented

- The nature and amount of concentrations of risk within or across categories of plan assets

*PwC observation: Although FAS 132(R) already requires certain disclosures regarding major categories of plan assets, FASB believed those disclosures were not specific enough to allow financial statement users to determine the types of assets held as investments and the related concentrations of risk that may arise from a lack of diversification.*

- Disclosures about fair value measurements similar to those required by FAS 157 including a reconciliation of the beginning and ending balances of assets measured using significant unobservable inputs (level 3)

Summary of emerging accounting, tax and regulatory issues in 2009
PricewaterhouseCoopers

*PwC observation: This provision is included because FAS 157 disclosures are not required for plan assets reported in the sponsor's financial statements. Such disclosures provide useful information about the valuation techniques and inputs used for fair value measurements of plan assets, the level within the fair value hierarchy in which the assets fall, and a reconciliation of the beginning and ending balances of fair value of assets measured using significant unobservable inputs (level 3).*

The FSP also reinstates a requirement for nonpublic entities to disclose net periodic benefit cost for each period presented (which was inadvertently eliminated from FAS 132(R) by the issuance of FAS 158). That requirement became effective upon issuance of the FSP. The requirements related to disclosures about plan assets are applicable on a prospective basis for fiscal years ending after December 15, 2009. Earlier application is permitted.

### FASB Staff Position No. FAS 157-3, *Determining the Fair Value of a Financial Asset When the Market for That Asset Is Not Active* (October 2008)

Given the depressed state of the securities markets, confusion exists regarding the use of market quotes and whether current market prices represent the fair value of investments in accordance with FAS 157 or are in actuality distressed sales. This FSP clarifies FAS 157's application in inactive markets by addressing:

- How an organization's own assumptions (i.e., expected cash flows and appropriately risk-adjusted discount rates) should be considered when relevant observable inputs do not exist

- How available observable inputs in a market that is not active should be considered when measuring fair value

- How the use of market quotes (e.g., broker quotes or pricing services for the same or similar financial assets) should be considered when assessing the relevance of observable and unobservable inputs available to measure fair value

The FSP was effective upon issuance (October 10, 2008). Any revisions resulting from changes in valuation techniques or their application should be accounted for as changes in accounting estimates.

### FASB Staff Position No. FAS 117–1, *Endowments of Not–for–Profit Organizations: Net Asset Classification of Funds Subject to an Enacted Version of UPMIFA, and Enhanced Disclosures* (August 2008)

This FSP has widespread importance to the not-for-profit sector, especially with respect to organizations with large endowments. Its purpose is twofold. First, in an era of increased public scrutiny of not-for-profits' endowment management and spending policies, the Board believed that users of financial statements (such as donors, credit rating agencies, and regulators) would benefit from enhanced disclosures regarding an organization's endowment and its policies for managing them. Second, the Board believed that organizations located in states that were adopting (or will soon adopt) a new model law governing investment, management, and spending from donor-restricted endowments (the Uniform Prudent Management of Institutional Funds Act or "UPMIFA") required guidance regarding the effect of that statutory change on the classification of net assets reported in their balance sheets.

*New disclosures required for all not-for-profits*

The FSP significantly expands the disclosures that all not-for-profit organizations must make with respect to their permanently-restricted gifts, term endowments, and quasi-endowments. The new disclosures apply to both "true" donor-restricted endowments (temporary and permanent) as well as board-designated funds functioning as endowments. They include:

- A description of the governing board's interpretation of the law that underlies the net asset classification of donor–restricted endowment funds

- A description of endowment spending policies

- A description of endowment investment policies, including the organization's return objectives and risk parameters, how those objectives relate to the organization's endowment spending policies, and the strategies employed for achieving those objectives
- The composition of an organization's endowment by net asset classification at the end of the period, in total and by type of endowment fund, showing donor–restricted endowment funds separately from board–designated endowment funds
- A reconciliation of the beginning and ending balances of the organization's endowment, in total and by net asset class, including investment return (separated between investment income earned and net appreciation/depreciation), contributions received, amounts appropriated for expenditure, reclassifications between net asset classes, and other changes

Appendix C of the FSP provides illustrative disclosures.

*PwC observation: These disclosures apply to all not–for–profit organizations, not just those operating in states where UPMIFA has been enacted.*

*Provisions affecting organizations in UPMIFA states*

When a donor's instructions regarding investing of or spending from endowments created by a gift are unclear, governing boards are faced with the task of interpreting the donor's instructions and acting accordingly. Virtually all states have enacted laws which provide guidance to assist governing boards in discharging their responsibilities in such situations, the most prominent of which was the Uniform Management of Institutional Funds Act (UMIFA) model law established in 1972. Because the complexity of investments and endowment management has increased, a new model law, UPMIFA, was drafted in 2006 to replace UMIFA, and individual states began enacting it shortly thereafter. The UPMIFA provisions of the FSP were issued to provide guidance on how this change in law would affect the financial reporting of donor-restricted endowments held in those states.

For financial reporting purposes, restricted net assets arise solely from restrictions imposed by donors; they do not arise from legal or contractual restrictions. UPMIFA's provisions governing "total return expenditure" from donor-restricted endowment funds are considered to be extensions of the donor's original instructions, not simply restrictions imposed by law. Thus, the financial reporting consequences of restrictions on spending imposed by UPMIFA laws align with the concept of reporting restrictions under the FAS 117 not-for-profit financial reporting model. Once UPMIFA becomes effective in a state, the only portion of a donor-restricted endowment fund that can be considered unrestricted is the portion that has been formally "appropriated for expenditure" by a not-for-profit's governing board. The remainder of the fund is restricted, both for legal and for accounting purposes.

The FSP requires that any portion of a donor-restricted endowment fund that is not classified as permanently restricted be classified as temporarily restricted net assets "until appropriated for expenditure by the organization." This involves implying a time restriction on the portion of a fund which previously would have been classified as unrestricted net assets prior to issuance of the FSP. The implied time restriction lapses only when and to the degree that a governing board appropriates an amount for expenditure from the fund after weighing the seven factors detailed in UPMIFA's prudent spending guidelines. If the donor-restricted endowment also carries a purpose restriction, the implied time restriction must be met (through appropriation for spending) before the purpose restriction can be met, in accordance with FASB Statement No. 116, *Accounting for Contributions Received and Contributions Made* (FAS 116).[3]

*PwC observation: Going forward, organizations in states subject to UPMIFA laws are likely to see a significant buildup in temporarily restricted net assets, and significantly smaller amounts of reclassifications from temporarily restricted to unrestricted net assets each year as a result of this change.*

---

[3] Paragraph 17, footnote 5.

Because UPMIFA eliminates the legal concept of "historic dollar value" and instead focuses on a fund as a whole, it imposes no duty to distinguish between temporarily and permanently restricted portions of funds. The FAS 117 net asset reporting model requires such distinctions to be made; thus, the FSP requires not-for-profits to determine (on a fund-by-fund basis) the portion of each donor-restricted endowment fund of perpetual duration that must be reported in financial statements as permanently restricted net assets.

If a state enacts a version of UPMIFA that explicitly requires the "purchasing power" of the original gift to be maintained, the original gift amount recorded in permanently restricted net assets must perpetually be adjusted. For financial reporting purposes, there is a significant difference between a statute that explicitly requires a portion of gains to be retained permanently and a statute that does not. An example of the former is Rhode Island's UMIFA law, which explicitly states that "The historic dollar value of an endowment fund shall be prudently adjusted from time to time to reflect the change, if any, in the purchasing power of the historic dollar value of the fund." The text of the model UPMIFA law does not include any similar statutory mandate to adjust the value of the fund to reflect the change in purchasing power. Recognizing that each state enacting an UPMIFA law might enact it with variations (as did Rhode Island with UMIFA), FASB stressed that organizations need to focus on the specific wording of the version of UPMIFA enacted in its state in determining whether it is legally required to maintain the purchasing power of its endowments.

*PwC observation: UPMIFA's prudent spending guidelines list "inflation" as one of the factors that an organization's board should take into account when making decisions about appropriating funds for expenditure. This appears to be consistent with an organizational policy of informally maintaining an inflation reserve by setting a spending rate that is lower than the expected rate of return, rather than a statutory mandate to retain appreciation. The FSP's basis for conclusions draws a clear distinction between an organizational policy of maintaining an inflation reserve and a statutory requirement to retain a portion of appreciation, stating that only the latter situation would result in adjusting permanently restricted net assets.*

UPMIFA also significantly changes an organization's ability to appropriate resources for spending from "underwater endowments." UPMIFA's predecessor (UMIFA) previously allowed spending of the net appreciation in excess of the historic dollar value of the underlying gifts. In "underwater" situations (i.e., when the fair value of the fund falls below the historic dollar value of the gift), UMIFA limited the ability to spend from the endowment until the fund recovered in value. UPMIFA provides more flexibility, allowing organizations to continue to appropriate funds for spending when funds are "underwater" if the governing board deems it prudent to do so after considering UPMIFA's seven prudent spending factors. However, the amount of permanently restricted net assets should not be reduced by investment losses or by spending in "underwater" situations.

*PwC observation: In substance, the changes brought about by UPMIFA merely provide organizations with short–term spending flexibility to deal with market declines that result in underwater situations. While the amount of assets associated with a donor-restricted endowment fund might fluctuate, the accountability to the donor for a permanent endowment remains unchanged.*

The FSP is effective for fiscal years ended after December 15, 2008 and requires retroactive application. The cumulative effect of any reclassifications between net asset classes resulting from adopting the FSP would be reported as a separate line item in the statement of activities/statement of operations, outside of any performance indicator or intermediate measure of operations, in the period in which UPMIFA becomes effective.

*PwC observation: For many organizations, the reclassification from unrestricted net assets to temporarily restricted net assets that will be required in connection with initial adoption of the FSP is expected to be significant.*

**FASB Staff Position SOP 94–3–1/AAG HCO-1,
*Omnibus Changes to Consolidation and
Equity Method Guidance for Not–for–Profit
Organizations* (May 2008)**

This FSP was issued to address conflicts in SOP 94–3, *Reporting of Related Entities by Not–for–Profit Organizations* (SOP 94–3) and the AICPA Audit and Accounting Guide Health Care Organizations (AAG–HCO) concerning consolidation and equity method guidance for not–for–profit organizations.

The FSP makes narrowly-focused amendments to the guidance for consolidation of related not-for-profit organizations. These pertain to the areas of sole corporate membership, majority voting interests, and temporary control.

*Sole corporate membership in another not-for-profit.* If a not-for-profit's articles of incorporation designate another not-for-profit as its sole "corporate member," AAG-HCO currently states that the sole corporate member generally would possess a controlling financial interest that requires consolidation unless it does not possess control. SOP 94-3 is silent regarding "sole corporate members." The FSP amends SOP 94-3 to conform to AAG-HCO in this regard.

*PwC observation: In effect, this explicitly requires all not-for-profit organizations to first consider "sole corporate membership" when evaluating whether consolidation is required. A sole corporate member is automatically deemed to have both control and an economic interest unless limitations have been placed on its ability to control.*

*Majority voting interest in the board of another not-for-profit.* The FSP also clarifies certain aspects of the guidance regarding possession of a "majority voting interest" in the board of a not-for-profit organization. First, it clarifies that the determination of whether a "majority voting interest" exists is made in relation to a not-for-profit organization's fully constituted board (i.e., the complement of board members provided for in its

charter or bylaws). If vacancies on that board cause another organization to temporarily possess a majority voting interest, that circumstance above would not require consolidation. Additionally, if a not-for-profit's articles of incorporation provide another organization the right to appoint a certain number of its board seats, those appointees do not need to be board members, employees, or officers of the appointing organization in order for a majority voting interest to exist.

*Temporary control exceptions.* The FSP eliminates the "temporary control" exception to consolidation that existed for certain relationships between not–for–profit organizations. Issuance of FASB Statement No. 144, *Accounting for the Impairment or Disposal of Long-Lived Assets* (FAS 144) had eliminated some, but not all, of the temporary control exceptions in SOP 94-3 and AAG-HCO; the FSP removes the exceptions.

The FSP also clarifies guidance on consolidation and application of the equity method with respect to investments in for-profit entities (including so-called "alternative investments").

*Consolidation of leasing special purpose entities (SPEs).* Several EITF issues[4] provide guidance on evaluating consolidation of SPE leasing entities. Not-for-profits (especially hospitals and universities) frequently use leasing SPEs, including SPEs that would be deemed "nonsubstantive" in nature and require consolidation under the EITF guidance. The EITF guidance was deemed nullified for entities that are within the scope of FASB Interpretation No. 46(R), *Consolidation of Variable Interest Entities* (FIN 46(R)). Because not-for-profits are excluded from the scope of FIN 46(R), the FSP affirms the continued applicability of the SPE leasing guidance to not–for–profit lessees in evaluating whether consolidation is required. The FSP also clarifies one specific aspect of EITF 90-15, stating that in order for a lessee not to be required to consolidate an SPE lessor, the majority owner(s) of record of the lessor must be an independent third party.[5]

---

[4] EITF 90-15, *Impact of Nonsubstantive Lessors, Residual Value Guarantees, and Other Provisions in Leasing Transactions (EITF 90-15); EITF 96-21, Implementation Issues in Accounting for Leasing Transactions Involving Special-Purpose Entities* (EITF 96-21); and EITF 97-1, *Implementation Issues in Accounting for Lease Transactions, Including Those Involving Special-Purpose Entities* (EITF 97-1)

[5] The FSP was silent on whether not-for-profit organizations should apply the SEC staff views expressed in EITF 90-15 (Questions 1-9) and Topic D-14, *Transactions Involving Special Purpose Entities*. However, it explicitly addressed one of the issues covered by Topic D-14; that is, in order for a lessee not to be required to consolidate an SPE lessor, the majority owner(s) of record of the lessor must be an independent third party.

Application of the equity method to alternative investments. The FSP clarifies that certain not-for-profit organizations must evaluate whether they are required to account for noncontrolling interests in companies such as LLCs and partnerships using the equity method. Those not-for-profit organizations include (a) all not-for-profit health care organizations and (b) all other not-for-profit organizations that do not carry their alternative investment portfolios at fair value as permitted by SOP 94-3.[6] Such not-for-profit organizations shall apply the guidance in FSP SOP 78-9-1 (*Interaction of AICPA SOP 78-9 and EITF Issue No. 04-5*) to determine whether their interests in for-profit partnerships, LLCs, and similar entities are "controlling interests" or "noncontrolling interests." They shall apply the guidance in EITF 03-16 (*Accounting for Investments in Limited Liability Corporations*) to determine whether an LLC should be viewed as similar to a partnership (as opposed to a corporation) for purposes of determining whether noncontrolling interests in an LLC or similar entity should be accounted for in accordance with SOP 78-9 (*Accounting for Investments in Real Estate Ventures*) for LPs or APB 18 (*The Equity Method of Accounting for Investments in Common Stock*) for stock corporations.

FSP SOP 94-3-1/AAG HCO-1 and the resulting amendments to SOP 94–3 and AAG–HCO are effective for fiscal years beginning after June 15, 2008.

### EITF 08-5, *Issuer's Accounting for Liabilities Measured at Fair Value with a Third-Party Credit Enhancement* (December 2008)

EITF 08-5 clarifies considerations associated with measuring the fair value of a liability that contains an inseparable third-party credit enhancement. All such enhancements must be separated from the liability when measuring or disclosing fair value under FAS 157.

*PwC observation: Insured municipal bonds would fall within the scope of EITF 08-5, because the bond insurance is a form of third-party credit enhancement. In order to properly measure the fair value of the municipal bonds, the effect of the bond insurance would need to be eliminated. When bonds are insured, the bond rating is based on the rating of the financial guarantor, rather than the borrower. For example, if a BBB-rated organization issues bonds insured by a AA-rated bond insurer, the bonds will be rated AA. Because EITF 08-5 precludes the organization from considering the bond insurance in the measurement of fair value, the fair value of the bonds would be determined using the borrower's underlying BBB rating.*

Practically, the requirement to fair value the debt without the credit enhancement presents some challenges. Most municipal debt issuers have historically obtained fair value information based on recent trade transactions. If trades were not proximate to the measurement date, the trades were adjusted to reflect credit spreads and yields using observable market data as of the measurement date. Under EITF 08-5, the market trades may be relevant inputs, but they will need to be adjusted since the trades are based upon the values of the debt instrument trading with the credit enhancement. Organizations will need to examine credit spreads and yields based upon their own credit standing as of the measurement date, which may be significantly different.

Other liabilities with credit enhancements may include derivatives (e.g., interest rate swaps) or other debt instruments (e.g., lines of credit or privately placed debt). Credit enhancements provided by a related party (e.g., parent or subsidiary) or the federal government (e.g., Perkins loans) are explicitly excluded from the scope of EITF 08-5.

EITF 08-5 is effective for reporting periods beginning on or after December 15, 2008 and should be applied prospectively. Early application is permitted.

*PwC observation: EITF 08-5 will primarily be relevant when making disclosures about the fair value of debt instruments under FAS 107, "Disclosures about Fair Value of Financial Instruments."*

---

[6] Par. 7 of SOP 94-3 grants an exception to applying the equity method to organizations that elect to carry their portfolio of alternative investments at fair value. It grants no similar exception to organizations that do not make this election.

■ 180 ■

**EITF 07–1,** *Accounting for Collaborative Arrangements* **(December 2007)**

EITF 07–1 addresses the appropriate accounting for "collaborative arrangements"—that is, for joint venture–like collaborations between two or more entities that do not involve the creation of a separate legal entity. An arrangement is within the scope of EITF 07–1 if the parties to the arrangement actively participate in the arrangement and are exposed to its risks and rewards, and the arrangement does not involve the creation of a separate legal entity. Prior to the EITF undertaking this project, many not–for–profit organizations relied upon a healthcare–specific AICPA Technical Practice Aid (TPA) 6400.33, *Accounting for a Joint Operating Arrangement*, for guidance in accounting for collaborative arrangements or joint operating arrangements that were not conducted in a separate legal entity. The TPA considered such arrangements to be "virtual joint ventures" and, accordingly, encouraged organizations to account for their respective interests using the equity method of accounting.

The EITF reached a consensus that using equity method accounting is not appropriate for arrangements that do not involve the creation of a separate legal entity (commonly referred to as a "virtual joint venture"). Instead, revenues generated and costs incurred by the participants should be reported in the appropriate line items in each participant's statement of operations/ statement of activities, pursuant to EITF 99–19, *Reporting Revenue Gross as a Principal versus Net as an Agent*. A line item such as "collaboration revenue" or "collaboration expense" would be used to report "sharing" payments made between the venture participants. The consensus also nullifies TPA 6400.33.

EITF 07–1 is effective for periods beginning after December 15, 2008, and requires retrospective application for arrangements in place as of the effective date.

*PwC observation: EITF 07–1 will impact not–for–profit organizations that have joint operating arrangements/ collaborative arrangements that are not conducted in a separate legal entity and which are accounted for by the equity method. If "virtual joint venture" arrangements are not restructured into a separate legal entity, implementation will require obtaining necessary current and historical financial data to present the arrangement on a gross basis for all comparative periods.*

**EITF 06–10,** *Accounting for Deferred Compensation and Postretirement Benefit Aspects of Collateral Assignment Split–Dollar Life Insurance Arrangements* **(March 2007)**

**EITF 06–4,** *Accounting for Deferred Compensation and Postretirement Benefit Aspects of Endorsement Split–Dollar Life Insurance Arrangements* **(September 2006)**

Many not–for–profit organizations purchase life insurance on key employees. In recent years, the accounting for the compensatory aspect of these arrangements has been subject to varying interpretations. Accordingly, these two EITF Issues focus on the accounting for arrangements in which an employer has agreed to share a portion of the value of the insurance policy with the employee. These arrangements are referred to as "split–dollar" arrangements. Two types of split–dollar life insurance policies exist: collateral assignment policies and endorsement policies. Generally, the difference lies in the ownership and control of the life insurance policy. In an endorsement arrangement, the employer owns and controls the policy, whereas in a collateral assignment arrangement, the employee owns and controls the policy.

Summary of emerging accounting, tax and regulatory issues in 2009
PricewaterhouseCoopers

The EITF concluded that the purchase of a split–dollar life insurance policy does not constitute a "settlement" of a postretirement benefit obligation as defined in FASB Statement No. 106, *Employers' Accounting for Postretirement Benefits Other Than Pensions* (FAS 106). Thus, an employer should recognize a liability for the postretirement benefit in accordance with FAS 106 or APB 12, *Omnibus Opinion—1967*. If, in substance, a postretirement benefit plan exists, FAS 106 should be followed. If the arrangement is, in substance, an individual deferred compensation contract, APB 12 would be applied. The accounting should be based on the terms of the substantive agreement with the employee. For example, if the employer has agreed to maintain a life insurance policy during the employee's retirement, the estimated cost of maintaining the policy during that period should be accrued. Alternatively, if the employer has effectively agreed to provide the employee with a death benefit, the employer should accrue a liability for the actuarial present value of the future death benefit as of the employee's expected retirement date. All available evidence should be considered in determining the substance of the arrangement.

For collateral assignment arrangements (i.e., those where the insurance contract is owned by the employee), the above guidance applies only if the life insurance arrangement is determined to provide a postretirement benefit. If the employer did not agree to maintain the life insurance policy postretirement or provide the employee with a death benefit based on the substantive arrangement, or the entity otherwise concludes that the arrangement does not provide a postretirement benefit, no obligation should be recorded.

*PwC observation: Determining whether the substantive arrangement provides a postretirement benefit may require significant judgment. A detailed understanding of the insurance contract, the substantive arrangement and the mutual understanding of the parties will be required.*

The accounting for the related insurance asset is also addressed. For endorsement arrangements (i.e., those where the insurance contract is owned by the employer), EITF 06–4 states that the asset should be determined pursuant to the guidance in FASB Technical Bulletin 85–4, *Accounting for Purchases of Life Insurance*. For collateral arrangements (i.e., those in which the policy is owned by the employee), EITF 06–10 states that the employer should recognize and measure the asset based on the nature and substance of the collateral assignment arrangement. In assessing the nature and substance, the employer should assess what future cash flows the employer is entitled to, if any, as well as the employee's obligation and ability to repay the employer. For example, a collateral assignment arrangement may provide that the employer is required to receive payment from the employee (or estate) of the premiums paid by the employer with interest. Alternatively, the arrangement might provide that the employee or estate must pay the cash surrender value of the life insurance contract upon the employee's death.

These consensuses are effective for fiscal years beginning after December 15, 2007. Entities should recognize the effects of applying the consensuses as a change in accounting principle through either a cumulative–effect adjustment to net assets as of the beginning of the year of adoption or retrospective application to all prior periods.

*PwC observation: As with any postretirement benefit arrangement, understanding the nature of the benefit promise between the employer and the employee is paramount. In order to determine the proper basis for the benefit accruals, organizations will need to consider all forms of communication with the employees related to these arrangements, not simply the formal plan documents or signed employee acknowledgements.*

Exposure drafts

## Proposed Financial Accounting Standard, *Subsequent Events* (October 2008)

Currently, most of the guidance on reporting subsequent events in financial statements resides in auditing literature[7] rather than accounting literature (and thus, is not part of the GAAP hierarchy). This proposed standard would move that guidance into the accounting literature and in doing so, would emphasize that the responsibility for preparation of financial statements in accordance with GAAP lies with an entity and its management, not with its auditors.

The current guidance describes two categories of subsequent events: those that provide additional evidence about conditions that existed at the balance sheet date ("Type One") and those that provide evidence with respect to conditions that arose subsequent to the balance sheet date ("Type Two"). FASB's proposed statement retains the two categories but renames them as "recognized" and "nonrecognized" subsequent events.

Under the current guidance, an auditor evaluates subsequent events that occur up until the date of the issuance of the auditor's report on the financial statements. FASB would require that preparers evaluate subsequent events up until the date the financial statements are either issued or available to be issued. The Board incorporated the concept of "available to be issued" primarily for entities whose financial statements are not audited or not widely distributed. Organizations will be required to disclose the date through which subsequent events review procedures were performed and why that date was selected; thus, a user that receives financial statements several months after their issuance will be alerted to the fact that events that may have occurred after that date which will not have been evaluated for their impact on the financial statements.

A final standard is expected to be issued in the spring of 2009; it will be effective for interim or annual periods ending after June 15, 2009.

## Proposed Financial Accounting Standard, *Going Concern* (October 2008)

This proposed standard would provide guidance regarding management's responsibility to evaluate an organization's ability to continue as a "going concern" when preparing its financial statements. Currently, the guidance related to going concern assessments is directed to auditors and resides in auditing literature.[8] FASB believes that guidance about the going concern assumption should also be directed to management, because management is responsible for preparing an entity's financial statements and evaluating its ability to continue as a going concern. Accordingly, the Board concluded that guidance pertaining to the going concern assumption should reside in authoritative accounting literature.

The exposure draft brings forward the going concern guidance from the auditing literature, subject to several modifications that are intended to facilitate convergence between US GAAP and International Financial Reporting Standards (IFRS). The most significant modification is a change in the time horizon used for the going concern assessment. Traditionally, auditors in the US used a time horizon that looked out 12 months beyond the date of the financial statements. FASB's proposed guidance would require management to consider information which is "at least, but is not limited to, 12 months" beyond the financial statement date when assessing whether the going concern assumption is appropriate. FASB wanted a more open-ended time horizon to avoid the inherent problems that a bright-line time horizon creates for events or conditions occurring just beyond the one-year time horizon (for example, a line of credit that expires 13 months after the balance sheet and will not be renewed). It also would require certain disclosures when financial statements are not prepared on a going concern basis or when there is substantial doubt as to an entity's ability to continue as a going concern.

A final standard is expected to be issued in the spring of 2009; it will be effective for interim or annual periods ending after June 15, 2009.

---

[7] AU Section 560, *Subsequent Events*

[8] AU Section 341, *The Auditor's Consideration of an Entity's Ability to Continue as a Going Concern*

*PwC observation: During the comment period, many expressed concern that the expansion of the time horizon is a significant change that will not be operational in the US. In response, FASB plans to add language indicating that the focus of the assessment would be on events occurring beyond twelve months which are reasonably foreseeable and materially affect the entity's ability to continue to meet its obligations as they come due without substantial disposition of assets outside the ordinary course of business, restructuring of debt, externally forced revisions of its operations, or similar actions, and on information which is available to the entity without undue cost and effort.*

## Proposed Financial Accounting Standard, *Disclosure of Certain Loss Contingencies* (June 2008)

This project was undertaken due to concerns that information disclosed about loss contingencies is "too little, too late" with respect to providing sufficient information to assist financial statement users in assessing the likelihood, timing, and amounts of cash flows associated with those contingencies. To address these concerns, FASB issued an exposure draft of a proposed standard which would amend FASB Statement No. 5, *Accounting for Contingencies*.

The exposure draft proposed expanding the population of loss contingencies that are required to be disclosed (by lowering the threshold for disclosure) and requiring disclosure of specific quantitative and qualitative information about those loss contingencies. This includes a description of each contingency and how it arose, the legal or contractual basis, the current status, anticipated timing of resolution, a description of factors likely to affect the ultimate outcome, the organization's assessment of the most likely outcome, and significant assumptions used. It also proposed requiring a tabular reconciliation of recognized loss contingencies to enhance financial statement transparency, and providing a "prejudicial exemption" that could exempt an organization from disclosing certain required information if its disclosure would be prejudicial to an entity's position in a dispute.

The comment period ended in August 2008. The Board encountered such significant resistance to the proposal that they directed the staff to prepare an alternative model that attempts to address the concerns raised by respondents. FASB hopes to issue a final standard in the summer of 2009.

*PwC observation: While an alternative model is being developed and field-tested, the original model continues to be field tested. It is likely that swift action will be taken once redeliberations begin, so it is recommended that organizations follow the status of the project closely.*

## Proposed Financial Accounting Standard, *Accounting for Hedging Activities* (June 2008)

In June 2008, FASB exposed for public comment an amendment to FAS 133 that would simplify accounting for hedging activities and make the accounting model and associated disclosures easier for users to understand. The proposal would replace FAS 133's current hedging requirements with a simpler "fair value approach" which focuses on individually measuring the change in fair value of the derivative and the change in fair value of the hedged item (or for forecasted transactions, the hypothetical derivative). The simplified approach would eliminate the shortcut method and critical terms matching, and would replace the current quantitative approach to assessing hedge effectiveness with a more qualitative approach. The comment period ended in August 2008.

Based on recent developments related to international convergence, it is unlikely that this proposal will be finalized as soon as was originally planned. FASB is working with the International Accounting Standards Board (IASB) on a joint standards project on reducing the complexity in the accounting for financial instruments, part of which would address hedge accounting issues. Thus, FASB has delayed redeliberations on the hedging project pending certain decisions related to the joint project. This will likely delay release of any revised hedge accounting guidance until late 2009 or 2010.

*PwC observation: Not-for-profit organizations that utilize hedge accounting should monitor these developments. Although new guidance would not be effective before 2010, derivative contracts entered into before then may be impacted by these changes.*

## Proposed Staff Position No. FAS 157-c, *Measuring Liabilities Under FASB Statement No. 157* (January 2008)

Applying the FAS 157 framework to liabilities has been challenging for many organizations. In January 2008, FASB issued a proposed FSP for public comment which would provide additional perspective on how to apply the FAS 157 framework to liabilities.

Among not-for-profit organizations, generally the only liabilities measured at fair value on a recurring basis are derivatives (e.g., interest rate swaps) that are out-of-the-money. Bonds and other debt are carried in the balance sheet at the amount the organization is required to repay; however the fair value of such liabilities must be determined for purposes of making the disclosures required by FASB Statement No. 107, *Disclosures about Fair Value of Financial Instruments.*

*PwC observation: FAS 157 requires an organization to incorporate risk of nonperformance when determining the fair value of a liability. The risk of nonperformance is the risk that an organization will not perform on its obligation. An addendum to PwC's "Guide to Fair Value Measurements" addresses how organizations can incorporate the risk of nonperformance into liabilities. Values of nonpublicly traded debt and derivatives (e.g., interest rate swaps) likely will require adjustment since often the fair value quotes and/or valuations obtained from brokers and financial organizations will not include the risk of nonperformance.*

FASB anticipates issuing a final FSP by the summer of 2009. The proposed FSP would be applied on a prospective basis and is expected to be effective on the later of (a) the beginning of the period that includes the issuance date of the FSP or (b) the beginning of the period in which an entity initially applies FAS 157.

## Proposed Staff Position No. FAS No. 144-d, *Amending the Criteria for Reporting a Discontinued Operation* (September 2008)

In an effort to converge guidance on discontinued operations in both US GAAP and IFRS, FASB issued a proposed FSP that would develop a converged definition of a discontinued operation together with the IASB.

Currently, the criteria in FASB Statement No. 144, *Accounting for the Impairment or Disposal of Long-Lived Assets* (FAS 144), for reporting a component as a discontinued operation are that (a) the operations and cash flows of a component have been (or will be) eliminated from the ongoing operations of the entity, and (b) the entity will not have any significant continuing involvement in the operations of the component after the disposal transaction. FAS 144 also states that a "component of an entity" may be a "reportable segment,"[9] an "operating segment,"[10] a "reporting unit,"[11] a subsidiary, or an asset group.[12]

*PwC observation: The proposed definition requires organizations to determine operating segments in accordance with FASB Statement No. 131, "Disclosures about Segments of an Enterprise and Related Information." Because not-for-profits were explicitly excluded from the scope of FAS 131, financial statement preparers may not be familiar with its complex requirements, and its application may prove challenging in practice.*

The proposed FSP would amend FAS 144 to narrow the definition of a discontinued operation to encompass only a component of an entity that is either (a) an operating segment that has either been disposed of or is classified as held for sale or (b) a business[13] or nonprofit activity that, on acquisition, meets the criteria for classification as "held for sale."

---

[9] As defined in FAS 131

[10] As defined in FAS 131

[11] As defined in FAS 142

[12] The lowest level for which identifiable cash flows are largely independent of the cash flows of other groups of assets and liabilities

[13] As defined in FAS 141(R)

*PwC observation: "Nonprofit activity" is a concept introduced in FASB's soon-to-be released, "Not-for-profit Entities: Mergers and Acquisitions" standard to serve as the not-for-profit analog to the "definition of a business" in FAS 141(R). A nonprofit activity is "an integrated set of activities and assets that is capable of being conducted and managed for the purpose of providing benefits, other than goods or services at a profit or profit equivalent, as a fulfillment of an organization's purpose or mission." The concept is important in distinguishing acquisitions that are business combinations from acquisitions of assets subject to liabilities when the acquirer is a portion of a not-for-profit organization (rather than a complete entity).*

The revised definition would narrow the ability for organizations to report discontinued operations by eliminating certain components[14] at a level below an operating segment (reportable segment, reporting unit, asset group) that previously were eligible for classification as a discontinued operation. However, it would also make it easier to determine whether a component that has been disposed of or classified as held for sale meets the criteria for reporting as a discontinued operation in the statement of operations/statement of activities (for example, by eliminating the provision that requires an analysis of cash flows and continuing involvement).

The FSP also would amend FAS 144 to expand the disclosure requirements around disposals/assets held for sale. Organizations would be required to disclose (either on the face of the statement of operations/ statement of activities or in the notes) information about all components that have been disposed of or classified as held for sale, regardless of whether the resulting income or loss qualifies for classification as a discontinued operations in the statement of operations/statement of activities.

FASB expects to finalize the FSP in the second quarter of 2009. The proposed guidance would be effective for fiscal years beginning after December 15, 2009 and for interim periods within those fiscal years. Earlier application would be permitted. The FSP would be applied retrospectively to all periods presented.

*PwC observation: Restricting the proposed definition to components that meet the definition of an "operating segment" may result in according discontinued operations treatment to disposals that do not represent a strategic shift in operations.*

**Proposed Staff Position No. FAS 107-a, *Disclosures About Certain Financial Assets* (December 2008)**

**Proposed Staff Position No. FAS 107-b/APB 28-a, *Interim Disclosures about Fair Value of Financial Instruments* (January 2009)**

FSP FAS 107-a proposes increasing the level of disclosure of fair value information related to financial instruments that are not measured at fair value on the balance sheet. After receiving numerous unfavorable comments from constituents on this proposal, FSP FAS 107-a was dropped and replaced with an alternate proposal, FSP FAS 107-b/APB 28-a. This proposed FSP would amend FASB Statement No. 107, *Disclosures about Fair Value of Financial Instruments*, and APB Opinion No. 28, *Interim Financial Reporting*, to require FAS 107 disclosures to be provided in interim as well as annual periods. The proposed FSP would be effective for interim and annual periods ending after March 15, 2009.

*PwC observation: Proposed FSP FAS 107-b was broadly supported and is expected to be ratified by FASB in the spring of 2009. The impact on not-for-profits is expected to be minimal.*

## Other FASB projects to watch

### Fair Value application and disclosure

In February 2009, FASB added to its agenda three short-term projects related to fair value accounting and disclosure:

* Determining fair value as it relates to distinguishing active and inactive markets, and identifying distressed sales

---

[14] Unless they are otherwise considered an operating segment or an acquired business/nonprofit activity.

- Measurement basis for interests in alternative investments based on net asset values (NAVs)
- Enhanced disclosure requirements for sensitivity of measurements and transfers between levels

All three projects address issues that have generated numerous questions from preparers. FASB anticipates completing the first two projects by the summer and the project on improving disclosures in time for year-end financial reporting.

*PwC observation: As discussed on page 28, during a meeting of FASB's Valuation Resource Group last year, the FASB staff indicated that it did not believe any additional guidance was needed on the NAV issue. Clearly, that view has now changed. FASB is aware of the large number of not-for-profit organizations that are struggling with the NAV issue and has indicated that they would like to issue guidance that is timely for the June 30, 2009 financial statement cycle.*

## Accounting for leases

The objective of this joint project of the IASB and FASB is to develop a new model for the recognition of assets and liabilities arising under lease contracts. This is one of the major convergence projects on FASB-IASB's Memorandum of Understanding (MOU). The MOU outlines the plan of the two Boards to achieve convergence on major projects by 2011.

The US lease accounting model focuses on distinguishing between capital and operating leases. A lease that does not meet the criteria of FASB Statement No. 13, *Accounting for Leases*, (i.e., it does not transfer substantially all benefits and risks of ownership) is classified by a lessee as an operating lease. The lessee does not recognize any elements of the lease on its balance sheet and only recognizes rental expense as it becomes payable. A capital lease, on the other hand, is treated like an asset purchase. The distinction between capital and operating classification is based on "bright-line" triggers.

Preliminary views under the joint project would replace this model with a "right-of-use" model. In a "right-of-use" model, the lessee recognizes an asset for its right to use the leased item and a liability for its obligation to pay for that item. In substance, a right-of-use model would virtually eliminate the concept of an operating lease and bring almost all lease contracts on-balance sheet.

FASB and IASB expect to publish a discussion paper this spring for public comment to set forth their preliminary views and solicit input from constituents. This is a first step in the plan to achieve convergence on the lessee side of lease accounting by 2011.

*PwC observation: Leases are a fundamental aspect of doing business for most organizations. Because they potentially have an enormous impact on financial statements, the implications of revising lease accounting are significant. Because lease structuring based on the accounting guidance has become so prevalent, there will likely be strong resistance to significant changes.*

## Revenue recognition

The objective of this joint project of the IASB and FASB is to issue a single statement on revenue recognition that applies across various industries for both US GAAP and IFRS. In December 2008, the Boards published a discussion paper, *Preliminary Views on Revenue Recognition in Contracts with Customers*, to set forth their preliminary views on a contract-based revenue recognition model. A discussion paper precedes development of an exposure draft. The discussion paper presents the basic model and its implications in order to seek input from respondents.

*PwC observation: This proposal would not affect the current revenue recognition model for contributions received by not-for-profit organizations. Those transactions are nonexchange in nature; the proposal focuses only on revenue received in exchange transactions.*

Summary of emerging accounting, tax and regulatory issues in 2009
PricewaterhouseCoopers

Currently, US revenue recognition guidance focuses on the concept of an "earnings process." The Boards' proposed model is radically different; instead, revenue recognition would be based on changes in "contract assets and liabilities." Simply put, a "contract asset" exists when an organization's rights to receive consideration under a contract exceed its obligations to provide goods or perform services. A "contract liability" exists when the obligations exceed the rights. Revenue is recognized when a "contract asset" increases or a "contract liability" decreases. Fundamental to this model is the need to measure an obligation to provide goods or perform services, which is referred to as the "performance obligation."

The Boards are working towards releasing an exposure draft in 2010. A final standard is not expected before 2011, with an effective date no earlier than 2012.

*PwC observation: Every industry within the scope of the revenue recognition project may be impacted to some extent. Entities that have historically followed industry-specific revenue recognition guidance under US GAAP (such as health care organizations) are likely to see pervasive changes.*

### Application Guidance for Pass-through Entities and Not-for-Profit Organizations, and Disclosure Modifications for Nonpublic Enterprises

This project would clarify what constitutes an "uncertain tax position" in financial statements of not-for-profit organizations and pass-through entities and provide guidance on disclosures required in financial statements of consolidated groups that include both taxable and nontaxable entities. It would also amend certain disclosure requirements for nonpublic entities (including nonpublic not-for-profit organizations). An exposure draft is expected to be issued in the first half of 2009.

*PwC observation: Although this project is directed in part to not-for-profit organizations, it is not expected to have a significant impact on current practice.*

# II. AICPA pronouncements and activities

In this section, we highlight certain activities of the American Institute of Certified Public Accountants and its senior technical committees.

## Accounting guidance

*The Accounting Standards Executive Committee (AcSEC) is the senior technical committee for financial reporting.*

### AICPA Audit and Accounting Guide Revision Projects

Currently, AcSEC has projects underway to overhaul the AICPA Audit and Accounting Guides *Health Care Organizations* and *Not-for-Profit Organizations*. These guides were originally issued in 1996, in conjunction with the effective dates of FAS 116 and 117. Over the ensuing 13 years, many new accounting and auditing issues have emerged, giving rise to the need for comprehensive revision of these guides.

*Healthcare Organizations Guide*

In 2004, a Healthcare Guide Task Force was formed to begin work on this guide overhaul project. To date, substantial progress has been made toward developing the new guide. All information related to financial statement display (which is scattered throughout various chapters of the current guide) has been gathered into one chapter on "Basic Financial Statements." The existing cash and investments guidance is being expanded to address accounting for alternative investments and for interests in investment pools sponsored by other not-for-profits. New chapters on "Derivatives" and "Tax–Exempt Debt" are being added, which will include information about interest rate swaps and SEC oversight of the municipal bond market. Information related to contributions and relationships with foundations (which currently is scattered throughout various chapters) is being gathered into one chapter. The current guidance on managed care accounting will be significantly expanded, and current guidance on continuing care retirement community revenue recognition will be clarified. All information specific to governmental (i.e., GASB) hospitals will be housed in a single chapter and expanded.

Because AcSEC can no longer issue authoritative standards, any conclusions reached during the project that conflict with existing GAAP in the current guide will require action by FASB (for example, issuance of an FSP) to change the existing guidance. Currently, areas identified where FASB will be required to take action include:

- Modifying revenue recognition guidance related to self–pay patients and charity care to more closely reflect the requirements of Staff Accounting Bulletin No. 104 (SAB 104), *Revenue Recognition*

- Modifying the required charity care disclosures

- Presentation and measurement of insured and self–insured malpractice liabilities and other risk exposures

- Discounting of accrued medical malpractice claims

- Estimated costs to be included in measuring loss contracts

- Presentation of contributions of long-lived assets

- Accounting for equity transfers between unrelated not-for-profit healthcare organizations

There are two remaining chapters with accounting guidance to be cleared by AcSEC before the guide is exposed for public comment. AcSEC hopes to expose the proposed new guide sometime in 2009.

*Not–for–Profit Organizations Guide*

In 2005, an NPO Guide Task Force began work on this guide overhaul project. The initial phase has focused on identifying technical issues where guidance may be needed, and discussing those issues with AcSEC. To date, issues discussed with AcSEC include:

- Accounting for special events held after year–end

- Ambiguous donor stipulations

- Correction of errors in net asset classes

- Contributions of non–financial assets such as media time

- Naming opportunities

- Promises to give funded after death
- Display of contributions made
- Remainder interests and noncash assets
- Contributed use of facilities
- Extending the requirement for reporting a statement of functional expenses
- Reporting program information in a statement of functional expenses
- Voluntary health and welfare organizations' statement of functional expenses
- Reporting not–for–profit interests in other entities
- Prepaid expenses, deferred charges and other similar costs
- Treatment of HUD capital advances
- Need for a performance indicator/measure of operations
- Display of investment expenses
- Consideration of subsequent events
- Remainder interests in real estate
- Disclosure and classification of segregated assets
- Related party disclosures
- Sales of contributed inventory
- Losses on donor-restricted endowment funds
- Gifts-in-kind received as contributions and subsequently contributed to others
- Unconditional promises to give long-lived assets
- Allocating a portion of purpose-restricted net assets to supporting services
- Incorporation of existing TPAs into guide
- Gifts of investment sold immediately upon receipt

During 2009, the Task Force plans to continue discussing specific issues with AcSEC. No timetable for a possible exposure draft of a revised guide has yet been identified.

*PwC observation: During the guide overhaul projects, the current guides are being updated for conforming changes on a more–or–less annual basis.*

**Codification and the AICPA Guides**

Currently, the *Health Care Organizations* and *Not-for-Profit Organizations* guides are level (B) GAAP within the US GAAP hierarchy. As discussed at page 2, FASB has undertaken a project to integrate all accounting standards currently within levels (A) through (D) of the GAAP hierarchy into one central, topically organized, electronically searchable site—the FASB Accounting Standards Codification™. When the Codification becomes effective (the target date is July 1, 2009), the GAAP hierarchy will be "flattened," and the Codification will become the single source of authoritative US GAAP.

While the specific level (B) industry specific accounting principles contained within the *Health Care Organizations* and *Not-for-Profit Organizations* guides will be merged into the Codification, the guides themselves will not. The best way to explain this differentiation is with an example. Chapter 4 of the *Health Care Organizations* guide discusses accounting issues related to investments. Most of this chapter is simply AcSEC's discussion of existing FASB (and GASB) standards from the standpoint of the healthcare organizations. While such discussions are informative, they do not result in any new accounting principles. The only unique level (B) accounting principles in Chapter 4 are the requirements for including (or excluding) various elements of investment return in the performance indicator (discussed in paragraphs 4.07 through 4.10), and the requirement in par. 4.02 to report "other investments" (such as real estate or certain oil and gas interests) at amortized cost. Those level (B) principles would become part of the Codification; the remainder of the information in Chapter 4 would not.

Once the Codification becomes effective, the Guides will, in essence, become an industry-specific commentary on FASB literature. The underlying accounting principles will remain the same—the only difference is that the source from which they derive their authority will hereafter be FASB, rather than AcSEC.

*PwC observation: The Codification consists of thousands of individual accounting principles that have been electronically linked, and accordingly its nature is somewhat fragmented. Because of this attribute, we believe the Guides' narrative discussions and industry-specific context will continue to be invaluable to both preparers and auditors.*

## TPA 1100.15, *Liquidity Restrictions*

In September 2008, the trustee of the Commonfund Short-Term Investment Fund announced its unilateral decision to place a freeze on withdrawals and initiate procedures for termination of the fund and an orderly liquidation of the fund's assets. Shortly thereafter, the AICPA staff issued this nonauthoritative Technical Practice Aid (TPA) to raise awareness of the potential accounting and auditing implications when a fund or its trustee imposes restrictions on an organization's ability to withdraw its balance in a money market fund or other short-term investment vehicle. Those implications may include:

- An inability to classify such amounts as cash equivalents

- Financial statement disclosure may be required in situations where restrictions create or lead to risks and uncertainties

- Balance sheet classifications and other events may trigger violations of debt covenants

- Subsequent event considerations may need to be made for liquidity restrictions imposed subsequent to the balance sheet date

- Going concern considerations may be triggered by an organization's inability to withdraw funds

- Communication with those charged with governance may be necessary

*PwC observation: If amounts previously reported as cash equivalents are subsequently determined to no longer qualify as cash equivalents as a result of imposition of such restrictions, the statement of cash flows will also be impacted. If prior year financial statements are presented for comparative purposes, the historical presentation of such amounts as cash equivalents would not change.*

## Draft Issues Paper, *FAS 157 Valuation Considerations for Interests in Alternative Investments*

Organizations with ownership interests in alternative investments face many challenges in applying FAS 157. In particular, the "exit price" concept under FAS 157 challenges an investor's decision to value these investments at net asset value (NAV) in an environment where many funds are imposing limitations on redemptions.

FASB's Valuation Resource Group, or VRG (a group formed to advise the FASB staff on certain implementation and valuation issues related to developing fair value measures used for financial reporting) has discussed the use of net asset value in valuing alternative investments. In those discussions, the FASB staff observed that it would be inconsistent with FAS 157 for an investor to presume that NAV automatically equals fair value. While the reported NAV may be a good starting point in determining fair value for an interest in an alternative investment, and in some cases ultimately may be determined to be a proxy for fair value, investors need to consider all relevant factors and attributes of the investment interest and assess the potential need to adjust that reported NAV to properly reflect the estimated exit price for the interest in accordance with FAS 157. At that time, the staff expressed its belief that FAS 157 provides reasonable guidance on adjusting NAVs in fair value calculations, and that the issue did not warrant any FASB action or further action. (Note: In February 2009, FASB decided to add a short-term agenda project to address issues related to the use of NAV in fair value measurements.)

Those views generated considerable debate and controversy among investors. In response to the uncertainty surrounding this issue, AcSEC assembled an alternative investments task force of representatives from various cross-industry AICPA expert panels as well as certain valuation specialists. In January 2009, AcSEC and the Task Force issued a draft issues paper, *FAS 157 Valuation Considerations for Interests in Alternative Investments*. The draft issues paper discusses how to estimate the fair value of alternative investments in accordance with the provisions of FAS 157. The draft issues paper also discusses the role of NAV in estimating fair value. Although the document does not indicate that NAV is fair value, it does provide guidance to assist in determining when NAV is an appropriate starting point and provides commentary on scenarios where adjusting off of NAV warrants consideration. Other areas discussed include:

- Determining the unit of account
- Determining the principal or most-advantageous market
- What inputs should be used when determining fair value, including NAV
- How should transactions in secondary markets be considered
- What features of an alternative investment fund should be considered (e.g., side pockets, redemption restrictions)

Currently, AcSEC and the Task Force are reviewing the comments received on the draft paper.

*PwC observation: To date, the AICPA's document is the most thorough exploration of measurement of fair value of an interest in alternative investments. Although the document does not indicate that NAV is fair value, it does provide guidance to assist in determining when NAV is an appropriate starting point and provides commentary on scenarios where adjusting off of NAV warrants consideration. Not-for-profit organizations that carry alternative investments at fair value should monitor the progress of this proposed Practice Aid.*

### Article—*Tax-Exempt Bonds—Accounting and Auditing Considerations in the Current Environment*

Defaults in subprime mortgages and consequent reduced value of many collateralized mortgage obligations resulted in the lowering of ratings of a number of bond insurers—ultimately leading, along with other factors, to a liquidity crisis in the municipal auction rate securities market during 2008. This triggered an unprecedented wave of municipal bond refinancings and debt restructurings.

Tax-exempt bond issuers were faced with a number of issues related to transaction accounting. Is an interest mode change an event that should trigger reporting a gain or loss? Is a refunding a modification or an extinguishment? If an organization purchases its own bonds at auction, can they be reported as an investment?

The refinancings and restructurings had a ripple effect into other areas of issuers' finances. Subjective acceleration clauses in liquidity facilities typically precluded variable rate demand obligations (VRDOs) from being classified as long-term debt. Replacing auction rate bonds (long-term debt) with short term VRDOs potentially created problems with liquidity covenants in debt or derivative agreements. Interest rate swaps became significantly out-of-the-money and as a result, triggered mandatory collateral postings or involuntary termination payments. Credit rating downgrades or covenant violations triggered technical defaults, which in turn triggered classification of debt as current or triggered cross-defaults in other agreements. Overall, such matters raised a host of issues with respect to assessing going concern.

The AICPA assembled an ad-hoc group of members of its Not-for-Profit, Healthcare, and State and Local Government Expert Panels to prepare a non-authoritative article reminding not-for-profit and governmental issuers of tax-exempt bonds of a number of GAAP considerations associated with balance sheet classification of VRDOs and other demand debt, accounting for refinancings and interest-mode conversions, termination of interest rate swaps, and other potential accounting and auditing matters relevant to issuers. The purpose of the article is not to answer all questions, but rather to point readers towards the accounting and auditing guidance that may be relevant to the issue.

The article can be downloaded from the AICPA's Web site at www.aicpa.org/download/acctstd/ARS_article14.pdf.

## Audit and attestation guidance

*The Auditing Standards Board (ASB) is the senior technical body designated to issue pronouncements on auditing and attestation matters. The Accounting and Review Services Committee (ARSC) is the senior technical body designated to issue pronouncements on compilation and review matters.*

### SAS No. 115, *Communicating Internal Control Related Matters Identified in an Audit* (September 2008)

This new auditing standard superseded SAS No. 112 to amend the definitions of the various kinds of deficiencies in internal control and the related guidance for evaluating them to conform more closely with the definitions and guidance used by the PCAOB for SEC registrants. The new definitions are as follows:

- A "deficiency" in internal control exists when the design or operation of a control does not allow management or employees, in the normal course of performing their assigned functions, to prevent, or detect and correct misstatements on a timely basis.

- A "significant deficiency" is a deficiency in internal control that is less severe than a material weakness, yet important enough to merit attention by those charged with governance.

- A "material weakness" is a deficiency in internal control which creates a reasonable possibility that a material misstatement of the entity's financial statements will not be prevented, or will not be detected and corrected on a timely basis.

SAS 115 also provides guidance on evaluating the severity of deficiencies identified, the consideration of compensating controls and the auditor's written communications related to deficiencies. It is effective for periods beginning on or after December 15, 2009.

### Reviews of Interim Financial Statements of Nonissuers (January 2009):

- **SAS No. 116,** *Interim Financial Information*

- **Statement on Standards for Accounting and Review Services (SSARS) No. 18,** *Applicability of Statements on Standards for Accounting and Review Services*

- **TPA 1900.01,** *Condensed Interim Financial Reporting by Nonissuers*

Early in 2009, the AICPA released a trio of documents related to performing reviews of interim financial statements of nonissuers (that is, of entities that are not SEC registrants). Together, these documents modify the professional standards governing whether such reviews should be performed under auditing literature (SAS) or under the literature applicable to unaudited engagements (SSARS).

SAS 116 amends SAS 100, *Interim Financial Information* (AU 722). Prior to issuance of SAS 116, "SAS 100" reviews were performed only on interim condensed financial statements[15] of SEC issuers (i.e., 10-Qs). An engagement to perform a review of interim financial information for a not-for-profit organization or a governmental entity was done under SSARS (standards for non-attest engagements) rather than auditing standards and could only be performed on a complete set of interim financial statements. Because SEC regulations underlaid much of SAS 100's guidance, the SAS 116 project focused on modifying SAS 100's precepts in order for them to make sense in the nonissuer environment.

Broadly speaking, SAS 116 now permits reviews of interim financial information of nonissuers to be performed under SAS (rather than SSARS) if all of the following conditions are met:

- The nonissuer's latest annual financial statements have been audited

---

[15] Such statements are presented in considerably less detail than a complete set of financial statements, particularly with respect to note disclosures.

Summary of emerging accounting, tax and regulatory issues in 2009
PricewaterhouseCoopers

- The nonissuer has controls over financial reporting that are sufficient to provide a reasonable basis for the preparation of reliable interim financial information (if such controls do not exist, a SAS 116 review should not be performed)

- The review is, in effect, an extension of the previous or current audit (so the accountant either has been engaged to audit the current financial statements, or has audited the latest financial statements and expects to be engaged to audit the current financial statements)

- The financials being reviewed (which can be either a full set of financial statements or condensed financial statements) cover a period of less than one year and are intended to provide a periodic update to the latest audited financials

- The interim financials are prepared consistent with the financial reporting framework used for the annual financial statements (e.g., US GAAP)

- If the interim financial information is in the form of condensed financial statements, those statements must:

  – Purport to be in accordance with an appropriate financial reporting framework (e.g., US GAAP). In connection with this condition, the AICPA staff issued TPA 1900.01, *Condensed Interim Financial Reporting by Nonissuers*, to clarify that in the absence of established accounting principles for form and content of condensed interim financial statements, it is appropriate for nonissuers to analogize to the guidance on form and content in Article 10 of SEC Regulation S-X

  – Include a note stating that the financial information does not represent complete financial statements and should be read in conjunction with the latest annual audited financial statements

  – Be accompanied by the latest annual audited financial statements, unless those statements are "readily available" (i.e., a third party user can obtain the financial statements without any assistance from the reporting organization)

*PwC observation: For organizations that issue tax-exempt debt, submitting continuing disclosure filings to the MSRB's new Electronic Municipal Market Access ("EMMA") System will satisfy the condition of audited financial statements being "readily available." For more information on EMMA (see page 49).*

Consistent with SAS 100, the results of the review engagement may be communicated either orally or in writing, as long as the reporting entity has not stated that the interim financial information has been reviewed by the independent public accountant (in which case a written report must be issued).

If any of these conditions are not met (for example, the latest annual financial statements were not audited; the interim financial statements are prepared under a different basis of accounting than the annual financial statements; the accountant was not engaged to audit the current year or the prior year financial statements; the form and content of condensed interim statements is not appropriate) an engagement to review the interim information would be governed by SSARS. The AICPA's Accounting and Review Services Committee (ARSC) issued SSARS No. 18, *Applicability of Statements on Standards for Accounting and Review Services*, to clarify that if the specific conditions in the revised AU 722 are not met, reviews of interim financials of nonissuers should be performed in accordance with SSARS.

SAS 116 and SSARS 18 are effective for reviews of interim financial information for interim periods beginning after December 15, 2009. Early application is permitted.

■ 194 ■

# APPENDIX D

The table below presents a snapshot of upcoming effective dates for selected pronouncements and technical bulletins recently issued by GASB. Each standard should be individually assessed to determine if it applies to your organization.

GASB pronouncements and technical bulletins

| | | Page | Year-end | | | | |
|---|---|---|---|---|---|---|---|
| | | | Mar 31, 2009 | Jun 30, 2009 | Sep 30, 2009 | Dec 31, 2009 | 2010 & Beyond |
| GASB 53 | Periods beginning after 6/15/09 | 33 | | | | | • |
| GASB 52 | Periods beginning after 6/15/08 | 35 | | • | • | • | • |
| GASB 51 | Periods beginning after 6/15/09 | 36 | | | | | • |
| GASB 49 | Periods beginning after 12/15/07 | 37 | • | • | • | • | • |
| GASB 45, Phase 2 | Periods beginning after 12/15/07 | 38 | • | • | • | • | • |
| GASB 45, Phase 3 | Periods beginning after 12/15/08 | 38 | | | | • | • |
| GTB 08-01, Pensions | Periods ending after 12/15/08 | 40 | | | | • | • |
| GTB 08-01, OPEB | Periods ending after 12/15/08—Concurrent w/GASB 45 | 40 | | | | • | • |
| GTB 06-01 | Concurrent with GASB 45 | 40 | | | | | |
| GTB 04-2 | Concurrent with GASB 45 | 40 | | | | | |
| **Exposure Drafts** | | | | | | | |
| Hierarchy of GAAP | Effective upon issuance | 42 | | • | • | • | • |
| Codification | Effective upon issuance | 43 | | • | • | • | • |

Summary of emerging accounting, tax and regulatory issues in 2009
PricewaterhouseCoopers

# III. GASB pronouncements and activities

*In this section, we highlight selected GASB pronouncements and activities that are particularly relevant for governmental business–type activities (BTAs) and which are already effective (or will be effective in the near future).*

## Final pronouncements and technical bulletins

**GASB Statement No. 53,** *Accounting and Financial Reporting for Derivative Instruments* **(June 2008)**

*Guide to Implementation of GASB Statement 53 on Derivatives—Questions and Answers* **(April 2009)**

This standard addresses the recognition, measurement, and disclosure of derivatives in financial statements of governmental entities. Although GASB 53's requirements are similar in some respects to the guidance in FASB Statement No. 133, *Accounting for Derivative Instruments and Hedging Activities* (FAS 133), GASB 53 is intended to be applied without any reference or analogy to FAS 133.

GASB 53 requires governmental entities to measure derivatives at fair value in their balance sheets. (An exception is provided for synthetic guaranteed investment contracts (GICs) that are fully benefit-responsive, which are permitted to be carried at contract value.) Changes in fair value are reported in the statement of revenues, expenses, and changes in net assets (SRECNA) as investment income or loss, unless the derivative effectively hedges an identified risk of adverse change in cash flows or fair values. In that situation, changes in fair value are reported as balance sheet deferrals until the derivative agreement terminates or ceases to be effective.

*PwC observation: GASB's Concepts Statement No. 4 (see page 41) incorporates two new elements of financial statements—deferred inflows and deferred outflows—to accommodate this aspect of the derivatives accounting model.*

Derivatives associated with hedgeable items must be tested for effectiveness. If an "effective hedge" exists, hedge accounting must be used; it is not elective. Effectiveness is determined by considering whether the changes in cash flows or fair values of the derivative substantially offset the changes in cash flows or fair values of the hedgeable item. Multiple methods of evaluating hedge effectiveness are allowed. Hedge accounting should be terminated if a hedging derivative fails the effectiveness tests, is terminated, or if other specified conditions occur. At that point, the entire balance sheet deferral would be "emptied" into the SRECNA unless the termination results from a defeasance of hedged debt. In that case, the write-off of the deferred inflows or outflows should be included in the calculation of the gain or loss on the refunding (which is subsequently deferred and amortized), rather than reported as a gain or loss.

*PwC observation: GASB 53 defines fair value as the market price in an active market. If a market price is not available, fair value should be based on expected cash flows (discounted) or formula-based methods or mathematical models.*

The disclosures previously required by GASB Technical Bulletin 2003-1, *Disclosure Requirements For Derivatives Not Reported At Fair Value On The Statement Of Net Assets*, were incorporated into GASB 53 along with additional disclosure requirements, including identification of the risks to which derivatives expose the organization.[16]

GASB 53 provides for the following scope exceptions:

- Normal purchases and normal sales contracts
- Insurance contracts accounted for under GASB 10, *Accounting and Financial Reporting for Risk Financing and Related Insurance Issues*
- Certain financial guarantee contracts
- Certain contracts that are not exchange traded
- Loan commitments

---

[16] Paragraphs 69-79.

GASB 53 is effective for reporting periods beginning after June 15, 2009, with earlier application encouraged. At initial adoption, organizations are required to restate all prior periods presented if it is practical to do so. If retroactive application is not practical, a cumulative-effect adjustment should be reported as a restatement of beginning net assets for the earliest period presented. A transitional evaluation of all potential hedging derivatives existing at the implementation date must also be performed (see illustration below).

In April 2009, GASB expects to publish an implementation guide to assist governments with applying the new standard. Additionally, GASB's Web site provides an excellent plain-English summary of the standard:

www.gasb.org/plain-language_documents/ Statement_53_plain-language_summary.pdf

*PwC observation: Some BTAs that apply paragraph 7 of GASB 20 have questioned whether the guidance in FAS 157 should be applied in measuring fair value of derivatives under GASB 53. The answer is no. GASB 53, paragraph 21 provides guidance on how GASB intends for the fair value of derivatives to be measured.*

### Illustration: Transitioning to GASB 53

In September 2007, BTA State University entered into an interest rate swap in connection with an issuance of debt. BTA must evaluate the transition reporting for this swap as part of its initial adoption of GASB 53 in its fiscal year ending June 30, 2010. As of June 30, 2010, the swap's fair value was $1.1 million; GASTB 2003-1 disclosures in the June 30, 2009 financial statements indicate that the swap's fair value at the end of the previous period was $1.2 million. BTA prepares single year financials statements.

First, BTA must evaluate the swap's effectiveness at June 30, 2010. If the swap is determined to be an effective hedge as of that date, it is deemed to have been effective since inception. In that case, BTA's balance sheet would report a derivative asset of $1.1 million and an offsetting amount of deferred inflows. There are no fair value changes to report in the SRECNA (because they are deferred in the balance sheet), and no adjustment of opening net assets would be required.

If the swap is not effective at June 30, 2010, BTA must perform a second effectiveness test, this time as of July 1, 2009 (using information from the June 30, 2009 note disclosures). If the swap was effective on that date, the swap is deemed to have been effective from inception to that point, with hedging terminated during fiscal year 2010. BTA's June 30, 2010 balance sheet reports a derivative asset of $1.1 million. No adjustment to the July 1, 2009 opening net assets would be required (because an offsetting amount of deferred inflows is presumed to exist at that date). Instead, the SRECNA would reflect a net derivative gain of $1.1 million in the current period change in net assets ($1.2 million gain from the termination of hedge accounting less the decrease in fair value during the year of $100,000).

If the swap is not effective at either June 30, 2010 or July 1, 2009, BTA's June 30, 2010 balance sheet would report the derivative asset of $1.1 million. The SRECNA would report an adjustment to the July 1, 2009 opening net assets in the amount of $1.2 million (the fair value of the derivative at that date), and a fair value decrease of $100,000 in the current period change in net assets.

**GASB 53 Implications for GASB 20, par. 7 BTAs**

GASB 53 uses the same basic definition of a derivative as is used in FAS 133 and, like FAS 133, it requires derivatives to be displayed at fair value on the balance sheet. However, it differs from FAS 133 in several significant respects. GASB 53 requires that governments assess all potential hedging relationships for effectiveness (that is, hedge accounting would be mandatory, not elective as it is under FAS 133). Multiple methods of evaluating hedge effectiveness are allowed. The effective portion of hedges is reported in special balance sheet accounts (deferred inflows and deferred outflows), rather than in the statement of revenues, expenses and changes in net assets. GASB 53 identifies the SIFMA (formerly the BMA) swap index and the AAA general obligation bonds index as benchmark interest rates for hedges of tax–exempt debt; FAS 133's benchmarks are LIBOR and the interest rates on direct treasury obligations.

*PwC observation: GASB 53 identifies LIBOR as a benchmark interest rate for hedges of taxable debt, but not as a benchmark rate for hedges of tax–exempt debt.*

**GASB Statement No. 52, *Land and Other Real Estate Held as Investments by Endowments* (November 2007)**

Many governmental enterprises hold land and other real estate as part of their endowment portfolios. GASB 52 requires assets held by permanent and term endowments to be reported at fair value. As a result, the reporting of real estate investments held by public sector endowments will be consistent with the reporting of similar investments held by private sector endowments that report "other investments" at fair value.

*PwC observation: GASB 52's scope extends only to investments held by permanent and term endowments. Land and other real estate investments held by "funds functioning as endowments" (i.e., quasi–endowments) will continue to be reported at historical cost. This is because activities of quasi–endowments present additional reporting issues and considerations that were deemed to be beyond the scope of this statement.*

To help users of financial statements better evaluate an endowment's investment decisions and performance, GASB 52 requires governments to report the changes in fair value as investment income. It also requires them to disclose the methods and significant assumptions employed to determine fair value, and to provide other information that they currently present for other investments reported at fair value. While the statement does not provide specific guidance on fair value measurement techniques, the Basis for Conclusions notes that the estimation of fair value depends on the unique facts and circumstances of the specific land or other real estate, and that methods and significant assumptions should consider cost–benefit constraints.

GASB 52 is effective for financial statements for periods beginning after June 15, 2008. Earlier implementation is encouraged.

*PwC observation: By carrying land and other real estate investments at fair value, governmental enterprises will be more comparable to each other and to their private sector counterparts, as well as to governmental pension plans, other post–employment benefit (OPEB) plans, external investment pools, and Internal Revenue Code Section 457 deferred compensation plans that already report land and real estate investments at fair value. Generally, reporting such investments at fair value provides more decision–useful information about their composition, current value and recent changes in value.*

**GASB Statement No. 51, *Accounting and Financial Reporting for Intangible Assets* (July 2007)**

This statement was issued to provide users of financial statements with more complete and consistent information about intangible assets. According to GASB 51, an intangible asset lacks physical substance, is nonfinancial in nature and has an initial useful life extending beyond a single reporting period. Intangible assets within the scope of GASB 51 include easements, computer software, water rights, timber rights, patents, and trademarks, among others.

*PwC observation: Goodwill is explicitly excluded from the scope of GASB 51. The Board concluded that the issues that would need to be deliberated in developing accounting and financial reporting requirements for goodwill extended beyond issues related to identifiable intangible assets.*

GASB 51 deems all intangible assets to be "capital assets" (except for those explicitly excluded from its scope, such as goodwill and capital leases) and extends to them all existing authoritative guidance related to accounting and financial reporting for capital assets (e.g., recognition, measurement, depreciation/amortization, impairment, presentation and disclosure).

*PwC observation: Among other matters, this will require intangible assets other than goodwill to be included in an entity's rollforward disclosure of capital assets by major classes.*

The provisions of GASB 51 are similar (but not identical) to those of FASB Statement No. 142, *Goodwill and Other Intangible Assets*. An intangible asset should be recognized only if it is considered "identifiable," meaning that the asset either: a) is capable of being separated or divided and sold, transferred, licensed, rented or exchanged, either individually or together with a related contract, asset or liability; or b) arises from contractual or other legal rights, regardless of whether those rights are transferable or separable from the entity or from other rights and obligations. GASB 51 establishes a "specified-conditions" approach to recognizing intangible assets that are internally generated (e.g., patents and copyrights, internally generated software).

GASB 51 also establishes specific guidance for the amortization of intangible assets, including determining the useful life of intangibles that are limited by legal or contractual provisions. If no factors exist that indicate a limitation on the useful life of an intangible asset, the asset has an indefinite useful life. Indefinite-lived intangibles should not be amortized unless their useful life is subsequently determined to be finite due to a change in circumstances. Like other capital assets, intangible assets within the scope of GASB 51 would be evaluated for impairment in accordance with the provisions of GASB Statement No. 42 (as amended by GASB 51).

GASB 51 is effective for financial statements for periods beginning after June 15, 2009, with earlier application encouraged. With certain exceptions (noted in paragraphs 21–23), the standard should be applied retroactively by restating financial statements for all prior periods presented. If restatement is not practical, the cumulative effect of the change should be reported as a restatement of beginning net assets for the earliest period restated.

*PwC observation: Until GASB 51 becomes effective, governmental enterprises that follow paragraph 7 of GASB 20 will continue to account for intangible assets in accordance with FAS 142, with impairment of goodwill and indefinite-lived intangibles assessed in accordance with FAS 142 and impairment of finite-lived intangibles assessed in accordance with FAS 144. Other governmental enterprises continue to account for intangible assets in accordance with APB 17 until they adopt the new standard.*

Because GASB 51's scope excludes goodwill, goodwill will continue to be accounted for in accordance with FAS 142 (for entities that apply paragraph 7 of GASB 20) and APB 17 (for all other entities).

## GASB Statement No. 49, *Accounting and Financial Reporting for Pollution Remediation Obligations* (November 2006)

This standard provides guidance on the accounting and reporting of obligations and costs related to existing pollution remediation, such as obligations to clean up spills of hazardous wastes or to remove contamination (e.g., asbestos). Pollution prevention or control is not within the scope of GASB 49.

*PwC observation: This statement is expected to have a significant impact on governmental organizations that have environmental contaminations, such as asbestos, on their properties. Originally, GASB's goal was to comprehensively examine environmental liabilities that related to past, current and future activities, but ultimately they narrowed the scope to focus on the issues they believed most needed guidance, namely existing pollution remediation obligations, including contamination. In the future, GASB may address other environmental issues, such as pollution prevention obligations and asset retirement obligations.*

GASB 49 does not require governments to search for pollution remediation obligations, but instead sets forth triggers that would signal that a government should determine if it has to estimate and report a remediation liability. Those five circumstances (called "obligating events") are when a government:

- Is compelled to take remediation action because pollution creates an imminent endangerment to public health or welfare or the environment, leaving the government little or no discretion to avoid remediation action

- Is in violation of a pollution prevention–related permit or license, such as a Resource Conservation and Recovery Act (RCRA) permit or similar permits under state law

- Is named, or evidence indicates that it will be named, by a regulator as a responsible party or potentially responsible party (PRP) for remediation, or as a government responsible for sharing costs

- Is named, or evidence indicates that it will be named, in a lawsuit to compel the government to participate in remediation

- Has legally obligated itself to commence or is already commencing cleanup activities or monitoring or operation and maintenance of the remediation effort. If these activities are voluntarily commenced and none of the other obligating events have occurred relative to the entire site, the amount recognized should be based on the portion of the remediation project that the government has initiated and is legally required to complete.

GASB 49 requires liabilities, expenses and expenditures to be estimated using an "expected cash flows" measurement technique. In addition, it requires disclosures about pollution clean-up efforts in the notes to the financial statements. The requirements of this statement are effective for financial statements for periods beginning after December 15, 2007.

*PwC observation: Some overlap exists between the scopes of GASB 49 and FASB Statement No. 143, "Accounting for Asset Retirement Obligations" (FAS 143). In applying FAS 143, governmental enterprises that follow paragraph 7 of GASB 20 must be careful to apply only those portions that do not conflict with requirements of GASB 49 or other GASB standards. Thus, they would not apply FAS 143's provisions concerning asbestos removal. They also would not apply any provisions related to "conditional" obligations unless those obligations are likely to occur, as discussed in NCGA Statement No. 4, "Accounting and Financial Reporting Principles for Claims and Judgments and Compensated Absences."*

*An interpretation of FAS 143, FASB Interpretation No. 47, "Accounting for Conditional Asset Retirement Obligations" (FIN 47), clarifies that the term "conditional asset retirement obligation" refers to a legal obligation to perform an asset retirement activity in which the timing and (or) method of settlement are conditional on a future event that may or may not be within the control of the organization. According to the "Statement 20 Guidance" page on GASB's Web site (www.gasb.org/st20guide.html), FIN 47 conflicts with the requirements of NCGAS 4 and FASB Statement No. 5 and, therefore, should not be applied by governmental organizations.*

## GASB Statement No. 45, *Accounting and Financial Reporting by Employers for Postemployment Benefits Other Than Pensions* (June 2004)

GASB 45 establishes standards for the measurement, recognition and display of OPEB expense and related liabilities (assets), note disclosures, and, if applicable, required supplementary information (RSI) in the financial reports of state and local governmental employers.

GASB 45 improves the relevance and usefulness of financial reporting by: a) requiring systematic, accrual-basis measurement and recognition of OPEB cost (expense) over a period that approximates employees' years of service, and b) providing information about actuarial accrued liabilities associated with OPEB and whether and to what extent progress is being made in funding the plan.

GASB 45 requires employers that participate in single-employer or agent multiple-employer defined-benefit OPEB plans (sole and agent employers) to measure and disclose an amount for annual OPEB cost on the accrual basis of accounting. Annual OPEB cost is equal to the employer's annual required contribution (ARC) to the plan, with certain adjustments if the employer has a net OPEB obligation for past under or over contributions.

The ARC is defined as the employer's required contributions for the year, calculated in accordance with certain parameters, and includes: a) the normal cost for the year, and b) a component for amortization of the total unfunded actuarial accrued liabilities (or funding excess) of the plan over a period not to exceed 30 years. The parameters include requirements for the frequency and timing of actuarial valuations, as well as for the actuarial methods and assumptions that are acceptable for financial reporting. If the methods and assumptions used in determining a plan's funding requirements meet the parameters, the same methods and assumptions are required for financial reporting by both a plan and its participating employers. However, if a plan's method of financing does not meet the parameters (e.g., the plan is financed on a pay-as-you-go basis), the parameters nevertheless apply for financial reporting purposes.

For financial reporting purposes, an actuarial valuation is required at least biennially for OPEB plans with a total membership (including employees in active service, terminated employees who have accumulated benefits but are not yet receiving them, and retired employees and beneficiaries currently receiving benefits) of 200 or more, or at least triennially for plans with a total membership of fewer than 200. The projection of benefits should include all benefits covered by the current substantive plan (the plan as understood by the employer and plan members) at the time of each valuation and should take into consideration the pattern of sharing of benefit costs between the employer and plan members to that point, as well as certain legal or contractual caps on benefits to be provided. The parameters require that the selection of actuarial assumptions, including the healthcare cost trend rate for postemployment healthcare plans, be guided by applicable actuarial standards.

A sole employer in a plan with fewer than 100 total plan members (including employees in active service, terminated employees who have accumulated benefits but are not yet receiving them, and retirees and beneficiaries currently receiving benefits) has the option to apply a simplified alternative measurement method instead of obtaining actuarial valuations. The option also

Summary of emerging accounting, tax and regulatory issues in 2009
PricewaterhouseCoopers

is available to an agent employer with fewer than 100 plan members, in circumstances in which the employer's use of the alternative measurement method would not conflict with a requirement that the agent multiple–employer plan obtain an actuarial valuation for plan reporting purposes.

Employers participating in cost–sharing multiple–employer plans that are administered as trusts or equivalent arrangements are required to recognize OPEB expense for their contractually required contributions to the plan on the accrual basis. Required disclosures include identification of the way that the contractually required contribution rate is determined (e.g., by statute, contract or on an actuarially determined basis). Employers participating in a cost–sharing plan are required to present as RSI, schedules of funding progress and employer contributions for the plan as a whole if a plan financial report, prepared in accordance with GASB 43, is not issued and made publicly available and the plan is not included in the financial report of a public employee retirement system or another entity.

*PwC observation: GASB 45 is likely to impact almost all governmental enterprises, and based on the facts and circumstances, amounts of liabilities and their impact on net assets could be material. It is important for organizations to understand the reporting guidance and engage technical experts early to prepare the necessary actuarial valuations. For organizations that participate in pooled arrangements (e.g., with a state system), it is important to understand the accounting and reporting requirements applicable to employers participating in cost–sharing multiple–employer plans. In instances where a public college or university participates in pooled arrangements, the public college or university should consider verifying with the state's comptroller the terms of the plans and whether there is a requirement or expectation to "push down" the accounting from the state to the public college or university.*

Employers that participate in defined–contribution OPEB plans are required to recognize OPEB expense for their required contributions to the plan and a liability for unpaid required contributions on the accrual basis. GASB 45

also includes guidance for employers that finance OPEB as insured benefits and for special funding situations.

The requirements of GASB 45 are effective in three phases based on a government's total annual revenues in the first fiscal year ended after June 15, 1999. Governments with annual revenues of $100 million or more (i.e., phase 1 governments) have already implemented GASB 45. For phase 2 governments (i.e., those with total annual revenues of $10 million or more but less than $100 million), the statement is effective for periods beginning after December 15, 2007, and for phase 3 governments (total annual revenues of less than $10 million), the statement will be effective for periods beginning after December 15, 2008. Component units should implement these requirements no later than the same year as their primary government.

Simultaneously with the implementation of GASB 45, governmental enterprises should implement the provisions of GASB Statement No. 47, *Accounting for Termination Benefits*, for any termination benefits provided through a defined–benefit OPEB plan. In addition, they should implement the OPEB-related provisions of Technical Bulletins issued to clarify narrow aspects of the standard. These include Technical Bulletins 2008-1 (on determining the ARC adjustments), 2006-1 (related to Medicare Part D prescription drug coverage) and 2004-2 (pertaining to the timing of reporting of contribution expense). Discussions of those Technical Bulletins follow.

*PwC observation: Some governmental organizations account for their OPEB liabilities in accordance with FASB Statement No. 106. Once GASB 45 becomes effective, FAS 106 should no longer be applied. When transitioning to GASB 45, those organizations should consider the guidance in question 8.69.3 of GASB's Comprehensive Implementation Guide for assistance in determining whether their "qualifying" trusts under FAS 106 will meet the requirements for a qualifying "trust or equivalent arrangement" under GASB 45. Because GASB 45 generally provides for prospective implementation, those organizations should also reverse any OPEB liabilities previously recognized under FAS 106.*

## GASB Technical Bulletin No. 2008–1, *Determining the Annual Required Contribution Adjustment for Postemployment Benefits* (December 2008)

This Technical Bulletin clarifies a narrow aspect of the requirements of GASB Statement No. 27, *Accounting for Pensions by State and Local Governmental Employers* (GASB 27), and GASB 45. A key component of the actuarial calculations performed for benefit plans is the determination of the ARC (that is, the amount that should be contributed to the plan each year). If an employer historically has contributed an amount less than the ARC, then future actuarial calculations will include an amount to compensate for the shortfall, and vice-versa. For accounting purposes, the portion of the ARC calculation related to past under- or overpayments has been recognized in prior years; therefore, an adjustment needs to be made to avoid double-counting. Statements 27 and 45 assume that the exact amount of this adjustment will not be known and provide a methodology to reasonably approximate the necessary adjustment.[17] However, some actuarial valuations separately identify the exact amount that is included in the ARC calculation related to under- and over-payments. GTB 08-1 clarifies that in those situations, the ARC adjustment may be set equal to the exact amount (in other words, there is no need to approximate an adjustment).

For pensions, the provisions of GTB 08-1 are effective for periods ending after December 15, 2008. For OPEB, they should be applied simultaneously with the government's initial implementation of GASB 45 or for periods ending after December 15, 2008, whichever is later.

## GASB Technical Bulletin No. 2006–1, *Accounting and Financial Reporting by Employers for Payments from the Federal Government Pursuant to the Retiree Drug Subsidy Provisions of Medicare Part D* (June 2006)

Medicare Part D is a federal program that provides prescription drug benefits to eligible Medicare recipients. Employers that provide postretirement prescription drug coverage benefits may receive federal subsidy payments related to Medicare Part D prescription drug coverage. GTB 06-1clarifies how state and local governments or plans should report those federal subsidy payments. It further clarifies that the accounting and reporting for OPEB is not affected by the Medicare Part D payment. Therefore, the calculation of the long–term obligation related to OPEB, the annual OPEB cost and a government's annual required contribution for OPEB would not be reduced by the federal payments that are expected in the future.

Most of the provisions of GTB 06–1 were effective upon issuance. However, the provisions that relate to OPEB reporting should be applied simultaneously with a government's implementation of the OPEB standards.

*PwC observation: GASB's reporting requirements for these payments differ from FASB's guidance applied by private sector entities. Private sector organizations net the subsidy payments against the related other post–employment benefit costs and liabilities, as required by FSP No. FAS 106–2.*

## GASB Technical Bulletin No. 2004–2, *Recognition of Pension and Other Postemployment Benefit Expenditures/Expense and Liabilities by Cost–Sharing Employers* (December 2004)

GTB 04–2 clarifies the requirements in GASB 27 and GASB 45 regarding accounting for employers' contractually required contributions to cost–sharing pension and OPEB plans. Per GTB 04–2, expenses related to contractually required contributions are recognized in the period they are due "for," rather than the period they are due "in." For example, OPEB expenditures that are "for" (i.e., related to) December's payroll should be recorded in December, even if they are not due until February 1.

The provisions of GTB 04–2 are already in effect for pension transactions. For OPEB transactions, the technical bulletin should be applied simultaneously with the implementation of GASB 45.

---

[17] See paragraph 13 of GASB 27 and paragraph 16 of GASB 45.

## GASB concepts statements

*GASB's Concepts Statements are intended to provide a conceptual framework of interrelated objectives and fundamental concepts that can be used as a basis for establishing consistent financial reporting standards. Concepts Statements do not themselves represent specific standards that must be applied in the preparation of financial statements; rather, they provide GASB with the basic conceptual foundation for considering the merits of alternative approaches to financial reporting and help the Board develop well–reasoned financial reporting standards. They also assist preparers, auditors and users in understanding the fundamental concepts underlying financial reporting standards.*

### Concepts Statement No. 5, *Service Efforts and Accomplishments Reporting* (November 2008)

### Request for Response, *Suggested Guidelines for Voluntary Reporting of SEA Performance Information* (July 2008)

Because the performance of governmental organizations often cannot be measured in terms of sales, profits or return on investment, the need exists for other types of information to be provided regarding a government's performance in providing services to its constituency. "Service efforts and accomplishments" (SEA) reporting provides more decision-useful information about a government's efficiency and effectiveness than can be provided by traditional financial statements alone. In November, GASB issued CON 5 to significantly amend its Concepts Statement No. 2 on that same topic. CON 5 provides a useful framework to assist GASB in considering suggested guidelines for voluntary reporting of SEA performance information by state and local governmental entities.

Simultaneously, GASB issued a revision of CON 2 which incorporates all of the CON 5 amendments as well as amendments made by Concepts Statement No. 3, *Communication Methods in General Purpose External Financial Reports That Contain Basic Financial Statements*, in 2005.

GASB also continues to work on developing conceptually-based guidelines for voluntary reporting of SEA information. Such guidelines would describe the essential components of an effective SEA report and the qualitative characteristics that are appropriate for reporting SEA information. In July, GASB issued a "request for response" document to solicit feedback from constituents that voluntarily choose to report on their SEA.

*PwC observation: SEA reporting is entirely voluntary; it is not GASB's intent to prescribe performance measures that must be used in performance reporting.*

### Concepts Statement No. 4, *Elements of Financial Statements* (June 2006)

This concepts statement establishes definitions for the seven elements of financial statements of state and local governments. Elements of financial statements are the fundamental components of financial statements. The elements of a statement of financial position are defined as follows:

- **Assets** are resources with present service capacity that the government presently controls

- **Liabilities** are present obligations to sacrifice resources that the government has little or no discretion to avoid

- A **deferred outflow** of resources is a consumption of net assets by the government that is applicable to a future reporting period

- A **deferred inflow** of resources is an acquisition of net assets by the government that is applicable to a future reporting period

- **Net position** is the residual of all other elements presented in a balance sheet

The elements of the resource flows statements are defined as follows:

- An **outflow** of resources is a consumption of net assets by the government that is applicable to the reporting period

- An **inflow** of resources is an acquisition of net assets by the government that is applicable to the reporting period

These definitions are primarily based on the inherent characteristics of each element. Central to most of these definitions is a "resource," which in the governmental context is an item that can be drawn on to provide services to the citizenry.

*PwC observation: Prior to completing its work on CON 4, GASB had relied on the financial statement elements defined in FASB Concepts Statement No. 6: assets, liabilities, equity/net assets, revenues, expenses, gains, losses, comprehensive income, investments by owners and distributions to owners. GASB's elements framework adds two new balance sheet elements that do not appear in the FASB framework—"deferred outflows" and "deferred inflows." The CON 4 project was closely linked to GASB's derivatives project, because the two new balance sheet elements defined above are an essential component of GASB's model for reporting hedging derivatives (see page 33).*

## GASB exposure drafts

**Proposed Governmental Accounting Standard, *The Hierarchy of Generally Accepted Accounting Principles for State and Local Governments* (August 2008)**

In the United States, GAAP—the body of authoritative accounting principles used in the preparation of financial statements—is referred to as a "hierarchy" because the various standards it contains have

varying levels of authoritativeness. Currently, the GAAP hierarchy used in the preparation of financial statements for state and local governments resides in professional auditing literature.[18] This has come under criticism, as the guidance is directed solely to auditors, rather than to preparers of financial statements. The current hierarchy has four levels of "authoritativeness" ranging from most authoritative (level A) to least authoritative (level D).

In August 2008, GASB issued an exposure draft of a proposed standard that would move the existing multi-tiered hierarchy from the auditing literature to accounting literature "as is," subject only to modifications needed to make the language more responsive to the governmental environment. The proposed standard would become effective upon issuance. GASB expects to issue a final standard in May 2009.

*PwC observation: SAS 69 established three separate US GAAP hierarchies: one for the private sector, one for state and local governments, and one for federal government entities. All three standards boards (FASB, GASB, and FASAB) have undertaken projects to move their respective hierarchies into authoritative accounting literature. The private sector transfer was completed with the issuance of FASB Statement No. 162 (see page 5). FASAB issued an exposure draft of a proposed standard in December 2008.*

*Many private sector pronouncements are considered level A or level B GAAP for governmental BTAs. As discussed on page 1, all private sector pronouncements are being integrated into the "FASB Accounting Standards Codification™" that, once effective (scheduled for July 1, 2009), will supersede all of the existing private sector standards. The implications of that change for the state and local GAAP hierarchy are being dealt with in a separate GASB project, "Codification of Pre-November 30, 1989 FASB Pronouncements" (see page 47).*

---

[18] AICPA Statement on Auditing Standards No. 69 (SAS 69), *The Meaning of Present Fairly in Conformity With Generally Accepted Accounting Principles.*

**Proposed Governmental Accounting Standard, *Codification of Accounting and Financial Reporting Guidance Contained in the AICPA Statements on Auditing Standards* (August 2008)**

In addition to the GAAP hierarchy, other guidance used in the preparation of financial statements for state and local governments also resides in professional auditing literature. In August 2008, GASB issued an exposure draft of a proposed standard that would move guidance on related party transactions, subsequent events, and going concern considerations from the auditing literature into accounting literature "as is," subject only to modifications needed to make the language more responsive to the governmental environment. This emphasizes that the responsibility for preparation of financial statements in accordance with GAAP lies with an entity and its management, not with its auditors.

Related party transactions. AU 334, *Related Parties*, acknowledges that "…accounting principles ordinarily do not require transactions with related parties to be accounted for on a basis different from that which would be appropriate if the parties were not related" and that "…financial statements should recognize the substance of particular transactions rather than merely their legal form." The proposed standard does not propose modifications to that guidance.

Subsequent events. AU Section 560, *Subsequent Events*, explains that events or transactions that affect the financial statements sometimes occur subsequent to the balance sheet date but before financial statements are issued. It describes two categories of subsequent events: those that provide additional evidence about conditions that existed at the balance sheet date ("Type One") and those that provide evidence with respect to conditions that arose subsequent to the balance sheet date ("Type Two"). "Type One" events require adjustments to the financial statements, while "Type Two" events may require disclosure in the notes to the financial statements. Under the current guidance, an auditor evaluates subsequent events that occur up until the date of the issuance of the auditor's report on the financial statements. The proposed standard would bring forward the "Type One" and "Type Two" guidance and would require that preparers evaluate subsequent events up until the date the financial statements are issued.

Going concern. AU Section 341, *The Auditor's Consideration of an Entity's Ability to Continue as a Going Concern*, states that "continuation of an entity as a going concern is assumed in financial reporting in the absence of significant information to the contrary," and provides guidance to auditors related to making going concern assessments in connection with a financial statement audit. The proposed standard indicates that preparers of a governmental entity's financial statements have a responsibility to evaluate whether there is substantial doubt about the government's ability to continue as a going concern for a reasonable period of time (not to exceed one year beyond the date of the financial statements). It identifies certain factors that could indicate that there may be substantial doubt about a governmental entity's ability to continue as a going concern and provides examples of information that a preparer might disclose in the notes to financial statements if the conditions warrant such disclosures.

*PwC observation: Questions as to whether the liquidation basis of accounting or some other measurement should be used for a governmental entity when its ability to continue as a going concern is remote are being dealt with in a separate project, "Chapter 9 Bankruptcy Filings" (see page 45).*

The proposed standard would be effective upon issuance. GASB expects to issue a final standard in May 2009.

*PwC observation: Subsequent to issuance of this exposure draft, FASB issued two similar exposure drafts: "Subsequent Events" and "Going Concern" (see page 20). FASB, like GASB, is moving this guidance into its own literature. If the proposed GASB and FASB standards are finalized in their current forms, differences between FASB and GASB guidance will exist, primarily due to FASB's efforts to align its guidance with International Financial Reporting Standards. For example, FASB would require preparers to disclose the date through which subsequent events were considered, while GASB standards would not impose such a requirement. GASB would require evaluation of the going concern assumption for a period not to exceed one year beyond the date of the financial statements; FASB is proposing a more open-ended time horizon. FASB has proposed replacing the "Type One" and "Type Two" terminology with the terms "recognized" and "unrecognized." It is unlikely that GASB will incorporate any aspects of FASB's proposals in finalizing its proposed standard.*

## Other GASB guidance and projects to watch

### Comprehensive Implementation Guide Update

Each fall, GASB publishes an update of its Comprehensive Implementation Guide. This project would update the most recent edition of the Guide to incorporate the impact of pronouncements issued since its issuance and to address additional issues that came to the attention of the GASB staff in the intervening period.

*PwC observation: The Comprehensive Implementation Guide can be ordered through the GASB's Web site at www.gasb.org.*

### Financial Instruments Omnibus

*Note: GASB plans to issue an exposure draft this summer and a final standard by the end of 2009.*

This project was undertaken to consider significant issues that have been identified in practice since the issuance of GASB Statement No. 31, *Accounting and Financial Reporting for Certain Investments and for External Investment Pools*, and what potential revisions to existing reporting and disclosure guidance may be required. Identified issues include:

- Investment reporting (specifically external investment pools, unallocated insurance contracts, and reporting realized gains and losses)
- Investment disclosures (specifically interest rate risk associated with mutual funds and custodial credit risk of deposits that participate in deposit placement services)
- Derivatives (including the scope of the derivatives standard and measurements relating to swap terminations)

### Public/Private Partnerships

*Note: GASB plans to issue an exposure draft this spring and a final standard in early 2010.*

Arrangements referred to as "public/private partnerships" (PPPs) have proliferated in recent years. Although this term has been applied to a wide variety of transactions (from contracting out of social service programs to complete privatization of public assets), this project was initially prompted by increasing interest in arrangements through which a government enters a long-term contract with a private company or not-for-profit organization to operate and maintain (and sometimes to build) a major public facility. PPPs often result in governments transferring certain rights and responsibilities associated with the underlying property (including the right to collect revenues and the responsibility of operation and maintenance) and the responsibility to provide certain services to the private sector entity. For example:

- A hospital authority transfers its assets, liabilities and hospital operations to a not-for-profit hospital system through a lease and management agreement, with the hospital authority's ongoing operations being limited to issuing conduit debt for the not-for-profit hospital system and serving as a "pass-through" for governmental grants.

- A state university leases land to a third-party developer for construction of a dormitory building, with the building being leased back to the university or the units being leased directly to university students and faculty by the developer.

This project was undertaken to consider whether existing authoritative guidance is sufficient to address issues associated with accounting for these arrangements, or whether new guidance is needed. GASB plans to issue an exposure draft of a proposed standard in the spring of 2009, hold public hearings during the summer, and issue a final standard in early 2010.

*PwC observation: In 2006, the International Public Sector Accounting Standards Board (IPSASB) added a project on PPPs to its agenda. GASB staff are also serving as staff for the IPSASB project. While public attention has been largely focused on efforts to converge FASB and IFRS private sector guidance, this is an example of similar convergence efforts taking place within the international governmental sector.*

## Chapter 9 Bankruptcy Filings

*Note: GASB plans to issue an exposure draft this summer and a final standard before the end of 2009.*

Recent high-profile bankruptcy filings involving governments impacted by the economic downturn have raised questions about the accounting implications associated with municipal bankruptcy filings. This project will provide guidance on recognition and measurement issues in financial statements of governmental entities that have formally petitioned for, or have been granted, protection from creditors under Chapter 9 of the US Bankruptcy Code.

Chapter 9 bankruptcy is available exclusively to a "political subdivision or public agency or instrumentality of a State." It provides a financially distressed government with protection from its creditors while it develops and negotiates a plan for reorganizing its debts. Although similar to other chapters in the Code in some respects, Chapter 9 is significantly different in that it contains no provision for liquidation of the government's assets and distribution of its proceeds to creditors. If a petitioning government files under Chapter 9, in general it remains "business as usual." Reorganization of the government's debt is typically accomplished by extending debt maturities, reducing the amount of principal or interest, or refinancing the debt.

The principal financial reporting guidance applicable to non-governmental entities in bankruptcy is AICPA Statement of Position (SOP) 90-7, *Financial Reporting by Entities in Reorganization Under the Bankruptcy Code*. The SOP applies to Chapter 11 bankruptcies, which are typically used to reorganize a business. It provides for "fresh-start" reporting using reorganization values based on the notion that the entity that emerges from Chapter 11 bankruptcy is different from the entity that petitioned the court due to establishment through reorganization of a new controlling interest. That concept would not apply in the governmental environment.

## GASB 14 Reexamination

GASB 14, *The Financial Reporting Entity*, was issued nearly twenty years ago. It establishes the criteria governing which of a governmental entity's related parties should be formally incorporated into its financial statements, along with how to report joint ventures, jointly governed organizations, and other arrangements. The project will determine the effectiveness of the current standards, focusing on whether users, preparers, and auditors believe that the governmental reporting entity includes (and excludes) the appropriate related organizations. The reexamination will also consider whether the financial information of included organizations is displayed and disclosed in the most appropriate and useful manner. Specific issues being reexamined include:

* The appointment of a voting majority criterion when it results in component units being blended and there is little to no financial relationship between the entities

* Whether the "fiscal dependency" criterion is appropriately positioned in the standard

* Whether the "misleading-to-exclude" criterion is still needed now that GASB 39 has been issued

* How to address inadequate discussions of component units in notes to the financial statements

* Whether the provisions for determining "major component units" are appropriate

* How investments in component units should be displayed in the financial statements

* Clarification of how to report minority interest investments in component units

* Clarification of fiduciary responsibilities and fiduciary activities

At one time, the project scope also included establishing standards for reporting by departments and other reporting units that are less than a complete legal entity. However, in early 2009 GASB voted to not continue with that portion of the project. An exposure draft of a proposed standard is expected to be released in early 2010.

*PwC Comment: Much of the guidance in GASB 14 focuses on the extent to which operational overlaps exist between traditional governments. It does not focus on issues related to legal ownership of one government by another or on the corporate-type parent-subsidiary structures used by many BTAs. Often, BTAs with corporate-type structures use a "consolidated" financial statement presentation for their wholly-owned or majority-owned subsidiaries (based on GASB 14's concept of "blending").*

*Consistent with the focus of the original GASB 14 project, much of the project research thus far has focused on relationships involving traditional governments (e.g., states, cities and counties). The extent to which GASB will consider providing guidance concerning corporate-type legal structures in this reexamination is not yet clear.*

## Postemployment Benefits

GASB has undertaken a comprehensive research project to evaluate the effectiveness of its pension accounting and reporting standards and consider whether the standards need to be amended. Because the standards for retiree health insurance and OPEB take the same basic approach as the pension standards, the Board is also considering OPEB in the project's scope.

The Board plans to release an Invitation to Content (ITC) this spring on key issues such as postemployment benefit liability measurement and recognition, pension plan reporting, and cost-sharing arrangements. The questions in the ITC will focus primarily on pensions. However, conclusions that the Board may reach with regard to pensions during a later stage of the project (and considering the feedback on the ITC) also may be applicable at least in part to OPEB, based on the conclusion that pensions and OPEB are conceptually similar. The Board plans to hold public hearings this summer and, after considering the input received from the ITC and the public hearings, issue an exposure draft in the summer of 2010.

## Fair Value measurement

The move towards fair value measurement in the private sector appears to be having a ripple effect in the governmental sector. For example, many BTAs that apply paragraph 7 of GASB 20 (who must apply all FASB standards unless they contradict or conflict with GASB pronouncements) are struggling with questions on the extent to which they should apply FASB's standard on fair value measurement (FAS 157). Fair value has not been extensively employed as a measurement attribute in the governmental financial reporting model outside of investments and (once GASB 53 becomes effective) derivatives. GASB standards provide guidance for measuring fair value of those items,[19] but to date there has been no comprehensive examination of the role of fair value measurement in governmental financial reporting. This project would further the appropriate use of fair value reporting by considering alternative methods of measurement and information that should be disclosed. It is still in the research stage.

*PwC observation: According to the "Statement 20 guidance" page on GASB's Web site (www.gasb.org/st20guide.html), FAS 157 applies only when a governmental entity is making a fair value measurement required by an applicable FASB pronouncement.*

## Codification of Pre-November 30, 1989, FASB Pronouncements

Standards issued by FASB and its predecessors prior to November 30, 1989 must be applied by governmental BTAs unless they conflict with or contradict GASB standards. As a result, preparers must identify which provisions within those FASB standards (sometimes only a few provisions within a particular pronouncement) are applicable. The difficulty in doing so is compounded by the fact that the pre-1989 FASB literature is "frozen in time" and must be applied in its pre-1989 state, even if it has been superseded or amended since then. Further, the question of whether certain guidance is "conflicting and contradictory" can be subject to differing interpretations. This project would definitively determine which provisions of pre-1989 FASB standards apply to governments and do not conflict with or contradict GASB standards, and consider whether those standards should be incorporated into GASB literature. It is still in the research stage.

*PwC observation: The need for this project is made more urgent by the fact that FASB's original pronouncements will be superseded once the "FASB Accounting Standards Codification™" becomes effective (see page 1).*

---

[19] GAS 31, paragraphs 7, 10, and 11, and GASB 53, paragraph 21

# IV. Other accounting issues

*This section contains information on issues of general interest.*

## Convergence with International Financial Reporting Standards (IFRS)

In October 2002, FASB and the International Accounting Standards Board (IASB) signed a memorandum of understanding (the "Norwalk Agreement") which formalized their commitment to a common goal—one set of high quality accounting standards for international use. In 2005 meetings, FASB and IASB reaffirmed their commitment to the convergence of US GAAP and IFRS.

As a result, IFRS continues to gain momentum in the United States. In November 2008, the SEC took a major step toward international convergence by issuing for public comment a proposed "road map" for transition by US public companies to the use of IFRS. The road map sets a date of 2011 for the SEC to decide whether to proceed with rulemaking that would require SEC registrants to begin using IFRS beginning in 2014. The roadmap would also allow for early adoption for certain issuers beginning with filings in 2010.

While some developments appear to be taking the United States in the direction of mandatory adoption of IFRS by US issuers beginning in 2014, others seem to signal a slowing of the pace of transition. The election of President Obama and the subsequent appointment of his top economic advisors may impact the timing of IFRS implementation. Mary Schapiro, the newly appointed chairperson of the SEC, has stated that she favors a slowing down of IFRS adoption by US companies. Additionally, the SEC has estimated that eligible early adopters making the transition from GAAP to IFRS will spend approximately $32 million over their first three years of filings. The SEC has already received numerous transition complaints ranging from the difficulty of maintaining two sets of books while in transition to potentially applying IFRS to previously reported information upon adoption.

In the summer of 2008, FASB hosted a forum to dialogue with constituents about whether and how to move US financial reporting to IFRS. The forum consisted of a panel discussion between FASB board members and invited guests including financial statement users, representatives from small and large private and public companies, auditors, educators, not-for-profits, regulators, and other representatives of facets of the US economy that would be affected by such a move. While the use of IFRS for public companies was generally supported, many concerns were raised regarding the future of financial reporting by nonpublic and not-for-profit entities.

- Will FASB transfer all standard-setting for all US private sector organizations to the IASB or will they transfer just the standard-setting for SEC registrants? If standard setting for not-for-profit organizations is not transferred, how will consistency of financial reporting between not-for-profit and for-profit organizations that operate in the same business be affected? For example, not-for-profit healthcare entities need for-profit oriented standards as well as not-for-profit-specific standards in order to generate meaningful financial statements. How are investors served if different standards are being followed for similar transactions?

- If standard-setting for not-for-profit organizations is transferred and the IASB does not amend its charter to include not-for-profit organizations, would these organizations have to produce financial statements using principles developed solely for for-profit entities? For similar transactions, this should not be a problem, but to the extent that transactions are unique to not-for-profit organizations or involve unique not-for-profit economics, the resulting financial statements may not appropriately reflect the economic substance of operations.

- If the IASB amends its charter to include not-for-profit organizations, how would a definition of a "not-for-profit organization" be developed that could be used across all jurisdictions? Currently, no such definition exists and accounting practices vary greatly across jurisdictions.

Summary of emerging accounting, tax and regulatory issues in 2009
PricewaterhouseCoopers

*PwC observation: Questions surrounding IFRS and not-for-profit organizations are likely to remain unanswered in the near-term. Private companies (including not-for-profits) will most likely remain in the background of the IFRS discussion while the issues surrounding SEC registrants are resolved. In the meantime, not-for-profit organizations should continue to monitor the activities of FASB, IASB and SEC for IFRS developments that may eventually impact private companies.*

## SEC mandates use of new municipal disclosure system

Many not-for-profit and governmental issuers of tax-exempt municipal securities are required to file disclosure documents with Nationally Recognized Municipal Securities Information Repositories (NRMSIRs). Currently, information filed with NRMSIRs is made available to investors for a fee.

In December 2008, the Securities and Exchange Commission amended SEC Rule 15c2-12 to mandate the use of a new "Electronic Municipal Market Access" (EMMA) system for continuing disclosure filings. Effective July 1, 2009, EMMA will become the sole NRMSIR for filing municipal bond official statements, annual and quarterly financial information and material event notices, replacing the four existing NRMSIRs. Similar to the SEC's Electronic Data Gathering, Analysis and Retrieval (EDGAR) system that makes annual, quarterly and material events information of SEC registrant companies publicly available, EMMA will make municipal disclosure information available to the public via an internet Web site at no cost.

*PwC observation: The SEC views EMMA as "a giant step toward bringing municipal disclosure up to the level of corporate disclosure."*

Implications of the rule change include:

- Effective July 1, 2009, organizations subject to continuing disclosure requirements will submit their financial statements, material event notices, and other filings directly to EMMA, rather than to the four NRMSIRs or to Disclosure USA (an "electronic post office" for submission of municipal documents)

- Organizations that previously submitted continuing disclosure information in hard copy format will now be required to submit such information electronically

- The general public will, for the first time, have ready access to disclosure documents for municipal debt issuers, instantly and without charge

- Organizations will have the ability to view their submissions online and free of charge, which was not previously possible with the former NRMSIRs

- EMMA will facilitate underwriter due diligence on new bond offerings by providing the ability to readily verify an organization's timely compliance with its continuing disclosure covenants

EMMA can be accessed at www.emma.msrb.org. For more information on the rule change, see www.sec.gov/rules/final/2008/34-59062.pdf.

## SEC seeks regulatory authority over municipal market

During the past two years, the SEC repeatedly has asked Congress for authority to regulate the municipal securities market. Presently, its authority is limited to bringing actions against issuers who make material misstatements in official statements or financial statements filed with NRMSIRs, and regulating the brokers and dealers who engage in securities transactions. The SEC's primary concern is that individual investors own nearly two-thirds of the $2.7 trillion of municipal securities outstanding (directly or through funds), but neither the SEC nor any other federal regulator has the authority to regulate the type and quality of disclosures they receive relative to those investments.

# APPENDIX D

The credit crisis may change all that, however. Problems with municipal bond insurers, the failure of the auction rate securities market, and widely-publicized stories about issuers in financial distress are focusing scrutiny on the municipal market. In testimony before the House Committee on Oversight and Government Reform last October, former SEC Chairman Christopher Cox stated, "Knowing what we now know, I would have begun this campaign [to bring municipal finance disclosure at least up to par with corporate disclosure] on my first day on the job."

Nearly two years ago, Chairman Cox and staff of the SEC's Divisions of Corporate Finance, Enforcement and Market Regulation, and of the Office of Chief Accountant sent a white paper to Congress outlining their ongoing concerns about investor access to full and accurate information regarding their municipal securities holdings (www.sec.gov/news/press/2007/2007-148wp.pdf). That white paper and a subsequent speech by Chairman Cox outlined what a municipal regulatory regime might entail, including:

- Private companies (including hospitals, universities, and other not-for-profit organizations) who issue municipal bonds through conduit financings would have disclosure requirements similar (but not identical) to SEC registrants.
- Offering documents and periodic reports provided to investors would contain information similar to what they're accustomed to seeing for publicly-traded securities.
- Financial statements, material events notices, and other continuing disclosure filings would be available to investors free of charge and on a timely basis through an easily accessible venue similar to the SEC's EDGAR system.

*PwC observation: Should this occur, it would bring most organizations that issue municipal bonds— including healthcare, higher education, and governmental entities—under some degree of direct SEC regulation.*

Chairman Cox did not envision a wholesale application of the regulatory model for SEC registrants to municipal securities issuers. For example, he did not envision the Division of Corporate Finance reviewing municipal offering statements and continuing disclosure filings. In his view, the regulatory regime should be tailored to accommodate the unique character of municipal bond issuers and special attributes of the municipal securities market.

Chairman Cox stepped down from his post when President Obama took office in January 2009. At that time, only one element of the proposed regulatory structure had come to pass -- the establishment of the new EMMA system for municipal disclosure filings (see page 49). The extent to which incoming Chairperson Schapiro will continue to advance those initiatives is unclear. Recently, she indicated that she plans to take a "deep dive" into municipal securities in the coming months. However, Commissioners Luis Aguilar and Elisse Walter have each recently made speeches calling on Congress to close the "regulatory loophole" and provide investors in municipal bonds with better information and more protection.

*PwC observation: It is unlikely that anything will happen quickly on the regulatory front, as Congress in the past has stubbornly refused the SEC any regulation over this market due to concerns about impinging on "states rights." However, the ball is definitely moving in that direction again. Given the interdependence of the capital markets that was illustrated so eloquently by the "domino effect" of the credit crisis events, the case is much more compelling now than in years past.*

Summary of emerging accounting, tax and regulatory issues in 2009
PricewaterhouseCoopers

# V. Regulatory issues

*This section highlights issues affecting the regulatory environment as well as changes to the professional literature and regulatory standards.*

## Adoption of the American Recovery and Reinvestment Act of 2009

On February 18, 2009, the Office of Management and Budget (OMB) issued government-wide guidance related to carrying out the programs and activities contained in the American Recovery and Reinvestment Act of 2009 (Recovery Act) (www.recovery.gov).

Further guidance will be issued by OMB and each Federal agency over the next several months. Given the relatively short time period (fiscal 2009—fiscal 2012) for awarding the funding, organizations should check the Web site frequently for further guidance, as it becomes available.

The Single Audit/A-133 will be impacted:

- Beginning with September 30, 2009 year ends, the Federal Audit Clearinghouse must make all Single Audit reports publicly available. Currently, a Freedom of Information Act (FOIA) request must be filed to gain access to a particular A-133 report.

- Federal Offices of Inspector General (OIGs) must conduct audit quality reviews with an emphasis on the Recovery Act funds. Audit results will be posted on the Web site.

- OIGs must identify programs and recipients that are high risk using risk-assessment techniques and conduct audits, inspections and investigations of the recipients so identified.

- OMB can designate certain programs as high risk and mandate they be audited as part of a recipient's normal A-133 audit.

- Recovery Act funds must be tracked separately by recipients.

- Prime recipients of Recovery Act funding will be required to submit new quarterly reports within 10 days of each quarter's end. The report will include extensive financial and project related information.

- The A-133 report schedule of expenditures of federal awards will identify Recovery Act funding with newly issued CFDA numbers.

- OMB is drafting further A-133 guidance to include in the 2009 Compliance Supplement due to be released tentatively in April 2009. OMB is likely to issue supplements to the 2009 Compliance Supplement as further compliance requirements are developed.

*PwC observation: A significant number of organizations are likely to receive project and program funding that is part of the Recovery Act. The overall principles of transparency and accountability will place a fresh spotlight on recipient compliance policies, processes and procedures. Organizations need to consider this added focus when accepting Recovery Act funding and the need to enhance existing compliance policies, processes and procedures to manage the added risk that comes with Recovery Act funding.*

## Changes to the professional literature and regulatory standards

### Yellow Book 2007 revision

In July 2007, the Government Accountability Office (GAO) posted the 2007 revision to "Government Auditing Standards," also known as "GAGAS" or "the Yellow Book," to its Web site (www.gao.gov). The 2007 revisions were comprehensive and include:

- Clarification of the use of terms "must," "should" and "may" when describing the auditor's responsibility

- A new chapter on ethics

- Adoption of AICPA Statement on Auditing Standards No. 112, *Communication of Internal Control Related Matters Noted in an Audit*. The new definitions of significant deficiency and material weakness that have been incorporated into the Yellow Book are likely to affect the auditor's risk assessment for major programs under OMB A-133. They also are likely to affect the number and type of control deficiencies reported in Yellow Book audits. The revised Yellow Book incorporates SAS 112 effective for financial statement audits conducted under GAGAS for years ending after December 15, 2006.

- Additional disclosure requirements related to the restatement of previously issued financial statements (e.g., discussion of the specific internal control deficiencies that contributed to the restatement)

- Expanded discussion of the use of "matter of emphasis" paragraphs in an auditor report (e.g., uncertainties about an institution's financial future)

- Many edits to modernize and incorporate current thinking concerning best auditing practices

- Expanded and updated performance audit standards

The 2007 Yellow Book revisions go into effect for audits of periods beginning after January 1, 2008. Printed revisions of the Yellow Book are available from the Government Printing Office (866-512-1800).

In January 2008, the GAO also issued a guidance document, *Government Auditing Standards: Implementation Tool—Professional Requirements for Use in Implementing Requirements Identified by "Must" and "Should" in the July 2007 Revision of Government Auditing Standards.*

*PwC observation: The changes to the Yellow Book are substantial. They reflect the changing audit environment in which greater transparency and accountability are expected from auditors and organizations. Broadly, the proposed Yellow Book revisions are part of the GAO's overall objective to support "the Congress and the nation in facing the challenges of a rapidly changing world while addressing the nation's large and growing long-term fiscal imbalance."[20]*

*The guidance document allows the auditor and other interested persons to focus on the most significant requirements contained in the Yellow Book. However, we recommend the guidance document not be used as a substitute for reading the Yellow Book because the Yellow Book contains explanatory material in addition to the minimum requirements.*

### New AICPA auditing standard

The AICPA superseded its Statement on Auditing Standards (SAS) 112, *Communication of Internal Control Related Matters Noted in an Audit* and replaced it with SAS 115 of the same title.

This new SAS impacts the audits of not-for-profits as well as other types of organizations that require an audit under the Yellow Book. It also impacts grant audits conducted under various state regulations, because some states follow the federal reporting guidelines. OMB and federal agencies have previously considered the impact of SAS 112 on OMB Circular A-133 and specific federal agency program audit regulations and guides, and the use of SAS 112 had been mandated when auditing major federal programs under the provisions of OMB Circular A-133.

SAS 115 includes the following changes from SAS 112:

- The PCAOB revised definitions of significant deficiency and material weakness contained in the PCAOB Auditing Standard No. 5, *An Audit of Internal Control over Financial Reporting that is integrated with an Audit of Financial Statements* were incorporated

- The list of control deficiencies that are also considered to be material weaknesses has been revised

- There is no longer a list of control deficiencies that ordinarily would be considered at least significant deficiencies

- The effective date of SAS 115 is fiscal years ending on or after December 31, 2009 and earlier implementation is allowed

The GAO has issued interim guidance on the implementation of SAS 115 before the Yellow Book is amended to incorporate SAS 115. This guidance can be found at www.gao.gov/govaud/YbK01.htm. The OMB has not, as of the date of this document, issued guidance on the application of SAS 115 to OMB Circular A-133 audits. Similarly, other federal agencies have not yet updated their audit guides for SAS 115. Therefore, it is not appropriate to use SAS 115 for Circular A-133 audits until such time as Circular A-133 and other audit guides are amended.

---

[20] GAO's Strategic Plan: 2004-2009, page 1

Summary of emerging accounting, tax and regulatory issues in 2009
PricewaterhouseCoopers

*PwC observation: SAS 115 definitions of significant deficiency and material weakness may appear on the surface to allow more flexibility on determining what is a significant deficiency or material weakness. However, a complete reading of SAS 115 demonstrates the criteria concerning severity of a finding has not changed in substance.*

## OMB A-133 Compliance Supplement

OMB is currently drafting the 2009 Compliance Supplement, which is expected to be issued in the second quarter of 2008. Changes anticipated include:

- Various program updates to several individual Catalog of Federal Domestic Assistance (CFDA) sections and the addition of some new program sections in part four
- Some clarifications and updates to the 14 compliance requirements in part three
- No significant changes to the research and development cluster in part five
- Several technical updates made throughout the Student Financial Aid cluster

*PwC observation: Organizations should review the 2009 Compliance Supplement, when it becomes available, with their auditor to determine the impact of these changes on the scope of their 2009 A-133 audit. The Compliance Supplement will be posted to OMB's Web site at www. whitehouse.gov/omb.*

## The Higher Education Opportunity Act

In August 2008, the Higher Education Opportunity Act (Public Law 110-315) (HEOA) was enacted by Congress. HEOA reauthorized the Higher Education Act of 1965, as amended. HEOA also makes numerous changes to existing Department of Education student financial aid programs, authorizes new programs and makes changes to other laws.

In December 2008, the Department of Education issued a "Dear Colleague" letter GEN-08-12 which contains a summary of the provisions of HEOA. The effective date of the HEOA is August 14, 2008 unless otherwise noted for any of the HEOA specific sections. However, some of the changes will require the Department of Education to issue specific regulations. Some of those regulations will be issued through the negotiated rule making process.

*PwC observation: The summary included with the "Dear Colleague" letter is approximately 220 pages and includes an 11 page detailed index and a chart summarizing the changes by specific effective date. It may take as long as two years before final implementing regulations for each of the changes included in HEOA are available. As indicated in the "Dear Colleague" letter, the Department of Education HEOA Web site (www. ed.gov/heoa) should be reviewed periodically for further guidance the Department of Education may issue before final regulations are available.*

## Data Collection Form

The Single Audit Clearinghouse made available, in August 2008, the Data Collection Form to be used for fiscal 2008, 2009 and 2010. Although the form itself has not changed significantly, the process for filing the data collection form and related A-133 report has changed.

The data collection form must be filed electronically beginning with fiscal 2008 year end reporting and the related A-133 report must be filed electronically with the data collection form via a pdf upload.

The Clearinghouse has posted to its Web site (http://harvester.census.gov) an instruction manual which includes a description of the process for obtaining a password code by both the auditee and the auditor in order that the form may be electronically signed.

*PwC observation: This new electronic filing process will eliminate the need for mailing hard copy reports to the Clearinghouse. In addition, built-in edit warnings will help to reduce errors in preparation of the data collection form. Time needed to read the manual and obtain the password codes should be factored into the filing timetable to ensure adequate time is available in order that the due date for the filing is not missed.*

# APPENDIX D

## Current regulatory environment

### Time and effort reporting

Time and effort reporting continues to be a challenging area, particularly for organizations that receive funding from the Department of Health and Human Services (HHS) and the National Science Foundation (NSF). In most federal awards, personnel costs, including direct labor charges, fringe benefits and the related indirect costs, represent the largest charges to the government. Federal agency offices of Inspector General (OIG) and the Department of Justice are aggressive in bringing charges for noncompliance with labor cost requirements and for overcharging for labor costs on federal awards.

The OIG work plans, which set the direction for the OIG's audits, include among the areas OIG offices plan to focus on:

- Effort reporting: Are the organizations accurately reflecting the portion of researchers' efforts spent on grants?
- Administrative and clerical salaries: Are organizations appropriately charging administrative and clerical salaries to federally sponsored grants and cooperative agreements?
- Cost transfers: Are cost transfers supported by documentation that fully explains the reasons for the transfer? Have responsible grantee officials certified the correctness of the new charges?
- Compensation of graduate students: Is compensation for graduate student researchers' who receive tuition remission as a component of compensation consistent with guidelines?

*PwC observation: Organizations that receive federal awards should pay particular attention to these areas of audit focus. When federal agencies find that organizations have not complied with effort reporting, multimillion-dollar repayments and fines can be and have been imposed.*

*Federal recipients should review their time and effort reporting systems—and strengthen them where needed. Some specific areas to address include:*

- *Timeliness of certification*
- *Access to a suitable means of verification for the person certifying the effort*
- *Accountability of time incurred at other related and unrelated entities*
- *Reconciliation of actual effort to the effort committed via award documents*
- *Review of central administration policies, in particular for effort reporting and cost transfers*

*In addition, symptoms of potential deficiencies in time and effort reporting systems might include:*

- *Missing or incomplete effort reports*
- *A high volume of cost transfers*
- *Multiple documents recording faculty effort*
- *Incentive pay agreements*

*In particular, research institutions with the following characteristics should continue to be aware of the potential risks associated with their time and effort reporting systems in the current environment:*

- *"Collaborative" research agreements with other institutions*
- *Rapid growth in clinical research*
- *Recent system implementations*
- *Closely affiliated faculty practice plans*
- *Pre- and post-award processes that are outdated and understaffed*
- *Closely affiliated hospitals and research institutions*

Summary of emerging accounting, tax and regulatory issues in 2009
PricewaterhouseCoopers

## Faculty and institutional conflicts of interest

Organizations have been required under federal regulations to implement research conflict of interest policies and procedures to protect the integrity and objectivity of research efforts. Federal requirements from the OMB, the NSF and the National Institutes of Health (NIH) have historically required that institutions identify, manage and disclose conflicts of interest among research faculty to sponsoring agencies. Recently, the management and reporting of conflicts of interest has been called into question. An audit of the NIH by the HHS found that existing NIH regulations governing the reporting of conflict of interest matters do not require organizations to provide adequate information about conflicts and how these would be managed by the reporting institution. There was also a lack of follow up by the NIH to request further information from organizations.

In June 2008, three professors at a major research university were questioned by Senator Grassley as they allegedly failed to disclose compensation of at least $1 million each from pharmaceutical companies. Senator Grassley has subsequently contacted 20 other organizations over financial conflicts of interest and initiated an investigation of 30 other scientists. The core of this issue gets at scientists, investigators and researchers failing to disclose accurate and timely information and the inability of organizations to identify and accurately report conflicts of interest.

## Impact on educational organizations

From these recent actions by Senator Grassley and the disparity of reporting noted in the audit findings, a new regulation was proposed by the Senate Appropriations Committee to "step up" oversight of financial conflicts of interest among organizations. The draft legislation would require drug and device makers to disclose payment amounts greater than $500 per year to doctors, scientists and researchers in a National Registry. In the future, it is possible that organizations and sponsoring agencies will be mandated to verify disclosure accuracy through this National Registry.

The individual organization will be required to communicate and enforce conflict of interest disclosure requirements among its faculty. The actual or perceived failure of an institution to identify, effectively manage and disclose conflicts of interest may lead to a damaged reputation, federal sanctions and a loss of future award funding from outside agencies. To address these issues and risks, organizations have implemented the following practices:

- Established policies to address federal requirements surrounding the identification, management and disclosure of conflicts of interest to sponsoring agencies.

- Implemented procedures to ensure conflict of interest disclosure requirements have been satisfied by faculty and investigators prior to funds being released to perform research.

- Created a centralized administrative group to evaluate and maintain disclosure information reported by faculty, assist with the development of management action plans and report required information to sponsoring agencies.

- Engaged an active executive oversight committee to approve policy modifications, provide guidance on how conflicts should be managed, and approve and monitor institutional compliance with federal regulations.

- Monitored faculty and investigator compliance with agreed-upon management action plans.

By implementing the above practices, organizations have been able to align themselves to more effectively comply with federal regulations.

*PwC observation: Organizations will need to be proactive and consider launching a full review of their practices within this area to include not only personal conflicts of interest among each faculty member, but also conflicts of interest between the organization and other entities it collaborates with. This review should encompass not only the resolution of conflicts, but the manner in which these are summarized and reported to senior management.*

Faculty, organizations and sponsors of research each share responsibility to protect the integrity and objectivity of research. To achieve these objectives and protect all stakeholders, organizations should consider the following leading practices:

- Reexamine existing policies and procedures to identify and address deficiencies and unmitigated key risks in conflicts of interest identification, management and reporting.

- Communicate conflicts of interest policies, procedures and objectives to new faculty during the "HR On-boarding" process.

- Educate faculty and other key stakeholders on the concerns expressed recently by Congress and federal agencies and the potential significance to the institution.

- Implement periodic training for existing research faculty and investigators to reiterate policies and procedures and raise awareness of current issues.

- Utilize an automated system (e.g., web-based) to facilitate submission of information by faculty and allow organizations to better identify, manage and report conflicts of interests.

- Solicit periodic confirmations from faculty that information reported to the institution is current and accurate and that faculty are in compliance with any management plans to address conflicts of interest.

### Federal award reporting requirements

OMB Circular A-110 Section 52 requires the submission of a "Financial Status Report (FSR)." Federal awarding agencies establish the frequency of submission, generally not more than quarterly and at least annually. For example, according to the NIH Grants Policy Statement, reports generally should be submitted within 90 days after the close of the annual budget, except for awards under the NIH Streamlined Non-Competing Award Process (SNAP) program, which requires an FSR to be submitted within 90 days of the end of the award or competitive segment.

Federal agencies are concerned with the higher delinquency rates associated with both financial and technical reports because they have resulted in significant delays to award closeouts. This problem is pervasive throughout the research industry and all federal agencies.

For instance, in 2004, HHS, NIH Office of Inspector General and the National Science Foundation OIG issued reports detailing the late reporting, which is in the double digits. The HHS and NSF OIG reports include similar recommendations to NIH and NSF program management officials:

- Develop automated reminder systems
- Improve ability for electronic submission of documents
- Focus more attention on late reporting
- Consider withholding future funding until the researcher and/or organization is caught up on late reports

PwC observation: Financial Status Reports may be late for many reasons. For example, reporting deadlines may be too tight, especially for complex awards involving subrecipients. Also, federal agencies sometimes cannot respond in a timely manner to requests from organizations for additional information. However, federal agencies have been known to withhold funding to principal investigators when the delinquency rate is particularly high. Organizations must work with the federal agencies to strike a reasonable balance. The completeness and accuracy of reports should not be sacrificed for better timeliness.

Summary of emerging accounting, tax and regulatory issues in 2009
PricewaterhouseCoopers

56

## Other regulatory issues

### Federal Funding Accountability and Transparency Act

On September 26, 2006, President Bush signed into law the Federal Funding Accountability and Transparency Act of 2006 ("the Act"). This bill required the OMB to develop a searchable Web site that taxpayers can access at no charge that will enable them to determine certain information about the grants, contracts, loans and cooperative agreements their tax dollars are funding. The Web site is now available at www.usaspending.gov.

The Act also required that by January 1, 2009, all primary award recipients will be required to submit information on all subawards and subcontracts to federal agencies for inclusion on this new Web site. A federal agency plans to pilot a program to determine the best way to implement a cost-effective process to submit subaward and subcontract data. The pilot program was delayed. The implementation date for posting of subaward date by prime award recipients to the Web site has also been delayed.

Regarding the reporting of subawards, prime award recipients can allocate as indirect costs reasonable costs for the collection and reporting of subaward data.

*PwC observation: Implementation of this Act allows the general public access to detailed information about the federal awards an organization is receiving and the tax dollars being spent on it.*

*Organizations should follow the developments with the reporting of subaward and subcontract information in order to plan for the effort that will be required to gather and submit to this new Web site subaward and subcontract data.*

### National Single Audit Sampling Project

The Department of Education and several other federal agencies, including HHS, NSF, DOD and HUD, designed a statistically valid approach to performing quality control reviews of single audits. Congress provided several million dollars to fund this effort, called the National Single Audit Sampling Project. The quality control reviews conducted under this project began in early 2005 and were concluded in the first quarter of 2007. A report summarizing the results of this initiative was issued by the President's Council on Integrity and Efficiency (PCIE) to OMB and provided to Congress as well as federal agency officials in June 2007.

The report noted several audit quality issues in varying degrees of significance that the PCIE recommends be addressed by both the accounting profession and federal regulators, including OMB. The recommendations include enhanced training requirements and revisions to the Single Audit Act standards and guidance.

In response to the findings included in this report, the AICPA Governmental Audit Quality Center (GAQC) created several task forces to develop solutions to audit quality issues and act upon the recommendations noted in the report. Similarly, several federal agencies have also formed task forces.

The AICPA task forces have over the past year drafted several audit practice aids to be used by auditors performing single audits. In 2009, the practice aids will be finalized and made available by the AICPA.

The OMB task forces are working on recommendations to improve Circular A-133 and the OMB plans to publish the recommendations in the Federal Register for comment. Among the potential changes to Circular A-133 that may be recommended is the mandate that extensions of the A-133 report filing due date not be granted by the federal agencies; therefore, an entity that files it's A-133 report late, would automatically be considered a high risk auditee.

# APPENDIX D

*PwC observation: The AICPA created the
Governmental Audit Quality Center to promote
and improve the quality of audits conducted under
the Yellow Book. Membership in this center is
voluntary and requires a CPA firm to adhere to
several stringent audit quality practices. Presently,
the GAQC member firms audit federal award recipients
that account for more than 80% of federal awards to
not-for-profit organizations that require a single audit.
The GAQC Web site (www.aicpa.org/gaqc) includes
more information regarding Governmental Audits
and Audit Quality.*

*Organizations should make every effort to submit
their A-133 reports to the Clearinghouse on a timely
basis. If your organization has had difficulties in the
past, we advise you to contact your auditor and work
out a plan to submit current and future years' A-133
reports on time. It is expected that OMB will issue
its view on this matter in 2009.*

# VI. Tax issues

*In this section, we address tax matters impacting tax–exempt organizations, including the IRS's Exempt Organization Implementing Guidelines for fiscal year 2009, legislative activity, and the redesigned Form 990. We also include information regarding items of continuing interest to tax–exempt organizations, including FIN 48, partnership investments, state reporting requirements, and international activities.*

## New issues

### The Redesigned Form 990 for 2008

Following a lengthy overhaul of the Form 990, Return of Organization Exempt From Income Tax, that had been in place for nearly 30 years, the IRS issued the official version of the Form and instructions at the end of 2008. According to the IRS, the redesigned Form 990 was based on the three guiding principles of transparency, compliance, and minimizing taxpayer burden. Organizations will begin using the new Form for years beginning in 2008. The 2008 Form 990, as well as other key information describing the redesign, is available on the IRS's Web site, http://www.irs.gov/eo.

#### Basic Structure of the New Form 990

The 2008 Form 990 consists of an 11–page core form that each filing organization must complete. In addition, the Form utilizes 16 schedules designed to require reporting of information only from those organizations that conduct particular activities.

#### Key Focus Areas of the Redesigned Form

Governance and Management: The redesigned Form 990 focuses on how an organization is governed through its policies and procedures. While many of the new questions on the Form 990 are not mandated by law, they highlight what the IRS and others might consider to be best practices for tax–exempt organizations. For example, the Form not only inquires as to the existence of a written conflict of interest policy, but also the monitoring and enforcement of that policy. It also inquires as to the existence of whistleblower and document retention policies.

The redesigned Form contains many new definitions and asks detailed questions regarding governance of the reporting organization. For example, the Form 990 asks whether a copy of the Form was provided to the organization's governing body before the Form was filed. The instructions provide that an organization may answer "Yes" to this question only if it provides the final version of its Form 990 to each board member in paper or electronic form prior to its filing with the IRS. However, the instructions also provide an example which clarifies that the requirement is merely to make the Form 990 available to each board member, and that the entire board is not required to review and/or approve the Form 990. Nevertheless, in addition to answering this question, an organization must disclose the review process, if any, by which the organization's officers, directors, trustees, board committee members, or management reviewed the prepared Form 990, including specifics regarding who conducted the review, when they conducted it, and the extent of any such review.

Compensation: Compensation on the 2008 Form 990 will be reported consistently with the Forms W–2 and 1099 issued during the fiscal year covered by the return. This represents a significant change from the prior Form 990, which allowed compensation to be reported either on a calendar year basis or an organization's fiscal year.

On Form 990, all of the organization's current officers, directors, trustees and key employees must be disclosed, along with their compensation from the reporting organization and related organizations. Disclosure also is required for certain former officers, directors, trustees, and key employees. The redesigned Form 990 has redefined who is a "key employee," and it is likely that organizations now will disclose more individuals and their compensation.

Additional detail regarding compensation arrangements of officers, directors, trustees, key employees, and the five most highly compensated employees who are not officers, directors, trustees, or key employees must be disclosed on Schedule J, *Compensation Information*. For example, organizations are required to disclose the provision of certain benefits including who received the benefit, whether it was included in compensation, and whether there is a written policy regarding the organization's payment or reimbursement of those benefits. The benefits include first-class or charter travel, travel for companions, tax indemnification and gross-up payments, discretionary spending accounts, housing allowances or residence for personal use, business use of personal residence, health or social club dues or initiation fees, or personal services (e.g., maid, chauffeur, chef). While these are permissible benefits, organizations should consider the impact of public disclosure. The redesigned Form 990 makes it clear that the annual accrual of deferred compensation (e.g., a Section 457(f) plan) needs to be disclosed in addition to disclosing the amount of deferred compensation when it is paid.

Hospitals: In response to Congressional pressure, the redesigned Form 990 requires additional reporting for hospitals, especially with regards to charity care and certain other community benefits. The IRS has defined "hospital" for Schedule H, Hospitals, purposes (not for Schedule A, Public Charity Status and Public Support, purposes) as an organization that is licensed, registered, or similarly recognized by a state as a hospital. Each legal entity that is classified as a hospital and files Form 990 will file one Schedule H for all of the health care facilities it operates. Schedule H is generally consistent with the Catholic Health Association community benefit reporting model. Hospitals have one year of transition relief for completing most of Schedule H.

Tax–Exempt Bonds: Schedule K, *Supplemental Information on Tax Exempt Bonds*, requires an organization to report detail on its tax-exempt bonds on an issue-by-issue basis, including proceeds, private business use, and arbitrage. Schedule K also asks whether the reporting organization has adopted management practices and procedures to ensure the post-issuance compliance with regard to its tax-exempt bond liabilities. Reporting will be required for each tax-exempt bond that was issued after December 31, 2002 and that had an outstanding principal amount in excess of $100,000 as of the last day of the tax year. Bonds issued after December 31, 2002 to refund bonds issued before January 1, 2003 may be excluded from Schedule K's private business use analysis (Part III), but they will still be reported in Parts I, II, and IV. In order to accurately track private business use, organizations will need to retain relevant documentation supporting their use of bond-financed facilities. Organizations with tax-exempt bonds have one year of transition relief for completing most of Schedule K.

*PwC observation: Organizations should proactively prepare for the redesigned Form 990's new reporting requirements by taking steps including:*

- *Review the redesigned Form 990 and the instructions in detail and consider how the changes will impact the reporting organization;*

- *Identify where collection of new data might be required and determine how the data will be gathered;*

- *Modify existing financial and information data systems to accommodate new data collection and reporting requirements;*

- *Implement policies and procedures that are consistent with their desired responses to questions on the redesigned Form 990;*

- *Draft responses to the redesigned Form 990 and relevant Schedules to identify information gaps and to ensure succinct and accurate representation of the organization;*

- *Consider having the audit or finance committee review and comment upon the Form 990 and providing copies of the final version of the Form 990 to the full board prior to filing; and*

- *Be aware of possible future guidance on the 2008 Form 990. While the 2008 Form 990 will not change, the IRS could issue FAQs to address certain common questions.*

Summary of emerging accounting, tax and regulatory issues in 2009
PricewaterhouseCoopers

## IRS Compliance initiatives

The IRS has continued its initiatives to focus on specific issues that it believes may be troublesome. In an effort to maximize the use of its resources and focus its efforts in the areas that it believes are problematic, the IRS continues to issue compliance questionnaires.

College and University Compliance Questionnaire: The most recent compliance questionnaire was the College and University Compliance Questionnaire, Form 14018. The IRS sent the questionnaire to 400 public and private colleges and universities of varying sizes and responses were due February 6, 2009. The IRS anticipates that the responses to the questionnaire will provide them with a better understanding of how colleges and universities:

- Report revenues and expenses from trade or business activities,

- Classify activities as exempt or taxable,

- Calculate and report income or losses on Form 990-T,

- Allocate revenues and expenses between exempt and taxable activities,

- Invest and use endowment funds, and

- Determine the types and amounts of executive compensation.

Upon receipt of responses to the questionnaire, the IRS will analyze the responses, conduct examinations focused on unrelated business income and executive compensation on a sample of the organizations, and issue a report on the project. Senator Grassley noted that the questionnaire's release is long overdue and issued a written statement in which he urged the IRS to quickly compile the results and issue its report.

Tax-Exempt Bonds Compliance Report: As a follow-up to its compliance questionnaire on tax-exempt bonds, the IRS issued an interim Tax-Exempt Bonds Compliance Report in 2008. The IRS distributed the Tax-Exempt Bonds Compliance Questionnaire to evaluate post-issuance compliance and record retention practices of organizations with outstanding tax-exempt bonds. The IRS sent the questionnaire to 207 IRC Section 501(c)(3) organizations with outstanding tax-exempt bond liabilities. After receiving responses and analyzing the data from 192 of the organizations, the IRS issued its interim report, which identified gaps in post-issuance compliance.

While almost all of the responding organizations said that they had implemented written post-issuance compliance policies and procedures, the IRS believes that only about 16% of the respondents had written specific procedures and another 33% had implemented ad hoc processes. The IRS has made clear that such inconsistencies warrant further inquiries in this area in the near future, including conducting additional field compliance checks.

Hospital Compliance Report: In February, the IRS released its nonprofit hospital compliance report based upon over 500 hospitals' responses to a 2006 IRS compliance questionnaire and also results from the IRS's examination of 20 hospitals regarding their executive compensation practices. The report goes into a detailed analysis of the data as sorted by the hospitals' demographics, including population levels and health insurance coverage levels, and their annual revenue. Based upon their analysis, the IRS found that the average percentage of a hospital's total revenue spent on community benefit was 9%. Uncompensated care was the largest reported community benefit expenditure, representing an average percentage of 7% of total revenue and accounting for 56% of aggregate community benefit expenditures. With regard to executive compensation, the IRS found that nearly all examined executive compensation was upheld as established pursuant to the rebuttable presumption of reasonableness, with hospitals using comparability data and independent personnel to review and establish compensation amounts.

The IRS expressed frustration in their report with the community benefit and reasonable compensation standards and how difficult they are to administer. Nevertheless, the IRS stated that refining or revising the community benefit standard could "seriously impact" hospitals because of varying practices and financial capabilities. Rather than changing the standard, the IRS is looking to Schedule H of the redesigned Form 990 to reduce variations in reporting community benefit measurements. In direct response to the IRS's report, Senator Grassley, a proponent of a bright-line test to determine whether hospitals qualify for tax-exempt status, expressed disappointment that the IRS didn't provide guidance with regard to defining community benefit and uncompensated care in their study. Senator Grassley additionally was disappointed that the IRS did not include community benefit and compensation data on for-profit hospitals in the study. He has promised to ask the IRS to conduct another study on this topic in the future.

*PwC observation: While a relatively small number of organizations have received the IRS's questionnaires, all tax-exempt organizations should review the questionnaires and consider how they would complete the applicable questions. For example, while the IRS sent the College and University Compliance Questionnaire only to colleges and universities, the IRS asked for detail regarding unrelated business income, endowments, and compensation, which impact many tax-exempt organizations. Executive compensation will continue to be a hot-button issue this year for tax-exempt organizations in general. If an organization has tax-exempt bonds, it should ensure that it not only has written post-issuance compliance policies and procedures but that it also follows such policies and procedures. Hospitals should be alert to whether the traditional community benefit standard for determining tax-exemption will remain in place or whether a more bright-line test will emerge.*

## Legislative update

Congress remains interested in tax-exempt organizations, focusing on specific areas where it sees a potential need for reform, including hospitals' provision of charity care and college and university endowment earnings. Senator Grassley, ranking member of the Committee on Finance, has actively suggested legislative reforms geared towards tax-exempt organizations.

Hospital Charity Care: In addition to the IRS's charity care initiative via Schedule H of the redesigned Form 990, Congress is examining the practices of tax-exempt hospitals with respect to the provision of charity care and community benefit. Healthcare represents a significant area of federal tax policy, and legislators want to understand how the benefits afforded to hospitals by their tax-exempt status are helping the public.

Senator Grassley's on-going interest in charity care and community benefit provided by nonprofit hospitals led to his request for a Government Accountability Office (GAO) report on how nonprofit hospitals satisfy the community benefit standard to maintain their tax-exempt status. In his request, he expressed concerns that hospitals and legislators are inconsistently interpreting and applying the community benefit standard. The GAO issued a report, "Nonprofit Hospitals: Variation in Standards and Guidance Limits Comparison of How Hospitals Meet Community Benefit Requirements," which largely confirmed Senator Grassley's concerns. In response to this report, Senator Grassley has suggested that the IRS needs a "bright-line test" for determining whether hospitals are qualifying for their tax-exempt status.

One of the GAO report's key findings was that the IRS's community benefit standard allows broad latitude regarding what constitutes community benefit. While a few states have put additional parameters around community benefit, including a specific definition, requirements for provision of community benefits, and reporting requirements, those requirements and definitions can vary substantially in scope and detail.

Summary of emerging accounting, tax and regulatory issues in 2009
PricewaterhouseCoopers

The GAO report also found that while the hospital industry has consistent definitions for certain of their charitable activities, there is inconsistent treatment of bad debt and the unreimbursed cost of Medicare. Some hospital associations include both bad debt and the unreimbursed cost of Medicare in community benefit, whereas others do not. The IRS has included sections in Schedule H of the 2008 Form 990 to allow hospitals to provide data on both bad debt and the unreimbursed cost of Medicare. These expenditures, however, are not integrated into the charity care and other community benefits analysis.

*PwC observation: Tax–exempt hospitals should be aware of the Senate Finance Committee's interest in charity care and community benefit reporting. Further, while Schedule H of the redesigned 2008 Form 990 grants hospitals transition relief for the most part, hospitals should consider doing a mock Schedule H to determine where there could be reporting issues. A broad spectrum of groups, including the media, the general public, local jurisdictions, the IRS, and Congress all undoubtedly will use the schedule as a way to collect information about hospitals' operations.*

Higher Education Endowments: In light of rising tuition costs, members of Congress have raised concerns regarding college and university endowment practices. At a roundtable discussion, entitled Maximizing the Use of Endowment Funds and Making Higher Education More Affordable, witnesses spoke before the Senate Finance Committee in three panels regarding:

- Understanding College Costs examined the causes and implications of rising college costs and tuition;

- What is an Endowment? examined the legal, fiduciary, and accounting definitions of an endowment for purposes of determining a mandatory payout; and

- Are Mandatory Payouts Beneficial? examined the private foundation mandatory payout, its history and effectiveness, and the impact of such a requirement on college and university endowments.

This roundtable was not a surprise following Senators Grassley and Baucus' previous survey of 136 colleges and universities regarding their endowment spending and Senator Grassley's endorsement of a 5% minimum payout requirement for large college and university endowments, similar to the private foundation minimum distribution requirement. The IRS is also very interested in college and university endowments, as evidenced by their College and University Compliance Questionnaire.

*PwC observation: With the focus on the current economic crisis, it is difficult to predict with certainty the level of emphasis that Congress will place on issues affecting the tax–exempt community. Nevertheless, Congress, particularly the Senate Finance Committee, remains actively interested in hospitals and universities. Their emphasis on oversight and reform should serve as a reminder for organizations to remain alert to future oversight and the potential for legislative changes.*

Cellular Telephones and Other Listed Property: The proliferation of employer-provided cell phones and other mobile communication devices (e.g., Blackberrys) has become problematic because these devices are considered "listed property." For this category of property, the Internal Revenue Code and Treasury Regulations require employers and employees to follow burdensome documentation rules which require detailed information regarding each call. Failure to follow these rules can result in the employee being required to report cell phone reimbursements as taxable income. The IRS has included this issue as part of employment tax audits and, consequently, organizations are actively reviewing their current policies. There is particular concern as the rules are applied to officers and other disqualified individuals because of the risk of intermediate sanctions.

Cell phones and other mobile communication devices, however, may be removed from the definition of listed property with legislation introduced in both the Senate and House. Both Senate Finance Committee Chairman Baucus and Ranking Member Grassley have expressed their support of the cell phone legislation. Additionally, the most recent report issued by the IRS Advisory Committee on Tax Exempt and Government Entities recognized the significant administrative burden associated with cell phones. They suggested that while waiting for Congressional action to exclude cell phones from listed property, the IRS should issue interpretive guidance to the Internal Revenue Code. Such guidance would permit employers to perform a statistically valid sampling, as set out by the IRS, over a specified period of time that would be sufficient to the IRS upon examination. If the legislation does get passed, an employee will no longer be required to provide detailed documentation of cell phone calls to claim a business expense.

*PwC observation: While Congress may enact legislation to exclude cell phones and other mobile communication devices from the listed property designation, the designation still applies until, and if, the legislation is enacted. Tax exempt organizations should consider the impact of these rules on their accountable plan policies and the potential exposure to intermediate sanctions. Even if legislation is passed, organizations will still need policies and procedures in place for reimbursement of cell phones for business use.*

### IRS issues fiscal year 2009 work plans

Last November, the Internal Revenue Service released its fiscal year (FY) 2009 Exempt Organization (EO) Work Plan for the coming year. In addition to the annual Work Plan, EO concurrently issued its first Annual Report, with the goal of providing readers a "fuller picture of how EO conducts its operations." The Annual Report provides statistical information on the EO division itself and their work. The statistics include a chart showing that EO has almost doubled its enforcement contacts between FY 2004 and FY 2008 by instituting compliance checks.

The FY 2009 Work Plan, which may be found in their entirety at http://www.irs.gov/pub/irs-tege/finalannualrptworkplan11_25_08.pdf, focuses on two areas—education/communication and compliance initiatives.

Education and Communication: The IRS has promised to work with members of the tax-exempt organization sector to prepare them for filing the 2008 redesigned Form 990. They will do this by providing web-based training and speakers at various conferences. Later, as organizations submit Forms 990 to the IRS, the IRS plans to evaluate what is being reported and whether the Form is serving its intended purpose to increase transparency and promote accountability and compliance.

Compliance Initiatives: The IRS plans to commence several compliance initiatives in FY 09, two of which are focused on governance and charitable spending. Through its governance initiative, which goes hand-in hand with the redesigned Form 990 focus on governance, EO will develop a checklist for its examining agents to determine whether an organization's governance practices impacted the tax compliance issues identified during the examination. This is consistent with the IRS's belief that well-governed organizations are more likely to be compliant organizations. EO will also commence an internal training program regarding nonprofit governance. Last, EO will begin to identify Form 990 governance questions that could be used in potential compliance initiatives, including those involving executive compensation and transactions with interested persons.

A second initiative, called the Charitable Spending Initiative, will be a long-range study for EO to gather information about "sources and uses of funds in the charitable sector and their impact on the accomplishment of charitable purposes." EO will look at a variety of revenue sources and types of expenditures. They will commence with organizations with "unusual" fundraising levels and organizations that report low levels of program service expenses and also report unrelated trade or business activity.

In addition to the FY 2009 EO Implementing Guidelines, the Tax Exempt Bonds (TEB) division of the IRS publishes its own Work Plan. The Work Plan can be found at www.irs.gov/pub/irs-tege/fy_2009_workplan.pdf For FY 2009, TEB has highlighted Sec. 501(c)(3) and hospital/healthcare bonds as having a high risk for potential noncompliance.

Summary of emerging accounting, tax and regulatory issues in 2009
PricewaterhouseCoopers

Sec. 501(c)(3) bonds were categorized as high risk because of the low level of Voluntary Closing Agreement Program requests relating to post-issuance compliance and also because of information gathered through the IRS's Tax-Exempt Bond Compliance Questionnaire from the Fall of 2008. Hospital/healthcare bonds were categorized as high risk because of the increased tendency for hospitals to merge with other hospital systems or privatize. As a result of the high risk categorization, TEB has allocated additional resources for examinations of bonds held by both Sec. 501(c)(3) organizations and hospitals/healthcare organizations.

*PwC observation: The EO Implementing Guidelines provide an important roadmap to the IRS's planned activities that will impact tax-exempt organizations. For this reason and also because of other related IRS initiatives, it is important for tax-exempt organizations to be familiar with the Implementing Guidelines.*

## Items of continuing interest

### Applicability of FIN 48 to tax-exempt organizations

The FASB issued FIN 48 in an effort to clarify the accounting for uncertainty in income taxes recognized in an organization's financial statements pursuant to FASB Statement No. 109, *Accounting for Income Taxes.* As a result of FIN 48, tax-exempt organizations' financial statements will reflect anticipated tax liabilities related to uncertain tax positions that exceed a materiality threshold. Tax positions include determining whether income is unrelated; whether to file Form 990–T; allocating expenses between related and unrelated activities; and classifying an organization, transaction or other position in a tax return as tax-exempt. FIN 48 only applies to income taxes—federal, state, local and foreign—and therefore other taxes, such as sales and employment taxes, do not need to be considered for purposes of this analysis. Tax-exempt organizations that have outstanding tax-exempt bonds are required to comply with FIN 48 for fiscal years beginning after December 15, 2006. For those tax-exempt organizations that do not have outstanding tax-exempt bonds, compliance is required for years beginning after December 15, 2008.

FIN 48 prescribes a two–step process—recognition and measurement—for evaluating uncertain positions taken, or expected to be taken, that impact current or deferred income or liabilities. These steps are required not only for the current fiscal year, but also for all previous years for which the statute of limitations remains open.

The first step—recognition—is fulfilled by taking an inventory of all tax positions and determining whether it is more likely than not that each position would be sustained upon examination. "More–likely–than–not" is defined as a position having a more than 50% likelihood of success upon audit. If a position cannot meet the more–likely–than–not threshold, a liability may need to be recognized for financial statement purposes.

If a position does not have a more–likely–than–not chance of being sustained upon examination, the second step—measurement—is completed by determining the amount of liability to be recognized in the organization's financial statements.

As a result of this two–step process, there may be: 1) an increased liability for income taxes (including interest and penalties) payable or a reduction in an income tax refund receivable, and/or 2) a reduction in a deferred tax asset or an increase in a deferred tax liability reported on an organization's financial statements. Recognition and measurement of uncertain tax positions should be reassessed each tax year, and conclusions are subject to change based on changing facts and circumstances.

*PwC observation: The requirements of FIN 48, in conjunction with the IRS's current focus on unrelated business income, make it particularly important for tax-exempt organizations to analyze their sources of revenue and determine which sources may result in treatment as unrelated business income. As a preliminary step, organizations should inventory all revenue sources and document the positions they are taking for income tax reporting purposes, including revenue recognition criteria, expense allocation methodology, and allocation and apportionment of state and local taxes. However, FIN 48 clearly requires additional documentation processes and procedures.*

*It is also important to note that, while an organization's financial statements are not required to be attached to Form 990, the redesigned Form 990 will require disclosure of an organization's FIN 48 footnote from its financial statements. Consequently, the IRS and state taxing authorities, among others, will be able to access information regarding an organization's uncertain tax positions if a FIN 48 disclosure has been made in its financial statements.*

## E-Postcard filing requirement for small tax-exempt organizations

Small tax-exempt organizations, whose gross receipts are normally $25,000 or less, are required to electronically file Form 990-N, *Electronic Notice (e-Postcard) for Tax-Exempt Organizations Not Required to File Form 990 or 990-EZ*, on an annual basis. Questions on the Form 990-N are basic, including the name, address and EIN of the organization. Exceptions to this requirement include private foundations that are required to file Form 990-PF, organizations that are included in a group return, and Section 509(a)(3) supporting organizations that are required to file Form 990 or Form 990-EZ.

Organizations that do not file Form 990-N, Form 990 or Form 990-EZ for three consecutive years but were required to do so will lose their tax-exempt status unless they participate in the IRS' voluntary compliance program, which will be implemented in FY 2009 according to the EO Work Plan. The e-Postcard filings are maintained by the Urban Institute in partnership with the IRS and can be found at http://epostcard.form990.org/.

*PwC observation: The Form 990-N filing requirement was created as part of the movement to improve transparency within the non-profit sector. The Form 990-N filing requirement will not directly impact larger tax-exempt organizations. However, they should be aware of the requirement if they have small affiliated organizations that wish to retain their tax-exempt status.*

## Medical residents and exemption from federal insurance contribution act

The debate continues whether medical residents' services fall within the statutory exemption from Federal Insurance Contribution Act (FICA) taxes for "student" employment. The Internal Revenue Code provides that FICA taxes are imposed on wages received by individuals "with respect to employment." "Employment" is defined as any service performed by an employee for the person employing him or her, with enumerated exceptions. The "student FICA exception" provides that services performed by students are exempt from "employment," and thus, not subject to FICA tax, if: (1) the services are "performed in the employ of ... a school, college, or university . . .", and (2) such services are performed by students who are "enrolled and regularly attending classes at such school, college, or university."

Within the past year, two court cases, University of Chicago Hospitals v. US and US v. Mount Sinai, have examined this issue and both ruled in favor of teaching hospitals. However, the courts in each case stated that a case by case analysis is necessary to determine whether medical residents qualify as students and consequently meet the student FICA exception. While another year passes without any final closure on when and how this issue—which has been debated since 1998—will be resolved, the IRS continues to maintain that services performed by medical residents cannot qualify for the student FICA exception.

*PwC observation: As litigation continues on this issue, it is recommended that organizations, including teaching hospitals, continue to file protective refund claims to preserve their refund rights, as well as those of their medical residents. A properly completed and filed protective refund claim specifically recognizes that an issue may not be settled yet, but can preserve an organization's right to file a complete claim at a later date—without that claim being barred because of the expiration of the statute of limitations on the claim.*

Summary of emerging accounting, tax and regulatory issues in 2009
PricewaterhouseCoopers

## Limited partnership investments and state reporting requirements

The economic environment may have slowed overall investment activity, but tax-exempt organizations continue to diversify their endowment holdings through the use of alternative investments, particularly through limited partnership investments. When an organization invests in a partnership, the organization must "look through" the partnership to the underlying activities to determine if those activities would be subject to tax or other reporting requirements had they been engaged in directly by the tax-exempt organization. If the partnership is involved in an activity that would be an unrelated trade or business activity if it were directly carried on by the organization, income from the partnership's activity will be unrelated business income (UBI) to its tax-exempt partners. This "look through" concept applies at both the federal and state level in determining tax liability derived from the generation of UBI.

A partnership's activities may create state nexus, and consequently state tax liability, for its partners. Currently, over 35 states impose a tax on UBI, and several states are aggressively pursuing partners' unpaid tax liabilities. Consequently, an organization should be aware of each state's laws regarding UBI where the organization could have nexus due to their partnership investments. An organization should determine in which states it has tax filing obligations on an annual basis. Not only should tax returns be filed in the states where an organization has a liability, but an organization should also make state estimated tax payments to avoid the imposition of interest and penalties.

*PwC observation: It is important for tax-exempt investors to institute appropriate policies and procedures to assess and manage the federal and state tax obligations that arise from partnership investments. This includes maintaining a master list of all partnership investments to ensure that the organization receives a Schedule K-1 for each investment on an annual basis. As states are facing economic challenges, many are taking a harder look at where they can generate additional revenue, which makes paying close attention to state tax reporting obligations increasingly important.*

## International activities

Increasingly, colleges and universities are engaging in collaborations with institutions in foreign countries. These collaborations may include joint education and/ or sponsored research programs as well as consulting arrangements. Some involve the granting of dual degrees within the foreign jurisdiction. Although colleges and universities may be considered tax–exempt institutions for US income tax purposes, they may be subject to taxes and a variety of reporting requirements in foreign jurisdictions.

Various issues may arise as a result of foreign activities. For example, intellectual property developed out of these collaborations may result in foreign tax implications when the funds are repatriated. If employees work in the foreign jurisdiction for periods ranging from a couple of days to well over a year, they also could be subject to taxation in the foreign jurisdiction. In addition, the hiring of foreign workers in the foreign jurisdiction may have tax reporting and liability consequences. Finally, Schedule F, *Statement of Activities Outside the United States*, of the redesigned Form 990 requires organizations to disclose a variety of information if they are conducting activities outside the United States.

*PwC observation: It is important for institutions to understand the tax and registration requirements related to proposed activities before entering into agreements. Up-front planning is important not only to ensure tax compliance in the foreign jurisdiction and the redesigned Form 990, but also for the institution to properly assess the economic results of the project.*

*To control costs and avoid lengthy negotiations, organizations need to develop policies and procedures for compensating employees on international assignments. Organizations should review their specific activities to determine whether they create nexus and, thus, tax compliance obligations in the foreign jurisdiction and/or disclosure on Schedule F. In addition, tax treaties should be reviewed as they may be applicable. Other tax obligations such as withholding and employment taxes may arise. If there are tax liabilities associated with the foreign program, it may be possible to negotiate for the foreign collaborator to assume responsibility for any tax liability and for the organization to receive its payment net of tax.*

### Internal Revenue Code Section 403(b) plans

An Internal Revenue Code Section 403(b) tax-sheltered annuity (TSA) plan is a retirement plan offered by schools, hospitals, charities and certain other tax-exempt organizations. An individual Sec. 403(b) annuity can be obtained only under an employer's TSA plan. Generally, these annuities are funded by elective deferrals made under salary reduction agreements and non-elective employer contributions.

Effective for 2009, Sec. 403(b) plans are subject to annual 5500 reporting and audit requirements similar to Sec. 401(k) plans. Large plans (100 or more participants) are required to file audited financial statements. Small plans (fewer than 100 participants) are eligible to use the short Form 5500 and waive the audit requirement. ERISA requires comparative statements of net assets, therefore December 31, 2008 balances are subject to audit.

On or before December 31, 2009, the Sec. 403(b) plan sponsor must have adopted a written plan that is intended to satisfy the requirements of Sec. 403(b) (including the financial regulations) effective as of January 1, 2009. Even if it does not formally adopt a written plan until the end of 2009, the sponsor must operate the plan in accordance with a reasonable interpretation of Sec. 403(b), taking into account the financial regulations. Also, before the end of 2009 the sponsor must make its best efforts to retroactively correct any operational failure during the 2009 calendar year to conform to the terms of the written plan, consistent with the general correction principles set forth in the Employee Plans Compliance Resolution System (EPCRS).

*PwC observation: Because Sec. 403(b) plans are often large and have had many years of operations, initial audits may be challenging. They will need to address the accumulation of the opening participant balances, accuracy of participant transfers between/ among Sec. 403(b) and other qualified plans at a single employer, the completeness of participants (both active and deferred vested), among other considerations. Therefore, it is important that organizations with Sec. 403(b) plans commence focusing on the new requirements as soon as possible.*

# APPENDIX D

Contributors to this year's *Summary of emerging accounting, tax and regulatory issues* include:

John Mattie
Partner
john.a.mattie@us.pwc.com
Telephone (646) 471 4253

Bob Valletta
Partner
robert.m.valletta@us.pwc.com
Telephone (617) 530 4053

Gwen Spencer
Partner
gwen.spencer@us.pwc.com
Telephone (617) 530 4120

Ralph DeAcetis,
Managing Director
ralph.deacetis@us.pwc.com
Telephone (617) 530 4320

Kaye Ferriter
Managing Director
kaye.b.ferriter@us.pwc.com
Telephone (617) 530 4063

Martha Garner
Managing Director
martha.garner@us.pwc.com
Telephone (973) 236 7294

Tom Gaudrault,
Managing Director
thomas.k.gaudrault@us.pwc.com
Telephone (617) 530 4757

Brian Huggins
Senior Manager
brian.j.huggins@us.pwc.com
Telephone (973) 236 5612

Steve Luber
Senior Manager
steven.j.luber@us.pwc.com
Telephone (973) 236 4957

Dave Merriam
Senior Manager
david.r.merriam@us.pwc.com
Telephone (213) 217 3205

Jocelyn Bishop
Manager
jocelyn.bishop@us.pwc.com
Telephone (617) 530 4946

Erin Couture
Manager
erin.couture@us.pwc.com
Telephone (617) 530 4096

Jeff Thomas
Manager
jeffrey.l.thomas@us.pwc.com
Telephone (973) 236 5044

# APPENDIX D

Thought leadership publications referenced in this year's *Summary of emerging accounting, tax and regulatory issues:*

## Impact of FAS 157 on contribution accounting

The application of FAS 157, *Fair Value Measurements*, to contribution accounting poses unique complexities and has raised debate in the marketplace, Additionally, the considerations for electing the fair value option under FAS 159, *Fair Value Option for Financial Assets and Financial Liabilities*, vary by client and at times may not be clear. We offer these guides to help assist you in your adoption of these new fair value standards.

## Fair value options considerations

The application of FAS 157, *Fair Value Measurements*, to contribution accounting poses unique complexities and has raised debate in the marketplace, Additionally, the considerations for electing the fair value option under FAS 159, *Fair Value Option for Financial Assets and Financial Liabilities*, vary by client and at times may not be clear. We offer these guides to help assist you in your adoption of these new fair value standards.

## Guide to Fair Value Measurements – 2007

This PwC Guide discusses key concepts and requirements of FAS 157 and FAS 159 and outlines their impact on significant accounting areas such as investments, impairments, and business combinations. The Guide, which also addresses certain industry-specific issues, is intended to: clarify a complex area of accounting by bringing together in one publication the relevant PwC guidance on fair value measurements; provide an overall framework for the application of fair value measurements; address key questions and answers; and highlight our perspectives, which are based on our analysis of the guidance and our experience with applying it.

■ 233 ■

www.pwc.com/healthcare

The information contained in this document is for general guidance on matters of interest only. The application and impact of laws can vary widely based on the specific facts involved. Given the changing nature of laws, rules and regulations, there may be omissions or inaccuracies in information contained in this document. This document is provided with the understanding that PricewaterhouseCoopers is not herein engaged in rendering legal, accounting, tax, or other professional advice and services. It should not be used as a substitute for consultation with professional accounting, tax, legal or other competent advisers who have been provided with all pertinent facts relevant to your particular situation. Before making any decision or taking any action, you should consult a competent professional adviser.

© 2009 PricewaterhouseCoopers LLP. All rights reserved. "PricewaterhouseCoopers" refers to PricewaterhouseCoopers LLP (a Delaware limited liability partnership) or, as the context requires, the PricewaterhouseCoopers global network or other member firms of the network, each of which is a separate and independent legal entity. 'connectedthinking is trademark of PricewaterhouseCoopers LLP (US). PH-09-0330 CV JP

# *APPENDIX E

# Perspectives in Higher Education

2009

*PRICEWATERHOUSE(COOPERS*

# Introduction

In response to a convergence of many fiscal, operational, and regulatory challenges in the past year, educational institutions are being asked to do more with less, while meeting the increasingly high expectations of all stakeholders. These challenges have necessitated focused and rigorous fiscal management, monitoring of endowment spending policies, and more critical reviews of both short and longer term financing options, among other responses. Simultaneously, expectations are rising for institutions to make investments in areas such as student aid and service delivery, information systems and security, and compliance. The nature of these issues, individually and in the aggregate, requires a proactive approach to planning in order to maintain a competitive advantage in an ever-growing global education market. This briefing, the product of PricewaterhouseCoopers' Assurance, Tax and Advisory staff specializing in higher education, was created to share our insights on several of the key issues facing large research and educational institutions and the challenges of responding to them, both now and in the foreseeable future.

As a leading auditor and advisor to the higher education and not-for-profit industry, PricewaterhouseCoopers has had the opportunity to work with many of the nation's premier institutions in addressing the most pressing challenges educational institutions face today. While each client we serve is faced with its own, unique set of issues, all educational institutions are currently contending with a number of shared challenges.

A number of the more prominent issues in the higher education sector today, along with our perspective on each of these issues, have been highlighted in this briefing. Our conclusions are based on our firm's experience in working with universities and colleges nationwide to provide a range of audit, tax and advisory services. Our position as a market leader in providing these services to the higher education sector gives us a view into industry issues, and we capitalize on this insight to the benefit of our clients. With industry professionals in accounting and auditing, regulatory compliance, risk management, exempt tax services and advisory services, we are able to deliver to our clients a clear understanding of critical issues and guidance from experienced teams in the field.

This briefing is not meant to be comprehensive in nature. Drawing upon our understanding of the diverse nature of higher education institutions that have complex educational, research, and clinical activities, we offer this summary as a broad platform for discussing these topical issues in a proactive and collaborative manner.

We hope you find this briefing useful. Please do not hesitate to contact Tom Gaudrault at (617) 530-4757 or me at (646) 471-4253 with any questions or comments.

John Mattie
National Higher Education and Not-for-Profit Practice Leader

# Oversight of Financial Strategies

►Background

The economic events of the past year have placed a strain on the financial resources of many colleges and universities. As a result of budgetary shortfalls and liquidity concerns, institutional priorities and strategic plans are being revised on a frequent basis. Important financial decisions should be based on real-time management information and reliable financial reporting that is provided to key decision makers, including senior management and the Board of Trustees. This reporting includes not only current and forecasted balance sheet and operating statement detail, but also cash flow analysis and budget scenarios based on market projections.

In addition to more frequent internal reporting, a sharper focus is being placed on how internal financial management reports used to manage an institution, align with external financial reports given to lenders, rating agencies, federal funding providers, and others. This alignment between internal and external reporting has resulted in institutions taking a fresh look at the integrated management reporting packages utilized to manage financial strategies, and adapting appropriately to effectively meet the needs of all users.

►Impact on Educational Institutions

Readily available financial information is being requested by many constituents. This is requiring senior management, including the President, Chief Investment Officer, Chief Business Officer, Development Officers, and other members of senior management to work more closely together than ever before in developing, managing, and monitoring financial strategies. In turn, Trustees are more engaged in the development of financial plans and strategies, as well as overall monitoring of the budget process, and actual financial results.

In response to this heightened scrutiny on financial reports, institutions are determining the most effective way to present information to multiple users to assist in managing and monitoring institutional strategies. Crafting of financial dashboards — which include metrics, key ratios and comparable data — is evolving to fulfill the needs of internal and external parties.

Effective multi-year budgeting is receiving a greater level of attention, and the focus is shifting away from solely evaluating the operating budget to a process that includes all financial resources and expenses including restricted funds, capital outlays and investments. In regards to restricted funds, these are being more closely analyzed to determine which can be utilized to assist with subsidizing the operating budget. In line with this focus on overall budgeting, Trustees and external parties are requesting greater transparency surrounding all institutional cash inflows and outflows.

Cash flow forecasting and balance sheet projections are deemed more critical than ever as key components of a financial reporting package. Communication between multiple departments within an institution, including Investment, Business and Development Officers, is imperative to determine appropriate cash flow projections associated with such items as investment capital calls and lock-up periods, anticipated annual gift funds, construction financing, research funding, medical service billings, and other sources and uses of cash.

The frequency of financial reporting has led more institutions to prepare quarterly financial statements on a basis consistent with year-end reporting, or a modified version of generally accepted accounting principles (GAAP). A formal reconciliation aligning internal management reports with external GAAP financial statements is evolving as a best practice. Quarterly reporting and reconciliation are often presented to the Finance and/or Audit Committee of the Board of Trustees at interim periods during the year.

►PwC Perspective

Creating a culture of accountability whereby institutional objectives are communicated frequently, and all parties are involved in monitoring the objectives requires timely budgeting and financial reporting of results. Involvement of key members of senior management and Trustees with respect to information flow, monitoring of financial plans, and actual results is imperative given the challenges in the uncertain economic climate. Developing financial plans based on the concept of "all resources and expense reporting", rather than focusing strictly on the operating budget allows for broader knowledge of the overall operations of the institution. Creating timely and appropriate cash flow analysis, operating statements, balance sheets and financial dashboards will lead to better information sharing and create data that will allow for timely monitoring of the financial situation of an institution.

To enhance discipline and control around financial accountability, consideration should be given to preparing interim GAAP financial statements on a periodic basis during the year and establishing tools to align internal management reporting to external financial statements. Along with this, sensitivity analyses and contingency plans should be developed and shared with the Board of Trustees on a periodic basis.

# Endowment Payout Considerations

▶Background

Educational institutions design and utilize spending policies for their endowment funds to provide for current spending, while preserving an endowment's corpus and supporting spending in perpetuity. Consistent with institutional policies to periodically review asset allocation, it is also important to review spending policies. The two policies are interdependent, and a balanced interaction between the two is critical to the long-term success of any endowment.

One of the primary objectives that governs the management of most endowments is the pursuit of real (inflation adjusted) purchasing power of the corpus over time. If this objective is met, it should enable an educational institution to achieve a relatively constant level of real spending.

Over the past two decades, many educational institutions have been under significant pressure to grow spending by more than the increase in the underlying rate of inflation. This pressure to grow spending is even greater during weak periods in the economy when other sources of funding such as gifts and grants decline. These periods tend to coincide with weak periods in the financial markets, which places endowments, especially those with an equity oriented investment strategy, under additional stress at the exact time they are the least equipped to handle it.

Most educational institutions utilize a market value based spending policy. This policy typically does not generate stable and predictable spending levels. During years of growth, a market value based spending policy will produce more total dollars for the institution, but during years of losses, spending can quickly retract. This can make the annual budgeting process for the endowment difficult. Institutions whose spending policies rely solely on the beginning market value each year can subject themselves to more volatile spending levels from year to year. A partial solution to the problem has been to adopt a moving average market value which reduces spending volatility, but does place additional pressure on the corpus during declining markets.

Some institutions are adopting spending policies that are tied to annual inflation rather than market returns, or a combination that considers an inflation adjusted amount of a percentage of the previous year's spending and market returns. These methods allow spending to grow in relationship to a consumer price index and results in less spending over the long term than by using a percentage of the asset value, as inflation is expected to grow at lower rates than long-term market returns.

▶ Impact on Educational Institutions

Current market conditions are having a significant impact on institutions' endowment payout rates. On average, spending rates at educational institutions are between 4% and 6% of the endowment's value each year. Many institutions are revisiting their endowment spending rate and determining whether changes need to be made.

Educational institutions are experiencing several conflicting considerations when establishing or changing their endowment payout rates. Institutions that heavily rely on endowment spending for their operating budget are experiencing significant deficits in the current economic environment. These institutions are in the process of determining how to reduce the deficit through such means as identifying other potential revenue sources, decreasing operating expenses, increasing the endowment payout rate, or borrowing to finance annual operating needs. Boards are focusing on maintaining long-term purchasing power during a time of significant investment declines and "underwater endowments" (i.e., when the fair market value of an endowment fund has fallen below the original corpus of the gift). Adding to the focus on endowment spending, the Senate Finance Committee, through letters initiated in January 2008, expressed concern surrounding the exponential cost increases of higher education during a period of significant growth of college endowment assets. There are many critics that believe colleges and universities should be required to have a legally mandated payout rate of at least 5% of the endowment's market value, which correlates to the amount private foundations currently pay annually. This attention and focus was before the market declines over the past year but still remains an unresolved Senate Finance Committee agenda item. Finally, some states have recently enacted the Uniform Prudent Management of Institutional Funds Act (UPMIFA). Some states' enacted version of UPMIFA includes a presumption of imprudence as to spending rates in excess of 7% per annum.

### ▶ PwC Perspective

The significant investment returns during 1988 to 2007 have resulted in higher "true dollar" levels of spending and larger operating budgets. Many institutions are making tough decisions in order to effectively manage their operating budgets. Communication between senior administration and the Board is imperative. To respond to this, a prudent and standard best practice is establishing a Board Committee made up of members of the Budget, Finance, and Investment Committee(s) to prioritize and examine how annual expenditures and strategic initiatives will be funded in the short and long term, and what role endowment payout rates play over those short and longer term periods.

This is an opportune time for institutions to revisit the method and process of its spending rate policy and calculation. Educational institutions may want to consider alternative calculation methods for spending. Management should "stress test" these varying methods to determine the financial impact to the institution under various budget scenarios over a shorter and longer timeframe as part of their financial planning.

All institutions have been impacted by the economic downturn and declines in their investment portfolios. The goal of all educational institutions is to continue their central operating mission and to avoid budget deficits. This is not a new issue. There is no magic formula on how to handle the endowment payout rate. What is clear however is the role of endowment spending in supporting both recurring operations and strategic initiatives, both in the short and long term, needs to be assessed as an institution develops its financial plans in response to the economic events over the past year. How an institution determines its endowment payout formula in support of such plans requires careful consideration as an institution balances short term needs with longer term responsibilities.

# Liquidity and Financing Considerations

## ▶ Background

The economic challenges over the past year have affected colleges and universities as much as any other institutional investor, and possibly more given the reliance on investments to fund operations and student borrowings to finance tuition. Major ratings agencies have projected sharp deterioration in the financial outlook for private colleges in the next two fiscal years.[i] Rating agencies have always emphasized strong liquidity as a measure of high institutional performance and the ability to repay debt obligations, but liquidity has become perhaps the most significant factor in determining and maintaining ratings.

The concerns of rating agencies in assessing higher educational institutions relate strongly to liquidity and sustainability of operations, including:

- Less flexibility on the pricing of tuition and possible tuition declines, placing greater stress on funding of operations through investments;

- Declines in enrollment and a shift to lower-cost institutions due to financial concerns of students and their families;

- Delays in capital investment and increases in deferred maintenance;

- Increases in the proportion of debt relative to financial position;

- Decreases in philanthropy; and

- Reductions in state appropriations.

## ▶ Impact on Educational Institutions

A convergence of factors related to the global economic challenges over the past year directly affected the ability of higher education institutions to access the capital markets and maintain operating liquidity. Additionally, investment earnings have deteriorated precipitously, since average aggregate gains of 17% in fiscal year 2007.[ii] Some attribute the volatility of the earnings to a general move in the industry toward more aggressive investment in illiquid assets, such as

hedge funds, private equity and property. The historic returns on this strategy outperformed even the top percentile of corporate pension funds; however, certain risks associated with this investment model left institutions vulnerable when the downturn hit, particularly with respect to liquidity.[iii] Certain institutions failed to arrange credit lines to manage cash needs, and some endowments were simply too small to handle the diversification required for the successful implementation of the investment strategy. The loss of endowment value directly affected the ability of higher education institutions to maintain their existing ratings and access the capital markets.

The economy has also taken a toll on students, their families, alumni and other donors, resulting in decreased philanthropy and stress on tuition revenues. Fiscal year 2008 saw a decline of 2% in total charitable giving within the U.S., but gifts to educational institutions were down nearly 9%, adjusted for inflation.[iv] Additionally, industry sources suggest there will continue to be a migration of students to lower-cost alternatives, causing implications for enrollment and sustainability for many higher-cost institutions.

Public educational institutions and institutions with academic medical centers had their own unique financial challenges. As of April 2009, at least 36 states had cut or announced proposals to reduce higher education spending because of their own looming deficits.[v] The trend may cause increasing operational concerns for state-sponsored institutions. However, their access to capital may be less affected because rating agencies view state-sponsored institutions as more insulated from economic downturns because they are less dependent on endowments and are accustomed to weathering budget constraints

Academic medical centers have specific challenges as well. In many cases, the clinical operations have provided cash to support the academic and research missions. Currently, the financial condition of many healthcare providers nationwide has deteriorated, and the healthcare debate currently taking place in Congress leaves great uncertainty about the future impact of hospital funding. In the best of times, academic medical centers have been able to exploit their higher education endowments, combined with the cash and margins of healthcare providers, to obtain solid ratings and access to capital. In the current environment, academic medical centers are likely to feel capital constraints from both directions.

Across the U.S., educational institutions are more actively managing their investment strategies, particularly regarding alternative investments and more illiquid investments, as well as their impact on liquidity. There is also a greater focus on globalization within the investment strategy by increasing investments in foreign markets to absorb the declines in the U.S. economy. Institutions are employing a global perspective when making investment decisions and are becoming more flexible in order to react to market conditions as they occur.

▶ PwC Perspective

Financial strength of educational institutions is defined primarily by the balance sheet and liquidity, both of which will continue to face significant challenges as the economy begins its slow recovery. Rating agencies have spelled out the factors that are most likely to lead to downgrades. Broad factors related to financial stability and liquidity include those already discussed. Additional concerns relate to:

- Transparency and timeliness of financial reporting and disclosure;

- Active involvement of governance and oversight; and

- Effectiveness and timeliness of adminstration's response to and understanding of financial and operational issues.[vi]

A deepening divergence between financial stability and capital access for the "haves" and the "have nots" appears to be emerging. According to the Education Department's fiscal year 2008 test of financial strength, more than 100 institutions failed based on the composite score of debt load, expenses relative to income and overall resources.[vii] Based on early fiscal year 2009 trends, that number is likely to worsen. More colleges and universities will be faced with the need for a line of credit to support the aid they award, at a time when they are least likely to be able to access liquidity facilities at reasonable rates. In recent years, troubled institutions have

closed or merged with larger entities. The number of troubled institutions is likely to increase, which may lead the industry to see more merger and acquisition activity.

Despite the economic turbulence of 2009, higher education institutions are beginning to access the capital markets again. Several well-publicized issuances in late fiscal year 2009 contained not only funding for capital projects, but also portions for working capital and operations. While the re-entry to the capital markets is encouraging, it appears to be limited to the financially strong, and at higher interest rates than historical rates.

Administration and Trustees can implement a number of practical actions, not only to demonstrate their strengths to the capital markets but also to bolster their long-term sustainability:

- Institutions should focus on strong management of liquidity and investments, with an emphasis on understanding the risks associated with various models and planning for the downturns.

- Institutions must not only focus on short term issues, but also long term strategy. A clearly articulated strategy supported by a flexible business plan, with contingencies and exit strategies, can help guide operational and capital planning. Moreover, the business plan will provide the basis for active and timely monitoring of operational and financial results. The ability to monitor results, disclose concerns, and respond quickly to challenges will be viewed favorably by rating agencies and credit markets, even if the financial position is not as robust as it has been historically.

- Given the deepening division between the "haves" and the "have nots," the financial fallout of the economic events over the past year may generate more opportunity for business expansion through acquisition. Higher education strategies should consider topics such as acquisition as a means to broaden the academic mission, whether through affiliations or through mergers.

- In terms of accessing the capital markets, the right story can be as compelling as the right numbers. Institutions that can articulate their strategic vision, their connection to planned capital investment, and their demonstrated ability to respond to fiscal pressures will be able to access capital at the more favorable rates.

- Finally, the use of capital should be appropriate to the source. This means that colleges and universities will have to demonstrate not only to the capital markets, but also to themselves, that the uses to which they put capital dollars bolster long-term sustainability and support strategy.

---

[i] Source: Moody's Fiscal Year 2008 Private College and University Medians: Early Signs of Sector Weakening in 2008; Sharp Deterioration Expected in 2009 Data, Moody's Investor Services, June 2009.

[ii] Source: Educational Endowments' Investment Returns Were -24.1% in the Last Six Months of 2008, www.commonfund.org.

[iii] Source: Ivory-Towering Infernos: America's Universities Have Seen Billions of Dollars Go Up in Smoke, www.economist.com, December 11, 2008.

[iv] Source: U.S. Charitable Giving Estimated to Be $307.65 Billion in 2008, Giving USA, a publication of Giving USA Foundation, researched and written by the Center on Philanthropy at Indiana University, June 10, 2009.

[v] Source: How Are State Budget Cuts Affecting Spending for Higher Education?, www.universityparent.com, April 6, 2009.

[vi] Source: Moody's Outlines Factors That Could Lead to Credit-Rating Downgrades, Moody's Investor Services, May 1, 2009.

[vii] Source: More Than 100 Colleges Fail Education Department's Test of Financial Strength, The Chronicle of Higher Education, June 12, 2009.

# Revenue Enhancement and Expense Reduction Initiatives

## ► Background

Although the demand for higher education has increased significantly over the past two decades, institutions are faced with a number of financial challenges. Among these challenges are increasing operating costs, growing expectations from students for additional services, legislative pressures for public institutions and the fluctuations of public resources to support student and research activities. Additionally, with high unemployment and financial uncertainty, more and more families are seeking less costly alternatives for higher education, including public and community colleges. These and other factors are requiring institutions to look at more cost efficient ways of delivering service, and seek alternative revenue-generating opportunities.

## ► Impact on Educational Institutions

The most recent Moody's analysis of the industry says that "higher-education institutions are facing a range of challenges in the next year and a half." These challenges will impact the operations of private and public institutions and include:

- Declining value of endowments – According to NACUBO's 2008 endowment survey results, higher education endowments experienced an average rate of return of -3.0% for fiscal year ending June 30, 2008. Since then, endowments have been down by as much as 35%.[i]

- Availability of federal and state funding – state appropriations, for public institutions, increased by approximately 7.5% from fiscal year 2007 to fiscal year 2008. However, based on preliminary data, state funding grew by only 1% nationally for fiscal year 2009.[ii] The current administration's American Recovery and Reinvestment Act will increase federal research funding over the next two years. However, record federal spending to stimulate the economy will increase the federal budget deficit, which will impact the availability of federal funds for research over the long term.

Senior management and their Boards are developing focused financial plans that consider the budgetary and operating implications of the above

factors. These plans contemplate the implementation of certain short and longer term tactical strategies to reduce cost, improve efficiency of operations, and explore alternative revenue sources.

## ► PwC Perspective

Institutions should develop a two-pronged approach focused on cost reduction and revenue enhancements. This approach should identify measurable actions in the short term and plans to sustain such actions. Sensitivity analyses and plans should also be developed to identify other courses of action, should cost reduction and revenue enhancements not be achieved.

Specific cost reduction and revenue enhancement actions have included, and will continue to include, the following:

**Cost reduction** - Sustainable cost reduction is a systematic approach to eliminating cost through the use of strategically tailored industry leading practices surrounding people and organization, effective use of technology, and efficient and effective processes geared towards specific actions and results. A focus on processes requires a cultural change that is only achieved through leadership, communications, clear accountabilities, and execution and performance measurement.

The cost reduction tactics that institutions will continue to pursue have reached into all areas of operations, including human resources, academics, financial operations, facilities and others.

Within human resources, certain colleges and universities have acted by eliminating raises for tenured faculty and staff whose salaries exceed certain dollar thresholds and have provided modest salary increases for untenured faculty and lower-paid staff. Other institutions have held flat salaries for faculty and exempt staff for the next academic year and have initiated voluntary early retirement programs for others. Some institutions have created leadership committees to review and approve new searches for term, temporary or regular staff members, as well as for any necessary utilization of consultants, temporary employees, and independent contractors proposed in lieu of staff hiring.

In the academic program area, institutions have discontinued unnecessary or outdated programs while others have attempted to predict program demand based on historical trends and demographic data. Other institutions have implemented earlier payment deadlines to help forecast demand and provide a better picture of the classes that are filling up and which ones may be at risk of not attracting a sufficient number of students to enroll.

Many institutions have revisited their capital projects and considered delaying physical expansions and scaling back on others. Other institutions are redirecting capital dollars to reduce operating costs.

Along the supply chain, institutions are consolidating and streamlining purchases and are re-evaluating contracts with vendors and updating preferred vendor lists. Certain institutions have implemented purchasing cards to help staff obtain purchases faster and reducing the number of checks produced.

Institutions are also implementing energy management improvement programs, such as closing certain administrative buildings during breaks to capture energy savings. Other institutions are reconfiguring standard desktop computers to decrease the purchase price and to utilize a new energy-efficient power supply that will reduce desktop energy consumption.

**Revenue Enhancement** - This is usually a longer-term approach that can aid in averting or reducing the severity of a fiscally challenging situation. Organizations across all industries are taking efforts to address growth opportunities in a rebounding economy with a focus on increasing cash flow while holding down associated operational and administrative costs, streamlining processes and improving performance across the entire organization.

A number of institutions are focused on enhancing revenue streams by targeting the following: expanding globally, expanding fundraising, and increasing the number of proposals submitted to sponsors to increase research revenues. Others are focusing on collecting revenue due to the institution, while minimizing uncollectible accounts.

These institutions are being more diligent in managing accounts receivable aging.

Many institutions are expanding their programs globally and adding satellite campuses abroad to respond to the increasing global demand for higher education. Globalization brings its own set of operational and financial challenges to the business office. An institution needs to determine how to price tuition (considering U.S. and foreign currency fluctuations); how to comply with a myriad of tax and regulatory requirements in other countries; and what additional people and processes are necessary to support global education delivery structures. Educational institutions need to develop administrative structures and processes to support the expansion, such as a formalized global operations team or dedicated individuals focused on international operations.

Certain institutions are reviewing patent revenue relationships and streamlining their portfolio of rented office and storage space while others are identifying new revenue opportunities and enhancing existing revenue from external groups' fees for spaces and services across campus. Many institutions are evaluating fees and charges within their organizations to identify efficiencies through simplification of existing processes.

Institutions will need to continue to focus on cost reduction and revenue enhancement strategies, including those above, to generate the resources necessary to maintain effective operations and initiate critical strategies. Continued long-term focus will be required to achieve the desired budgetary effects in the current economic situation.

---

[i] Source: National Association of College and University Business Officers publication, 2008 NACUBO-Commonfund Endowment Study Follow-up Survey, http:www.nacubo.org/documents/research/NES2008 Follow-upSurveyReport.pdf

[ii] Source: State Higher Education Executive Officers (SHEEO) publication, State Higher Education Finance Early Release FY2008, dated February 9, 2009.

# Current Regulatory Environment

▶ Background

The current regulatory focus on educational institutions, particularly with respect to compliance, remains intense. The impact of several of the more recent initiatives that commenced last year, including the redesigned 2008 Form 990 and the new Electronic Municipal Market Access system (EMMA), will be felt fully this year. Other areas of attention, such as conflicts of interest and effort reporting, will likely continue at a fast pace as well. Additionally, academic medical centers are faced with the Recovery Audit Contractor (RAC) initiative. This program established by the Centers for Medicare and Medicaid Services is an audit initiative designed to identify and recover overpayments made to providers of healthcare services. According to a recent status report, Medicare has recovered more than $1 billion through the RAC program since 2005.

In light of such regulatory requirements, educational institutions are under on-going pressure to demonstrate their compliance and accountability. The impact of actual or perceived failure of an institution to identify and manage compliance functions could lead to a damaged reputation among various stakeholders and potential administrative and financial sanctions imposed by regulators.

The following is a brief summary of selected regulatory matters where educational institutions are currently focusing resources to ensure compliance and to manage the risks associated with non-compliance.

## The Redesigned 2008 Form 990

Educational institutions will begin filing the redesigned Form 990 for their fiscal 2009 year. Responding to Congressional pressure for non-profit accountability, the IRS redesigned the Form 990 to achieve greater transparency and compliance from reporting organizations. Key focus areas of the redesigned Form 990 include governance and management; compensation; transactions with the reporting organization; relationships among certain individuals; and tax-exempt bonds. While many of the new questions on the Form 990 are not mandated by tax law, they highlight what the IRS and others consider to be best practices for tax-exempt organizations. The IRS has announced that they are revisiting their examination selection criteria based upon responses to the new Form 990.

## Tax-Exempt Bond Compliance

In their work plan for fiscal 2009, the IRS's Tax Exempt Bonds (TEB) division has highlighted Internal Revenue Code Sec. 501(c)(3) bonds as having a high risk for noncompliance. Sec. 501(c)(3) bonds were categorized as high risk based on information gathered through the IRS's 2008 Tax-Exempt Bond Compliance Questionnaire and based on the low level of Voluntary Closing Agreement Program requests relating to post-issuance compliance deficiencies. As a result of the high risk categorization, TEB has allocated additional resources for examinations of bonds held by Sec. 501(c)(3) organizations. Organizations are challenged in these difficult economic times to maintain compliance with bond covenants associated with their external borrowings.

## Electronic Municipal Market Access

The Securities and Exchange Commission has mandated the use of the EMMA system for continuing disclosure filings. Effective July 1, 2009, EMMA has become the sole Nationally Recognized Municipal Securities Information Repository (NRMSIR) for filing municipal bond official statements, annual and quarterly financial information and material event notices, replacing the four existing NRMSIRs. Similar to the SEC's Electronic Data Gathering, Analysis, and Retrieval (EDGAR) system that makes annual, quarterly, and material events information of SEC registrant companies publicly available, EMMA will make municipal disclosure information available to the public via an internet website at no cost.

## Effort Reporting

Time and effort reporting continues to be a challenging area, particularly for organizations that receive funding from the Department of Health and Human Services (HHS) and the National Science Foundation (NSF). In most federal awards, personnel costs, including direct labor charges, fringe benefits, and the related indirect costs, represent the largest charges to the government. Federal agency Offices of Inspector General (OIG) and the Department of Justice are aggressive in bringing charges for non-compliance with labor cost requirements and for overcharging for labor costs on federal awards. The OIG work plans, which set the direction for the OIG's audits, include review of effort reporting, administrative and clerical salary charge-backs, support for cost transfers and graduate student compensation.

### Faculty and Institutional Conflicts of Interest

Institutions have been required under federal regulations to implement research conflict of interest policies and procedures to protect the integrity and objectivity of research efforts. Federal requirements have historically required that institutions identify, manage and disclose conflicts of interest among research faculty to sponsoring agencies. Recently, the management and reporting of conflicts of interest have been called into question. Senator Grassley has contacted several organizations over their conflict of interest policies and has initiated investigations of specific conflict of interest matters involving several scientists and institutions. At issue is the failure by scientists, investigators, and researchers to disclose conflicts accurately and timely, and the inability of institutions to identify and accurately report such conflicts. Senator Grassley additionally has expressed concern that the National Institutes of Health does not receive sufficient information concerning specific conflict of interest matters reported to allow it to adequately make conclusions regarding the severity of reported conflicts and the institutions' resolution of the specific matters.

From these recent actions by Senator Grassley and the disparity of reporting noted in the audit findings, new legislation was proposed by the Senate Appropriations Committee to "step up" oversight of financial conflicts of interest among organizations. The draft legislation would require drug and device makers to disclose payment amounts greater than $500 per year to doctors, scientists and researchers in a National Registry. In the future, it is possible that organizations and sponsoring agencies will be mandated to verify disclosure accuracy through this National Registry. Several states also have enacted or proposed legislation that requires enhanced reporting of compensation from pharmaceutical companies to medical professionals in an effort to promote greater transparency and accountability to the public.

### International Activities

Increasingly, colleges and universities are engaging in collaborations with institutions in foreign countries. These collaborations may include joint education and/or sponsored research programs as well as consulting arrangements. Some involve the granting of dual degrees within the foreign jurisdiction. Although educational institutions may be considered tax-exempt for US income tax purposes, they may be subject to taxes and a variety of other compliance and reporting requirements in foreign jurisdictions.

### Internal Revenue Code Section 403(b) Plans

Effective for 2009, Sec. 403(b) plans are subject to annual Form 5500 reporting and audit requirements similar to Sec. 401(k) plans. On or before December 31, 2009, the Sec. 403(b) plan sponsor must adopt a written plan that is intended to satisfy the requirements of Sec. 403(b) (including the financial regulations) effective as of January 1, 2009. Even if it does not formally adopt a written plan until the end of 2009, the sponsor must operate the plan in accordance with a reasonable interpretation of Sec. 403(b), taking into account the financial regulations. Also, before the end of 2009, the sponsor must make its best efforts to retroactively correct any operational failure during the 2009 calendar year to conform to the terms of the written plan, consistent with the general correction principles set forth in the Employee Plans Compliance Resolution System.

### ▶ Impact on Educational Institutions

Many educational institutions are challenged to respond to increasing regulatory requirements. The items noted above are only a select few of the many rules and regulations with which educational institutions have to comply. Compliance with these requirements for many educational institutions has been an ongoing challenge and has strained internal resources. Colleges and universities are addressing the substantial requirements by determining the need for implementing new policies and procedures and modifying existing financial and information systems to accommodate new data collection. Additional "compliance internal controls" and investment in personnel may be necessary to ensure and maintain ongoing compliance.

Institutions have also been assessing their policies and procedures relating to tracking, reporting and communicating information related to the charitable benefit they provide the community. Disseminating information in an easily understandable format for interested parties (creditors, donors, regulators, etc.), in addition to proactively responding to any inquiries or comments, continues to be important in the current environment.

## ▶ PwC Perspective

The attention being placed on educational institutions and the heightened expectations for improved accountability and compliance are ongoing and not expected to subside in the near future. As a result, educational institutions will need to continue their focus on enhancing internal controls over compliance. In the past, institutions often substantially satisfied regulatory requirements by holding individual schools and departments accountable for compliance, rather than placing responsibility on the institution's central administration. While decentralized accountability for compliance may not be adequate to ensure institutional compliance, centralized compliance is a costly endeavor. Nonetheless, the establishment of an organizational structure that supports and promotes accountability for institutional compliance is becoming a more common and prudent response to the continued regulatory requirements. Any increased effort in this area will likely require an additional investment in compliance resources, which unfortunately coincides with a period of tight budgets and an uncertain economic climate.

In addition to the development of an organizational framework for institutional compliance, educational institutions must continue to develop other proactive responses to the myriad of regulatory initiatives imposed on them in order to keep up with the pressure from regulators. Consideration should be given to the following steps to enhance overall compliance and reduce the financial, operational and reputational risks associated with non-compliance:

- Review current policies and procedures at the "local" school, department, and/or unit level. Consider how the results can be summarized in a manner suitable for reporting compliance results back to central institution management.

- Review Board compliance oversight polices currently in place and strengthen such oversight as needed to ensure that compliance controls are receiving an adequate level of attention.

- Consider educating key stakeholders at the institution on regulatory requirements and compliance initiatives.

- Consider utilizing information technology reporting tools to identify compliance exceptions that can be reported centrally and remediated on a real-time basis.

# Enhanced Transparency and Accountability

## ▶ Background

Transparency has different meanings in different situations—clear, easily analyzed, reliable, timely—but in the world of financial reporting, it means all of these together. In 2005, PricewaterhouseCoopers published a paper, *Enhancing the Transparency of Financial Reporting*, dedicated entirely to addressing the information different users of financial statements of a higher education institution might desire to have included, the reasons they want the information, and ways to satisfy their needs. Since 2005, there has continued to be a significant focus by the Financial Accounting Standards Board (FASB), regulators and other parties to require additional transparency in external financial reporting. Whether it is disclosures regarding fair value measures, pensions, derivative activities, or net asset classifications, all institutions are finding the minimum amount of information required to be disclosed, and the related effort to collect and report that information in their financial statements, continuing to increase. Primary users and other stakeholders, including bond rating agencies, donors, and other users of the financial statements, are asking for more information that provides a deeper understanding of an institution's liquidity, total on- and off-balance sheet financing, and exposure to credit and market risks with respect to the investment portfolio, among many other items.

## ▶ Impact on Educational Institutions

As the availability of credit has become more restricted and investment portfolio values have decreased, many institutions have found their normal sources of liquidity have diminished significantly. Bond rating agencies are assessing institutions in a different light, and are seeking more information to assist them in their rating processes. For instance, Moody's issued two special comment reports in March and April 2009, *Moody's Developing New Liquidity Ratios for U.S. Universities, Hospitals, & Other Not-for-Profits*[i] and *U.S. Colleges and Universities Rating Roadmap: Focus on Special Risks During Recession & Credit Crisis*,[ii] addressing their concern with the current

level of transparency in Institution's financial statements.

The first report focuses on new liquidity ratios Moodys has developed. Given the recent strain on cash, as well as the inability to quickly liquidate long-term investments, Moodys is focusing on institutional liquidity and believes that clearly identifying unrestricted cash and investments, as well as any potential restrictions on the liquidity of investments, are critical components of their evaluation of an institution's financial health. This level of disclosure is currently not included, nor required, in external financial statements. The second report by Moodys reaffirms its measures of financial stability (e.g., selectivity and yield rates, expendable resources to debt, unrestricted cash to puttable debt, and the percentage of variable rate debt (before interest rate swaps) to total indebtedness). Additionally, the report addresses mitigating factors that institutions can employ to respond to their current financial situation, including re-evaluating capital plans and operating budgets, restructuring debt to fixed rate, replacing letters of credit counterparties with more financially sound counterparties, terminating interest rate swaps with collateral posting requirements, liquidating long-term investments to generate liquidity, and revisiting asset allocations.

In addition to rating agencies, donors are also requesting increased transparency surrounding the gifts they make. Specifically, donors are requiring more information be made available about the ultimate use of their donations. In several situations, donors have requested the return of their gift when they believed it was not being used for the purpose intended. To prevent this, institutions are implementing additional procedures to inform donors of the budgeted expenditures to be charged to their gift and actual results. Donors are also expressing concern about how their contributions are being invested, including understanding the spending policies of an institution. Through a recent FASB Staff Position, additional disclosures are now required on endowment fund activities and spending policies.

### ►PwC Perspective

There is no one-size-fits-all answer or approach to what constitutes effective financial transparency, beyond required disclosures, in the external financial statements. Each institution must evaluate the needs of the users of its financial statements, weigh the pros and cons of providing additional information, and make informed decisions on how to enhance its financial statements.

Institutions should consider including additional disclosures in their financial statements regarding liquidity, such as a table with timeframes of how long it would take to liquidate certain investments. Additionally, while many of the financial measures utilized by rating agencies can be calculated from financial statements, institutions should take a fresh look at other information that may be helpful to external users. While it is not realistic to include disclosures in the financial statements that address individual donor gifts and how they are utilized, it may be useful for institutions to provide an understanding of the funds management processes that ensure that the instructions of the donors are being followed.

As financial reporting transparency requirements continue to increase, institutions should critically assess what additional information may be helpful to external users to understand and provide helpful perspective as to its financial health and strategies, both today and in the future.

---

[i] Source: Moody's U.S. Public Finance - Disclosure of Liquidity Information for Universities is Weak. Special Report, March 2009.

[ii] Source: Moody's U.S. Public Finance - U.S. Colleges and Universities Rating Roadmap: Focus on Special Risks During Recession & Credit Crisis. Special Report, April 2009.

# The Impact of the Stimulus Package

▶ Background

In an attempt to invigorate a faltering economy marked by rising job losses, falling GDP and uncertainty in the capital markets, President Obama signed the American Recovery and Reinvestment Act (the "Recovery Act") of 2009 on February 17, 2009. The purpose of the Recovery Act includes preserving and creating jobs to promote economic recovery, providing investments needed to increase economic efficiency, and to assist those most impacted by the recession. The Recovery Act provides $787 billion of funding with a majority going towards existing programs. Three quarters of the package is intended to enter the economy by September 2010. The package intends to make a short and long term impact in investments that create jobs and provide future resources through building infrastructure, promoting science and education, improving health care, and increasing clean energy use.

President Obama was clear that portions of the stimulus package must focus on education. Although House and Senate versions of the bill included different measures of aid for students, infrastructure, scientific research and job training, the final package will generally benefit all institutions of higher education in one form or another. Those institutions focused on research and development should see increased federal awards from a variety of different agencies, while student financial aid recipients will benefit from increased Pell and Work Study funding from the Department of Education.

▶ Impact on Educational Institutions

The Recovery Act has provided many federal granting agencies with additional financial resources that will impact higher education institutions. Amongst these federal agencies are the following:

- The Department of Education will increase the maximum Pell award for eligible students from $4,850 to $5,350 and provide $200 million towards work study programs.

- The National Science Foundation has increased funding by $3.0 billion, including $2.5 billion for research, $400 million for infrastructure and $100 million for education.

- The National Institute of Health has been allotted $10 billion, including $8.5 billion for research and $1.5 billion for university research facilities.

- The Department of Energy has been awarded $2 billion for research.

Additionally, academic medical centers will see the effects of the stimulus package through the federal government's investment of $36 billion in Medicare and Medicaid providers between 2010 and 2017. A key goal of the Recovery Act is to reduce long-term costs by modernizing healthcare through the use of information technology. Of the $36 billion stimulus funding, $33 billion is expected to flow to healthcare providers, with the majority of the funding to those that use government-certified Information Technology systems, including electronic medical record systems.

The Act also created a new form of bonds known as Build America Bonds ("BABs"). These bonds were created in the stimulus legislation to help state and local governments (and related entities) raise money for building projects by making it significantly cheaper for them to issue taxable bonds. The Act created two types of BABs. The first type provides a federal subsidy to investors equal to 35% of the interest payable by the issuer ("Tax Credit BABs"). The second type of BABs provide a direct federal subsidy that will be paid to state and local governments in an amount equal to 35% of the interest ("Direct Payment BABs"). Both types of BABs must be issued before January 1, 2011. Public universities have started to utilize these bonds to fund various construction projects.

The Act holds institutions receiving funding to a high standard of accountability and transparency with respect to the utilization of funds received, including additional federal reporting requirements placed on institutions receiving Recovery Act funding. Institutions must separately track and monitor recovery funds, as such funds cannot be commingled with non-Recovery Act funds. Additionally, the Recovery Act provides additional funding to federal agencies for performance of audits and reviews to assure accountability, consistency, controls, and transparency. These requirements will place a greater burden on institutions in receipt of Recovery Act funds to assess how such funds complement existing research and other institutional strategies, and what level of institutional infrastructure and resources are necessary to manage and monitor expenditures funded through the Recovery Act.

### ▶ PwC Perspective

Institutions will need to be proactively strategic in identifying areas in which additional funding can be utilized and submit proposals to federal agencies to take full advantage of the Recovery Act funds.

As institutions begin to receive additional funding, an evaluation will need to be performed of the current organizational and administrative framework (e.g., people, processes, and information systems) required for effectively monitoring and reporting expenditures made with Recovery Act funds. Institutions should consider:

- Appointing one individual to coordinate and monitor all Recovery Act related activity at the institution. This must include frequent monitoring of the Recovery Act website as the federal compliance rules and guidelines are fluid, and are being developed and published in draft form for retroactive application.

- Reviewing policies and procedures in place to monitor Recovery Act grants from non-Recovery Act grants and identifying any special requirements associated with the Recovery Act funds.

- Ensuring all funds provided by the Recovery Act are distinguishable from non-Recovery Act funds in financial systems, business systems (i.e., grant and contract writing systems), and reporting systems.

- Reviewing compliance programs to ensure they consider the unique aspects of Recovery Act compliance requirements. For example, institutions will be required to provide, on a quarterly basis, an estimate of the number of jobs created, and the number of jobs retained, as a result of the support of Recovery Act projects.

Institutions that are affiliated with academic medical centers should take additional steps to determine the impact of a nationwide health information technology system by reviewing the following:

- Analyzing the potential level of incentives and determining which factors will impact those payments.

- Evaluating and balancing the clinical, capital and IT resources required to accelerate health information technology programs and potentially reducing resources and costs in other areas.

- Monitoring the requirements around showing meaningful use of a certified electronic health record product.

Proactive consideration of these practices will assist institutions in complying with the new requirements of the Recovery Act while taking advantage of the additional resources available from granting agencies.

# Enterprise Risk Management

## ►Background

Now more than ever, organizations of all types and sizes are dealing with significant risk on a day-to-day basis. Risk is any issue that impacts an organization's ability to meet its strategic objectives. Risk can generally be categorized in the following five broad categories:

- Strategic - high-level goals, aligned with and supporting the institution's mission;

- Operational - effective and efficient use of the institution's resources;

- Reporting - reliability of the institution's external and internal reporting;

- Compliance - the institution's compliance with applicable laws and regulations; and

- Reputational - damage caused by any of the other four that spills over to how the institution is valued or perceived.

The degree to which each of these types of risks exists within an organization is dependent to a certain extent upon the size and complexity of the organization. All entities face risk; the challenge for management is to determine how much and what types of risk are acceptable when setting its strategic goals.

Enterprise Risk Management ("ERM") philosophies have been embedded in corporate culture for a number of years. The Committee of Sponsoring Organizations of the Treadway Commission ("COSO") defines ERM as "...a process, effected by an entity's Board of Directors, management and other personnel, applied in strategy setting and across the enterprise, designed to identify potential events that may affect the entity, and manage risk to be within its risk appetite, and to provide reasonable assurance regarding the achievement of entity objectives." ERM recognizes that risks cannot be avoided, but the vast majority of surprises can be minimized. ERM also embodies a mindset that the risk population of an entity is too broad and too deep

to be fully understood and managed from the senior management leadership suite.

## ► Impact on Educational Institutions

Many Board members of educational institutions that have been part of implementing ERM initiatives in the corporate environment are asking the following questions:

- Does the institution have a risk assessment methodology in place?

- Does it understand the key risks and what is being done about them?

- Is an ERM structure viable?

- How can the institution implement ERM and where does it start?

- How can an ERM infrastructure be sustained?

Many research universities with academic medical centers have compliance programs in place that embody many of the same principles of ERM and have begun to broaden those programs to address risk beyond compliance. In fact, some universities have begun to adopt ERM programs. Other universities have risk assessment methodologies in place in certain areas but they are not formalized nor do they include all types of risk that exist across the entire enterprise. For those universities that have less formal risk assessment programs in place, ERM can serve as an excellent platform from which to formalize and enhance already existing programs.

A current key challenge for universities is how best to adopt the provisions of ERM in a highly decentralized environment and at a time when most universities are resource and priority constrained.

## ►PwC Perspective

Within a college or university, it is more critical than ever before to understand the risk profile of an institution. ERM is not about eliminating risk; it is about understanding where risks are, what existing controls are in place to mitigate them, and what additional controls can or should be put in place to bring the risk to a more tolerable level. It is important to first have an understanding of the risk appetite of the university from both management and the Board's perspective.

The most successful ERM implementations involve the entire university, and cannot involve senior-level management only. Everyone has a role, and those roles should be clearly defined.

The Board, primarily through the role of the Audit Committee, is ultimately responsible for ensuring that ERM initiatives are being adhered to and carried out as appropriate. The Board should be monitoring to ensure the focus of ERM shifts as overall operational strategies change throughout an institution. Typically the Chief Financial Officer or Chief Risk Officer, or in certain cases the Office of General Counsel operationally owns the ERM process. It is important for whoever owns the process to ensure the appropriate people are involved across the institution. The most successful implementations include management representatives from every major department across campus. Many universities have established "Risk Steering Committees." Such committees are made up of a cross section of university management that coordinates the risk assessment, prioritization, and risk mitigation process across the institution. These committees have been successful setting the ERM strategy and agenda.

Internal audit departments have historically driven ERM initiatives in higher education. They have an important role—adding value to the ERM initiatives by giving their sense of the overall risk issues facing the institution, keeping the risk agenda on task, and ensuring that management takes responsibility for the ERM initiative and risk mitigation strategies.

Institutions should also consider how the ERM program will be monitored. Important questions include identifying who will be responsible for which mitigation strategies are implemented, and whether the strategies are operating effectively.

At the outset of the project, ERM can be very overwhelming. Certainly as one looks across an entire institution, there are multiple risks. It is important to start by assessing and prioritizing risk at some level in the institution. It is also helpful to focus on one category of risk at a time and to have a response plan or framework in place. For example, once an institution has identified all of the particular risks, a plan should be in place to determine which risks will be focused on first and mitigated, which will

be monitored, and which will be left as is. The response plan will help to keep an appropriate focus on those key risks which are most significant to the organization's ability to continue its strategic mission and meet its strategic goals.

It is also important to recognize that ERM is a continual and evolving process. In order for it to be successful, it has to be embedded in the overall institutional strategy and management philosophy of the institution, so that as new initiatives or strategies are proposed, risks are identified and dealt with appropriately within the context of an ERM framework, and complement strategic initiatives.

# Tuition Affordability

▶ Background

Tuition affordability remains a concern of students, parents, regulators, and other constituent groups. The price of attending college for a year is commonly compared to annual income, and as family income declines, paying for a college education is becoming a greater challenge. Although information released by the College Board in 2008 shows that over a working life, the typical full-time worker with a four-year college degree earns over 60% more than a worker with only a high school diploma[i], attaining this degree is becoming increasingly unaffordable for many families.

Although tuition increases this year are less than in prior years, paying for these increases is challenging for families. While time is needed to assess the complete economic impact on higher education and tuition affordability, families looking to cut costs and save money will likely be seeking more financial aid than ever before. Compounding the ability of families and students to pay for a college education, by October 2008, approximately two dozen lenders had stopped issuing or cut back on student loans.[ii]

▶ Impact on Educational Institutions

As institutions respond to the challenges that families are facing, several additional current factors that can impact tuition affordability include:

- Impact of additional funding for financial aid from the American Recovery and Reinvestment Act;

- Revised institutional endowment payout strategies in support of financial aid; and

- Accessibility of tuition financing and the availability of student loan lenders.

The American Recovery and Reinvestment Act will provide approximately $30 billion in new funding in 2009 and 2010, coming in the form of a $17 billion increase in Pell Grants and $13 billion in more higher education tax credits. Institutions are factoring in these forms of financial assistance when considering future awarding strategies.

Many institutions are determining how to fund financial aid-related endowments that may be underwater as a result of market conditions. From a strategic perspective, institutions are deeming the funding of these initiatives to be critical to maintaining affordable tuition for those who can not cover the full cost of education. Universities continue to work to maintain or increase their budgets for financial aid. For example:

- Institutional awards increased 8% in 2007-08 from the prior school year.[iii]

- Institutions have become the largest source of grant aid, accounting for 42% of all grants;[iii]

- Over 80% of entering first-time, full-time undergraduates receive an institutional grant award;[iii]

- 75% of private colleges have experienced increasing requests for institutional aid;[iii] and

- While only 11% of these institutions drew more funds from their endowments to accommodate these requests, an additional 17% were able to cut other areas of their budgets and shift funds to financial aid.[iii]

In addition, institution's often utilize the Federal Family Education Loan Program (FFELP), through which banks make federal student loans backed by the federal government. In 2008, when available capital from this program came into question and the private loan market became volatile, many institutions began to turn to the Federal Direct Student Loan program, which provides funds directly from the federal government rather than banks or other lenders. This was a move that many institutions felt would secure students' continued education. These Direct Loans currently account for about 30% of all federal student loans and may account for over half by late 2009.

► PwC Perspective

The trends in institutional aid imply that colleges and universities continue to be challenged to contain costs and commit financial aid to students of need. More than ever, as students and their families struggle through difficult economic times, university officials need to be vigilant in providing the most timely and thoughtful information to students, parents, donors, and Board members. Actions taken should foster discussion, specifically around the following:

- How tuition increases are established and their relationship to institutional costs;

- The willingness of the institution to provide grants and loans to students;

- The determination of endowment payout rates and the percentage of endowment payout that supports financial aid; and

- Strategies employed to raise endowment funds in support of need-based scholarships.

Universities should continue to be as transparent as possible, by explaining how the economy is affecting their own operations, what costs are necessary to support and manage the institution, and the investments that are required to support long-term institutional strategies—all while remaining focused on delivering the important message regarding the social, economic and other benefits that an education provides.

---

[i] Source: College Board publication, What Every Parent Should Know about Paying for College, from 2008 Trends in Higher Education Series.

[ii] Source: TIME news article, Colleges Getting Hit by the Credit Crunch, dated October 8, 2008.

[iii] Source: NACUBO and AGB publication, The Financial Downturn and Its Impact on Higher Education Institutions, dated October 24, 2008.

# Green Initiatives

▶Background

Green initiatives are increasingly becoming a key question of prospective and current students as they evaluate educational institutions. Measures of accountability are becoming standardized across the U.S. and are providing students with access to information, which increases their expectations of higher education institutions. The most recent annual survey conducted by the Princeton Review of "College Hopes and Worries (2009)" showed that 64% of participants in the survey would value having information about a college's commitment to the environment. Among the participants, 24% said such information would strongly or very much impact their or their child's decision to apply to or to attend the school.[i] In response to these expectations, such organizations as the Princeton Review and Kaplan have added "green ratings" to their evaluations of educational institutions in the U.S. These ratings have been established based upon the institution's practices, policies and course offerings. As comparable information becomes more readily available to prospective students and becomes more standardized across the U.S., colleges and universities are going to be held to an increasingly higher standard for leadership in the green movement.

Colleges and universities across the country are developing policies to formalize the green initiatives on campus. Many educational institutions have utilized the LEED ("Leadership in Energy and Environmental Design") metrics established by the United States Green Building Council ("USGBC") as a framework for developing institutional policies. For example, of the 39 institutions highlighted by the USGBC for their leadership in green building, 41% of the institutions required all new buildings to attain at least the silver level of LEED certification.[ii] According to the American Council on Education, 133 colleges and universities have built LEED certified buildings and the National Association of Independent Colleges and Universities ("NAICU") has reported that the number of campus projects registered for LEED certification has grown an average of 37% per year since 2002.[iii] Adopting institutional policies of sustainable building

standards has provided colleges and universities with a benchmark for publically reporting and evaluating their relative involvement.

Green building is only one way educational institutions can become involved in sustainable practices. Other areas of participation include maximizing water and energy efficiency, reducing carbon emissions, planting native landscapes and incorporating awareness and education into the curriculum. Educational institutions are uniquely positioned to be leaders in the efforts to educate the next generation on environmental concerns and best practices. Over 600 college and university presidents have pledged their commitment to the American College and University Presidents Climate Commitment to be leaders in the community by modeling ways to eliminate global warming emissions and by providing the knowledge and the educated graduates to achieve climate neutrality.[iv] Additionally, the College Sustainability Report Card, the only independent evaluation of campus and endowment sustainability, noted significant improvements across a wide array of areas of sustainable practices in terms of the aggressiveness of the programs and the number of educational institutions with programs.[v] However, while these initiatives are gaining momentum in educational institutions across the country, there are minimal controls in place to validate the information being voluntarily reported by the institutions and additional benchmarks for comparisons are needed.

▶ Impact on Educational Institutions

Given the current financial pressures faced by most institutions, it is difficult to consider new initiatives, particularly those with significant upfront costs. The ability of educational institutions to enact policies and incorporate change in operations can depend on the size of the organization, the size of the population the organization serves and its overall financial means. However, there are many different ways to incorporate green initiatives on campus. Some large colleges and universities have been able to assemble sustainability committees of faculty members and have hired sustainability coordinators, while some smaller organizations with fewer financial resources have been able to bring about change through volunteer and student-run initiatives. The College Sustainability Report Card, published by the Sustainable Endowments Institute, found that the most prevalent area of involvement of educational institutions is in food and recycling, which can be a largely student-run initiative.

Other ways that educational institutions are making change possible, despite financial constraints, include grants and rebates. President Obama has continually stated his commitment to address climate change and energy consumption. Through the American Recovery and Reinvestment Act, tax credits and grant funding are available for research in sustainable projects. Additionally, utility rebates can be a way of reducing overall costs of conservation programs. Given the constraints of educational budgets, it is important for educational institutions to consider incentive programs currently being offered to entice organizations to be involved in the green movement.

▶ PwC Perspective

Educational institutions' ability to integrate green initiatives successfully into the culture of the organization is increasingly being viewed as a strategic, compliance, operational, reputational and financial issue. Currently, voluntary reporting is the only source of information for interested stakeholders, including prospective and current students, parents, faculty, donors and local communities. Benchmarks and increased monitoring controls are needed to evaluate the impact the programs are truly having on the environment. In the interim, educational institutions should continue to develop strategies to inform the public of the ongoing efforts of the institution by participating in voluntary reporting mechanisms and work to balance the rising expectations of the current students and the students of the future with the demands of the university's infrastructure, operational and budgetary commitments.

[i] Source: Princeton Review 2009 Survey, College Hopes & Worries Survey.

[ii] Source: U.S. Green Building Council website.

[iii] Source: National Association of Independent Colleges and Universities website.

[iv] Source: American College & University President's Climate Commitment website.

[v] Source: The College Sustainability Report Card.org.

# Identity Theft

▶Background

Identity theft is the number one complaint to the Federal Trade Commission ("FTC"), impacting 4.6% of U.S. citizens each year with an estimated $50+ billion in losses. In just the first 3 months of 2009, the Identity Theft Resource Center ("ITRC") reported 133 data breaches nationwide, that potentially exposed 1.5 million records containing personally identifiable information (also referred to as "PII"), such as Social Security and credit card numbers. Of those breaches, 14.3% represented data breaches at higher education institutions. According to the ITRC, a non-profit organization that works to promote the understanding and prevention of identity theft, approximately 650 data security breaches at higher education institutions had been reported by the end of 2008, which reflected an increase of 47% over the prior year.

Universities collect and maintain large amounts of data from current students, former students, students not accepted by the institution, alumni and their families, faculty, employees and research subjects. This large amount of data makes higher education institutions targets of data breaches. Recently, a data breach into a university network led to the theft of information of 40,000 elderly residents based on a hosting arrangement between the University and an Office on Aging.

PII is a commodity in and of itself. On the black market, university-related PII is extremely valuable. In a May 2008 report published by the Malicious Code Research Center, the fees for providing stolen personal information can be lucrative. Typically, a stolen name and Social Security number can be sold for approximately $10; adding information such as a home address and date of birth could increase the asking price to $16-$17 each. Multiplied by thousands of names, identity theft has become a big business.

In addition to the personally identifiable information students provide at time of enrollment, campus health services centers also collect and maintain health insurance information and other medical information, such as immunization records and names of the physicians that students may have

seen for diagnoses or treatment. In 2009 a health-information data breach exposed not only students' information but also their parents and spouses who were linked to the insurance coverage. Medical identity theft itself is a $1 billion dollar business expected to grow exponentially in the coming years. Today, the value of a single health record can bring $50 to $60 on the black market. In 2005, an estimated 250,000 Americans were victims of medical identity theft, a 334% increase over 2001.

Recognizing the growing epidemic of identity theft, the FTC enacted the Identity Theft Red Flags Rule effective November 1, 2008. The anticipated enforcement date is November 1, 2009. The Red Flags Rule was designed specifically to reduce, prevent and mitigate the risk of identity theft. Institutions covered by the Rule are those that collect and use confidential consumer data and maintain account relationships that have regular account-related transactions. These include banks, creditors, certain healthcare services providers, as well as many colleges and universities. For example, if an institution participates in the Federal Perkins Loan program, is a school lender in the Federal Family Education Loan Program, or offers loans to students, faculty or staff, the institution could be considered a "creditor" under the Red Flags Rule.

The Red Flags Rule differs from other data protection / identity theft prevention requirements in that its focus is the use of fraudulently acquired data to obtain credit or other credit related services. Due in large part to their clean credit records upon entering college, students are often targets of identity thieves, as newly enrolled college students are prime targets of credit card issuers and other companies. Additionally, the Red Flags Rule places affirmative duties on financial institutions and certain creditors, such as higher education institutions, to focus on the "reasonably foreseeable risk to the safety and soundness" of the institution towards detecting, preventing and mitigating potential institutional risks posed by identity theft.

## ▶ Impact on Educational Institutions

Organizations required to comply with the Identity Theft Red Flags Rule will need to develop and implement a written identity theft prevention program. Under the Rule, covered organizations are required to conduct a targeted risk assessment based on specified criteria to identify certain classes of accounts and account-related activities that potentially may pose a risk of identity theft. Rather than viewing the Rule as requiring large expenditures in technology and people, universities should look to leverage existing processes that help to enhance data security and fraud reporting. Universities should consider that the risk of non-compliance may result in reputational and brand damage; potential loss of revenue; civil liability arising out of identity theft-related damages to current and former students, their families, and university employees; as well as the potential of significant regulatory penalties for failing to protect confidential data.

As a result of this new law and increased risk of identity theft and data breaches, higher education institutions are increasingly assessing risk. Many are adopting approaches to information security similar to those used by private industry companies, such as putting enhanced administrative, technical and physical security controls in place for the protection and sharing of information. Some of those safeguards include: limiting (i) access and use of admissions and matriculatation information, (ii) the ability to conduct global research and operations, and (iii) sharing of research data and results. Key initiatives include:

- Developing integrated frameworks that combine compliance, privacy, security and identity theft

- Inventorying and removing sensitive data from business and HR processes

- Enhancing administrative safeguards such as:
  - Integrated privacy and information risk management assessments
  - Incident response plans to cover privacy
  - Training
  - Employee background checks
  - Contractual safeguards with third parties that handle confidential information
  - Vendor assessments

- Reviewing and enhancing or implementing key identity theft safeguards such as:
  - Encryption of data in storage and transit
  - Access controls and identity management
  - Document retention compliance

- Data leakage prevention
- Use of alternative identifiers and social security numbers/other sensitive information masking

## ▶ PwC Perspective

Identity theft is an issue of concern to regulators and consumers, including students and their families, faculty and employees. Colleges and universities will need to determine the extent to which the Identity Theft Red Flags Rule applies to their operations. As many institutions seek to attract students and donors and maintain relevance in the age of technology, they have turned to tactics used by marketers over the years. In doing so, higher education institutions now fall under the watchful eye of regulators such as the FTC. To that end, protecting the information assets of the institution and complying with the growing specter of regulatory requirements are more important than ever. Higher education has often approached risk and compliance on a law-by-law basis and/or in vertical silos across the organization. To promote consistency, heighten compliance and potentially generate efficiencies and cost savings, colleges and universities have been developing integrated frameworks and new governance models and managing common controls across multiple laws, risks and parts of the institution. Additionally, colleges and universities that take affirmative steps to address identity theft and data mismanagement prevention often experience a marked reduction in the number of incidents of breaches and data mismanagement.

Electronic and interactive communications have added and accelerated the frequency and amount of information sharing at higher education institutions. Moreover, as students, education, research, collaboration, fundraising, campus satellites and other key future growth and strategic initiatives increasingly expand globally, the success of many of these initiatives relies on the ability to share information freely cross-border to non-U.S. locations. Further, with an increasing number of applicants, students, alumni, researchers, faculty and partners, educational institutions should assume greater stewardship of the personal data they are collecting. While the issue of privacy protection and identity theft prevention among institutions of higher learning is focused on heightened controls and data security, it will be the responsible handling of personal information that will enable institutions to use such information to achieve critical educational, research, development and community-related goals.

## Contributors

**Tom Gaudrault**
Oversight of Financial Strategies and the Impact of the Stimulus Package

**Shannon Smith**
Endowment Payout Considerations

**Ann Filiault**
Liquidity and Financing Considerations

**Lisa Franciosa**
Revenue Enhancement and Expense Reduction Initiatives

**Carlos Cevallos**
Revenue Enhancement and Expense Reduction Initiatives

**Kaye Ferriter**
Current Regulatory Environment

**Gwen Spencer**
Current Regulatory Environment

**Jocelyn Bishop**
Current Regulatory Environment

**Lee Ann Leahy**
Enhanced Transparency and Accountability

**Shea Fowler**
Enhanced Transparency and Accountability

**Ralph DeAcetis**
Current Regulatory Environment and The Impact of the Stimulus Package

**Caitlin Blundell**
The Impact of the Stimulus Package

**Ann Pike**
Enterprise Risk Management

**Tami Radinsky**
Tuition Affordability

**Katharine Grover**
Tuition Affordability

**Kimberly Rothrock**
Green Initiatives

**Laurie Smaldon**
Identity Theft

**Lydia Payne-Johnson**
Identity Theft

pwc.com

© 2009 PricewaterhouseCoopers LLP. All rights reserved. "PricewaterhouseCoopers" refers to PricewaterhouseCoopers LLP or, as the context requires, the PricewaterhouseCoopers global network or other member firms of the network, each of which is a separate and independent legal entity.

# Index